BESIDE OURSELVES

Our Hidden Personality in Everyday Life

Naomi L. Quenk

Davies-Black Publishing
Palo Alto, California

BESIDE OURSELVES

Published by Davies-Black Publishing, an imprint of Consulting Psychologists Press, Inc., 3803 East Bayshore Road, Palo Alto, CA 94303; 1-800-624-1765.

Special discounts on bulk quantities of Davies-Black Publishing books are available to corporations, professional associations, and other organizations. For details, contact the Director of Book Sales at Davies-Black Publishing, 3803 East Bayshore Road, Palo Alto, California 94303; 415-691-9123; Fax 415-988-0673.

Myers-Briggs Type Indicator and MBTI are registered trademarks of Consulting Psychologists Press, Inc.

The following publishers have generously given permission to use extended quotations from copyrighted works: From *The Inferior Function,* by Marie-Louise Von Franz. © by Marie-Louise Von Franz. Reprinted by arrangement with Shambhala Publications, Inc., 300 Massachusetts Ave., Boston, MA 02115. From Jung, C. G.; *Collected Works, Volumes 6, 8, 9i, 11, 16, 18,* and *The Visions Seminars.* Copyright 1976, 1960, 1959, 1969, 1954, 1976, 1976 by Princeton University Press. Reprinted by permission of Princeton University Press.

"Portrait of a Woman" by Pablo Picasso © 1993 ARS, New York/SPADEM, Paris

99 98 97   10 9 8 7
Printed in the United States of America

Library of Congress Cataloging-in-Publication Data
Quenk, Naomi L.
        Beside ourselves : our hidden personality in everyday life / Naomi L. Quenk.
        p.   cm.
Includes bibliographical references and index.
ISBN 0-89106-062-6
1. Typology (Psychology)   2. Myers-Briggs Type Indicator.
3. Jung, C. G. (Carl Gustav), 1875-1961.   I. Title.
BF 698.3.Q46 1993
155.2'64—dc20   93-4373
                                                                             CIP
First printing 1993

To Alex

Contents

Preface

I WAS INTRODUCED TO psychological type in 1960 on my first day of graduate school in the psychology department at the University of California at Berkeley. I took the *Myers-Briggs Type Indicator®* (MBTI®) personality inventory along with a number of other personality tests. At the time, the MBTI inventory was a little-known personality instrument used only by a few researchers. Later, when we received our test results, I was surprised that the description of my type, INFP, was so positive. Like most psychology students, I was oriented to the negative and the pathological.

Over the next several years I learned more about the MBTI inventory through the creativity studies at Berkeley's Institute for Personality Assessment and Research (IPAR). I used the instrument in my dissertation research, although it was not my central focus. I was impressed with its potential as a vehicle for exploring normal human behavior, which continues to be my primary focus in the field of personality. I began to administer the MBTI whenever I could.

In 1972 I joined the Longitudinal Study of Medical Students at the University of New Mexico School of Medicine, and was delighted to discover that the MBTI inventory was one of the major instruments being used. In addition to studying our research data on type, I had frequent and enlightening discussions about type theory and the MBTI inventory with my colleagues Gerald Otis and Wayne Mitchell. We also had the good fortune of collaborating with Isabel Myers and Mary McCaulley, who were following up Myers' earlier longitudinal study of medical students.

In 1975, the Longitudinal Study of Medical Students joined the newly formed Center for Applications of Psychological Type (CAPT) to conduct workshops on the MBTI inventory for the many medical educators who were interested in its potential as a career tool. We added workshops for other health professionals, psychotherapists, general educators, and various other professionals who were rapidly discovering the applications of typology.

During this time, I read Jung's book *Psychological Types* and was motivated to read more of his remarkable insights. Eventually, I read most of his writings. I became aware of the critical role that typology plays within Jung's system, and my depth and breadth of understanding vastly increased as I came to understand the overall Jungian context within which typology exists.

I first presented the inferior function, or hidden personality, aspect of Jung's typology when my husband (a psychologist and Jungian analyst) and I taught CAPT workshops for psychotherapists. Participants made immediate connections with some of their own persistently puzzling experiences. This was later followed by talks at various conferences and in other settings.

When the Association for Psychological Type (APT) began its MBTI training program in 1979, the inferior function was not a part of the curriculum, as it was considered advanced, esoteric, and irrelevant to a basic understanding of typology. However, when I noticed that participants in this intense workshop seemed to be expressing their inferior functions, I began to include it as a teaching segment. I hoped to augment people's appreciation of the breadth of typology and help them understand their own inferior function responses.

Many people had "aha" reactions, which are typical when people first become aware and conscious of a habitually unconscious occurrence. These people were now able to recognize puzzling and disturbing out-of-character experiences as manifestations of an unconscious but predictable part of themselves. Recognizing this provided them with a helpful perspective on the reactions they had during the training experience. The concept turned out not to be too advanced for an introductory workshop.

I now include the inferior function in most of my MBTI training workshops. My APT faculty colleague, Nancy Barger, added it to her training sessions and collected participant "stories," many of which are in this book. Others who teach typology have also included the concept in their presentations.

People had often suggested that I "write up" what I knew about the hidden part of our personality, the inferior function. Several years ago, while attending an uninspiring day-long seminar, I created the outline for this book. I later entered it into my computer, started inserting notes, and eventually it became a book. I hope that it succeeds in stimulating in readers the same kind of recognition, understanding, relief, and excitement that I have observed in people during my lectures.

This book resulted from trying to put a bad experience (the uninspiring seminar) to good use. This is also my goal for readers of the book. By recognizing the seemingly "negative" parts of themselves as necessary and healthy, I hope that readers will appreciate their own incredible complexity and the amazing ways in which a "normal" personality develops, functions, and thrives.

CHAPTER 1

Jungian Psychology
and Hidden Personality

"I don't know what's gotten into him. He's always been so sensible, and here he is imagining the most bizarre possibilities!"

"It was weird, my obsession with a brain tumor. All I had was an ordinary headache. I tried to talk myself out of it, but it was overpowering."

"To our amazement, she suddenly stood up, burst into tears, and stormed out of the meeting!"

"I never knew he had it in him! He was quite the life of the party, dancing with every woman, telling ribald stories....Not at all the straitlaced, conservative guy I'd known him to be."

"Here I was, an acknowledged expert in my field, and all I could think about was how stupid I sounded, how people must be bored and irritated with my lecture, and how foolish I was to put myself in such a humiliating position."

WE ALL HAVE TIMES when we are "out of character," feel outside and beside ourselves, and act in unexpected ways. And we've all observed such aberrations in others. Sometimes we are intrigued or even amused by these atypical behaviors; more often, however, we are puzzled, distressed, put off, and embarrassed by them. As a general rule, we rely on our past experiences to guide our expectations of others. We expect people to be consistent and predictable from one day to the next. If this were not the case, our relationships with the people we know would be just as unpredictable as our encounters with strangers.

Even though consistency in behavior is generally the rule, people do sometimes act in unexpected, seemingly capricious ways. To explain such deviations from "normal," we usually assume that there must be something "wrong" with the person. When the out-of-character behavior is extremely odd and unusual, we may attribute it to irrationality, instability, or downright craziness.

We Are All Personality Theorists

Each of us operates with some system for understanding people, whether we use a formal theory or just an implicit set of general guidelines. Most of us use our daily observations of other people and our own reactions to what we observe as a basis for generalizing, explaining, and predicting our own and others' behavior.

Whether formal or informal, personality theories attempt to organize observations of people by providing some kind of underlying framework for classifying and describing behavior. Formal personality theories, such as those put forth by psychologists, tend to use concepts and language that are not easily understood by most people. As a result, most of us devise our own system for making sense of people's attitudes, motives, and behaviors.

On rare occasions, the concepts in a formal personality theory are also meaningful and useful to people who are not specifically trained to understand psychological complexities. When that happens, we benefit from both the conceptual power of a carefully developed system as well as a straightforward and practical way of understanding our own personality and the personalities of others. Jung's theory of psychological type is an example of such a theory.

A Formal Theory
That Confirms Common Sense

Psychological type theory is accessible to an everyday understanding of personality consistency because it was formulated to describe and explain normal behavioral variations among "normal" people. Even though the style and language Jung used to describe his system can be confusing, others, most notably Katharine Briggs and Isabel Briggs Myers, have provided easily understandable clarifications and interpretations of Jung's

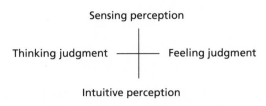

Figure 1   Opposite Jungian Functions

original work. Briggs and Myers' development and expansion of Jung's original theory is formalized in the *Myers-Briggs Type Indicator* (MBTI) personality inventory.

Jung's system focuses on how people go about gathering information about the world (perception), how they reach conclusions about what they have perceived (judgment), and what their sources of energy are (attitude or orientation). Based on many years of keen observation, Jung hypothesized two opposite ways of perceiving, *sensation* (or sensing) versus *intuition*, and two opposite ways of judging, *thinking* versus *feeling.* Figure 1 above shows these opposite functions or processes.

In addition to these opposite mental functions or processes, Jung described two opposite attitudes or orientations of energy, *extraversion* versus *introversion.* A person habitually uses each of the four functions in one of these two attitudes. Thus, one person might habitually extravert sensing perception, while another person might habitually introvert sensing perception. Myers added a fourth pair of opposites to those Jung proposed, a *judging* versus *perceiving* orientation toward the outer world. Combining the four individual preferences yields distinct **types**[1] of personality. The complex variations that result from combinations of these functions and attitudes are fully described in Chapter 3 of this book.

Jung and Myers assumed that people are born with a preference for one of each pair of opposites—that is, they have a preference for sensing (S) or intuition (N), thinking (T) or feeling (F), extraversion (E) or introversion (I), and a judging (J) or perceiving (P) attitude. These innate tendencies develop and reach their fullest potential over the course of a person's lifetime.

These opposite preferences, as defined by type theory, take many of our characteristics out of the realm of the puzzling and peculiar by describing them as orderly, rational, and predictable. We can readily recognize the

ISTJ	ISFJ	INFJ	INTJ
ISTP	ISFP	INFP	INTP
ESTP	ESFP	ENFP	ENTP
ESTJ	ESFJ	ENFJ	ENTJ

Figure 2 The Sixteen Types Identified by the MBTI

sixteen types that emerge when we combine the four pairs of opposite preferences because they appear in our daily lives.[2] People appreciate and use information that helps them understand personality characteristics and explains and predicts people's similarities and differences. The growing popularity of the typological approach attests to its usefulness in understanding the consistencies found among individuals of the same type. In fact, in a study that asked people to evaluate a number of personality instruments (Druckman & Bjork, 1991), the majority identified the MBTI personality inventory as providing the most insights and as having the greatest impact on their behavior and decisions. A chart listing the sixteen types that result in combinations of the four pairs of opposite preferences is shown above in Figure 2.

Though it may not be as readily apparent to people familiar with psychological type theory and the MBTI personality inventory, Jung's method not only addresses the consistency and predictability of our personalities but also our inconsistencies. The theory includes a rationale for our modes of being when we are out of character, not acting normally, or otherwise "beside ourselves." For Jung, even our inconsistencies are consistent, predictable, logical, and valuable.[3]

Our out-of-character predictability is a critical aspect of the dynamic character of psychological type theory. As a hidden part of personality, it is embodied in Jung's concept of the unconscious **inferior function,** especially in the often dramatic experience of "being in the grip of one's inferior function." When, how, and why this phenomenon occurs is the subject of this book.

Some Basic Concepts

During the early part of his career, Jung was a disciple of Sigmund Freud, whose insights into the nature of the human psyche, particularly the unconscious, have dramatically altered the way we think about ourselves. Later, Jung's thinking diverged significantly from Freudian psychology in ways that are directly relevant to the inferior function.

Jung viewed human personality from a broad perspective, so his system for understanding individual differences and similarities is quite detailed and complex. You won't need a comprehensive knowledge of Jung's theory to understand the subject of this book, but some background that places typology and the inferior function in the context of Jung's total system will be helpful.

The Psyche Can Balance Itself

Jung saw the human **psyche** as containing everything necessary to grow, adapt, and heal itself. He believed that people were capable of directing their own personality development and of recognizing and benefiting from both positive and negative life experiences. Clearly, not everyone successfully heals their psychological wounds or develops their personality maximally. But Jung focused primarily on the *potential* for growth and development of both individuals and humanity as a whole.

The Effects of a One-sided Approach to Life

Jung's clinical work with people demonstrated to him that one-sidedness was maladaptive. When a person devotes excessive energy to one thing, she ignores, rejects, or devalues its opposite. If one of the attitudes or functions embodied in psychological type theory is overemphasized, the opposite attitude or function will be neglected. When this happens, a person may risk having inappropriate perceptions or making poor judgments, since only one aspect of a situation is allowed into awareness. A person who uses only intuition may imagine the beautiful rooms he is going to add to his house while ignoring the leaking roof that is damaging his computer! Similarly, a person who ignores her feeling judgment in making a career decision may choose a career that is quite logical, but that she greatly dislikes.

As a general rule, when we overdo one function or attitude to the exclusion of its opposite, our use of it tends to become rigid, automatic, and stereotypical. Its exaggerated form appears as a caricature of a normal,

TABLE 1   **Adaptive Versus One-sided Type Preferences**

Preference	Adaptive Form	One-sided Form
Extraverted Attitude	Charming Enthusiastic Sociable	Boastful Intrusive Loud
Introverted Attitude	Deep Discreet Tranquil	Aloof Inhibited Withdrawn
Sensing Perception	Pragmatic Precise Detailed	Dull Fussy Obsessive
Intuitive Perception	Imaginative Ingenious Insightful	Eccentric Erratic Unrealistic
Thinking Judgment	Lucid Objective Succinct	Argumentative Intolerant Coarse
Feeling Judgment	Appreciative Considerate Tactful	Evasive Hypersensitive Vague
Judging Attitude	Efficient Planful Responsible	Compulsive Impatient Rigid
Perceiving Attitude	Adaptable Easygoing Flexible	Procrastinating Unreliable Scattered

effective mental process. Table 1 shows some of the typical adaptive qualities of type attitudes and functions and provides a comparison of how they appear in an exaggerated, one-sided form.[4]

The Principle of Compensation

Psychological opposites are essential for the whole of Jung's personality theory, just as they are for his type theory. This opposition provides a way for our psyches to correct one-sidedness. Jung called the mechanism for correcting one-sidedness **compensation.**

Jung borrowed Newton's third law of motion in proposing compensation as a way to regulate and balance our functioning: Every action force has a reaction force equal in magnitude and opposite in direction. Jung (1976a) concluded that

> whenever life proceeds one-sidedly in any given direction, the self-regulation of the organism produces in the unconscious an accumulation of all those factors which play too small a part in the individual's conscious existence. For this reason I have put forward the compensation theory of the unconscious as a complement to the repression theory. (p. 419)

Jung did not see compensation as necessarily disruptive. Rather, he viewed such seeming aberrations as having a complementary and not an oppositional role. Thus, while out-of-character inferior function experiences may be jarring, they play a critical role in encouraging and restoring the psyche's equilibrium by tempering a one-sided devotion to one or another typological function. Many examples of the compensatory nature of the psyche are included in Chapters 6 through 13.

Compensatory Messages in Dreams

The 40-year-old daughter of an army general held her father in high esteem. She admired his competence, self-confidence, and calmness in the face of all crises. She could consistently rely on him for support during difficult times. She was therefore surprised and disturbed when, while visiting him, she dreamed that she saw him walking down a dingy street in a poor part of town. His usually immaculate uniform was torn and disheveled, his hair was unkempt, his skin pasty, and his posture slouching.

This dream scene revealed her father as so out-of-character, so deviant from her conscious perception of him, that she was forced to explore its meaning. In doing so, she recognized that her 73-year-old father was now getting old, frail, and tired, and that by exaggerating his strengths, she was denying his more vulnerable side and his ultimate mortality. She was thus forced to have a more realistic perception of him, which led to a healthier, more adultlike relationship.

The Concept of Projection

Unconscious contents are charged with energy that must be discharged in order for a person to function comfortably and with minimal tension and distress. One of the most powerful and universal ways that human beings have of dealing with unacknowledged, unconscious thoughts and feelings is through **projection**. Because the inferior function is appropriately understood as an unconscious process that is subject to the mechanism of projection, an understanding of this concept is essential.

Simply described, projection involves attributing to others an unacknowledged, unconscious part of ourselves—something that lies outside of our conscious awareness. What we project onto others can be negative, repugnant, and undesirable—or positive, admirable, and wholesome. In either case, the "projector" unconsciously identifies someone who possesses at least *some* of the unconscious quality in question, but then exaggerates the degree to which that quality is actually present. The "added amount" of the quality comes from the projector's unconscious. The person being projected on is then seen as more hostile, lazy, talented, or admirable, for instance, than is really the case.

For the most part, projection is a normal psychological process that enables us to relate to each other by recognizing areas of similarity and mutually shared interests and values. We feel secure and comfortable when we see aspects of ourselves in others; similarly, we may be suspicious, fearful, and distrustful when we meet people who are extremely different from us. "Finding" ourselves in others thus serves as a connecting link to our shared humanity and prevents the isolation and loneliness we would experience if we were completely unique and disconnected from other people. If we withdrew all of our projections, we would become so completely detached and unaffected by the world that we could no longer function as members of human society.

In Jung's psychology, projection often accounts for our initial attraction to or rejection of others. A person may be a ready "host" for one or more aspects of our own unconscious. And like compensation, projection is one of the ways the psyche regulates itself. Equilibrium is maintained when people eliminate their contradictory ideas or feelings. Thus, a person who presents herself as extremely honest, strangely ignoring some of her own rather shady activities, may frequently and loudly complain about political corruption. Unable or unwilling to recognize her own immorality, she projects it on an easy target. Politicians provide a ready hook upon which she can hang her own unacknowledged morally questionable behavior.

The Growth Instinct

Jung suggested that we each have an instinct that pushes us to grow toward completion, to become the best possible version of ourselves. He referred to this goal as **individuation**, a state of self-awareness or self-actualization toward which we strive but rarely, if ever, achieve. Therefore, he saw the lifelong process of individuation as more important than a hypothetical, generally unattainable end point. Jung's psychology is therefore **prospective,** purposive, or goal-oriented—the goal being individuation.[5]

Jung looked at all behavior, including neurotic symptoms, as ways of stimulating an individual's growth toward wholeness. He was interested in personality development as it occurred over the life span and saw it as an ongoing process that continued during adulthood, midlife, and even advanced age.

The way we move toward wholeness or individuation is by expanding our knowledge and awareness of ourselves, which increases our ability to control and direct our lives. We are continually discovering our actualities and potentialities through living, working, relating to others, and contemplating our lives. But for psychologists like Jung and Freud, the major repository of valuable new growth-enhancing information was the unconscious realm of our personalities.

The Character of the Unconscious

Jung and Freud agreed that the unconscious contains repressed memories, experiences, and ideas. But in Jung's view, the unconscious also includes neutral contents, such as latent or dormant potentials that are yet to be realized.

Jung also described a second, deeper, nonpersonal layer of the unconscious. He labeled it the **collective unconscious.** It is this part of the psyche that makes us larger than our individual selves. It contains images related to common **archetypes**—human experiences and patterns such as birth, death, marriage, mother, father, hero, child, wise woman, and so on. These themes link us to other people and to our ancestors, providing the vital connection to our past, present, and future as individuals and as a species. Jung believed that the incorporation of such images into our awareness was vital to our completion through the individuation process.

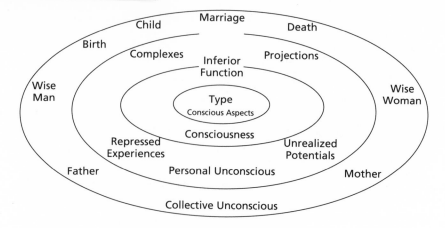

Figure 3   Map of the Psyche

The Inferior Function and Individuation

How does one gain access to the unconscious information required for human development? For Freud (1933), "the interpretation of dreams is the royal road to a knowledge of the unconscious activities of the mind" (p. 608). For Jung, the route to the unconscious is through the inferior function. In Jung's system, the inferior function is the undeveloped component of an individual's basic character or type. As we will see, of the four functions of type, three are capable of consciousness, while the fourth, the inferior function, remains largely unconscious. It therefore provides the first and most direct entry into information in the personal layer of the unconscious. This entry is the important first step toward acquiring the personal and archetypal information that encourages individuation. Figure 3 above shows a map of the psyche, including selected features specified by Jung and the location of the inferior function within that structure.

Both Jung and Freud saw dreams as important sources of unconscious information, and both devoted much attention to the skillful interpretation of their patients' dreams. Although even uninterpreted dreams may aid psychological awareness, incorporating a dream's meaning into one's waking life is a much more potent way of expanding one's **consciousness.** Interpretation enables the new knowledge dreams provide to be consciously integrated and used.

In much the same way, inferior function experiences may aid our personality development, even when we don't understand and interpret them. Their very strangeness can force us to have a new awareness. Our other "off" experiences are likely to be passing idiosyncrasies, temporary fads, and momentary passions that do not startle us with their excessiveness or jar us into a new perspective. Inferior function episodes, in contrast, alarm us with their "Jeckyl and Hyde" character, forcing us to examine the essence of our character and personality. These experiences can therefore be understood as our psyche's attempt to move us in the direction of completion and individuation. In fact, when people describe being "beside themselves," "not themselves," or "taken over by something," they often spontaneously mention the valuable insights, new information, or change of perspective that resulted from the experience. Such reported beneficial effects of inferior function experiences demonstrate the natural ability of the psyche to restore its own equilibrium.

Access to Information From the Inferior

The inferior function phenomenon is a normal, adaptive way of promoting personality development. It can be observed in everyday life and occurs in mild and mundane, as well as in extreme and debilitating, manifestations. Because it is a natural part of personality, we can all benefit from the insights that can be gained from encounters with our inferior. No special expertise is required. What is essential to understanding, however, is recognizing the characteristics of one's own and others' inferior functions and their adaptive place in our lives.

Just as most people readily recognize their own and others' personality types when they are first introduced to type theory, most people instantly recognize their own and others' expressions of the inferior function. In fact, the majority of examples and stories that appear in Part 2 of this book were contributed by people who were entirely ignorant about the inferior function and its characteristics at the time the episodes occurred. Their recognition came "after the fact," sometimes many years later when they heard a lecture or attended a workshop addressing type and the inferior function.

But intellectual knowledge about one's inferior function by no means guarantees awareness of what is happening while one is "in the grip." *When we are under the influence of something that is unconscious, we are, for the most part, unconscious of it.* We may have a dim suspicion that the inferior is involved in the episode, but we may also have insufficient conscious energy and perspective to be altogether sure. This is as true for me as it is for the other "aware" people whose stories are in this book. All we may know is that something is wrong, that we are feeling and appearing out of character and unbalanced, while wondering whether this experience of ourselves is the "real" us, and our former selves the aberration.

Earlier writing on the inferior function tends to emphasize its pathological appearance. With the exception of Jung's own work, Von Franz's (1971) discussion of the subject is currently the most complete available. It is an insightful and informative exposition, although there is less focus on integration of the inferior as an expected consequence of normal development than is true of my own approach. In a more recent book, Angelo Spoto (1989) focuses on the negative and destructive potential of the inferior for individuals and society.

If we come equipped with a psyche designed to maintain its balance and move toward wholeness, external intervention is only a helpful (if sometimes necessary) method of achieving that which we are by nature "designed" to achieve. Our psyche operates regardless of whether we "know the rules." Dreams can compensate for a one-sided attitude, even if they are not fully interpreted and understood. Inferior function experiences can also compensate for one-sidedness and thus add richness to our lives.

But just as we can learn a great deal more from a well-interpreted dream, so can an understanding of the character of our inferior function increase its power to expand our self-knowledge. And just as there are "big" dreams that feel—and are—more significant than everyday dreams, so there are more important inferior function episodes and less notable ones. We tend to remember striking dreams in great detail and for long periods of time. The same is true for powerful inferior function experiences.

The Positive Focus of Myers and Briggs

Jung's writings on typology describe the effects of extreme and one-sided use of preferences, and the examples he gives often point out the more negative aspects of a particular attitude-function combination. It was indeed a tour de force for Isabel Briggs Myers to extract and fully describe mature and adaptive functioning for each type. Her careful consideration of type dynamics was critical to this achievement.

Jung may have overemphasized the negative and maladaptive aspects of the inferior function. And, in adopting his pathology-centered approach, many Jungians miss the importance of the phenomenon for normal, everyday **adaptation.** Myers' primary focus on healthy adaptation perhaps led her to appropriately understate the more negative expressions of the unconscious inferior function. In doing so, she missed out on a very rich and fruitful aspect of normal functioning.

My goal is to bridge these two approaches by exploring the range of territories in which the inferior function appears. In this way, we can best understand this phenomenon as a natural response of normal people making their way through the stresses and strains of their complex inner and outer worlds. I therefore present the inferior function:

- As it is demonstrated in our everyday behavior—in characteristic sensitivities and typical projections onto others
- As it is revealed in our interests, hobbies, and ways of relaxing
- In the typical ways it is triggered or provoked and the forms it takes when it erupts
- In the experiences people report while they are "in the grip"
- In how the psyche returns to equilibrium
- As it appears during midlife and beyond

The Organization of This Book

This book describes the character and form of the eight inferior functions. Each is described in sufficient detail for readers to identify their own experiences of the inferior. There are ample examples of inferior function experiences, how they came about, and the benefits derived from them.

My goal in presenting the inferior function as a normal, adaptive aspect of life is to provide readers with a new and useful approach to some of their own and others' puzzling behavior. Such enhanced understanding should encourage people to explore new and exciting parts of themselves. Ultimately, this kind of expanded knowledge will increase our effectiveness within ourselves as well as in our relationships with others.

The remainder of the book is divided into two parts. Part One, "The Hidden Personality in Context," provides the information needed for understanding the dynamic character of typology in general. It begins with Chapter 2, which describes the most important aspect of Jung's type theory, *type dynamics,* the interactions among the functions of sensing, intuition, thinking, and feeling, along with their extraverted or introverted attitudes. Chapter 3 provides the method for determining the dynamics of any type formula and shows how different dynamic relationships affect attitudes and behaviors. These two chapters provide the background for understanding the specific dynamics of the inferior function, which is the topic of Chapter 4. Chapter 5 outlines the structure for approaching the hidden personality of the sixteen types described in Part Two, "The Hidden Personality in Action." It provides a detailed introduction to the contents of Chapters 6 through 13, which are devoted to each of the eight inferior functions. Chapters 6 through 13 begin with extraverted thinking types and end with extraverted intuitive types. Chapter 14 discusses the effects of the inferior on relationships, and, finally, Chapter 15 offers some concluding remarks and intriguing issues concerning the inferior function.

There are two Appendices to this book. Appendix A contains Myers' descriptions of the sixteen personality types, and Appendix B contains selected quotations from Jung's *Collected Works.* Included are statements about the inferior function and important comments about typology that are of general interest.

Finally, a glossary provides definitions for the terms used in this book.

A Caution to Readers

Most books about personality discuss what is wrong with people, how they became that way, and what they can do about it. People are depicted as having too much or too little of this or that important characteristic, as being afflicted by this or that dysfunctional environment, and as being defined by membership in one or another pathological group. We are told what should be different and why, who treated us badly or how we are treating others badly, and what kinds of corrective measures are required to change us or those close to us into well-adjusted, functioning people.

My fear is that people are so accustomed to being told what is wrong with them and how to change it, that readers will expect this book to be about getting rid of some bad, pathological, inferior part of their personalities. If that is your expectation, I hope you will be greatly disappointed!

- This book will *not* tell you what is wrong with your (or someone else's) personality.

- It *will* help you understand and appreciate yourself the way you are and help you identify other adaptive aspects of your personality and how they operate.

- It will *not* show you how to make the hidden and unconscious parts of your personality entirely conscious and under your total control.

- It *will* explain the importance of some unconscious aspects of your personality type and why they neither can nor should be made conscious.

- It will *not* teach you ways to become equally proficient or to have equal access to all of the personality elements defined by psychological type theory.

- It *will* explain the critical difference between developing skills in using all aspects of your personality type, and having all of those parts equally developed.

This book is not about abnormality and pathology. It explores a part of our personalities that often looks and feels abnormal and pathological, but is in fact natural, adaptive, and healthy. You are unlikely to discover that something you believe to be a "good" part of you is really insidiously destructive. Rather, you are likely to recognize that some of the characteristics that you find puzzling or distressing are adaptive and helpful.

PART 1

The Hidden Personality
in Context

•

CHAPTER 2

The Dynamics of Jungian Typology

THE DYNAMIC CHARACTER OF type theory is commonly overlooked by people new to typology and the MBTI personality inventory. This accounts for their often simplistic, categorical approach to the sixteen types. Similarly, psychologists familiar with **trait** approaches to personality often assume that the type system describes four personality dimensions whose effects are merely additive (McCrea & Costa, 1989). In ignoring the dynamic interactions critical to Jung's system, both laypeople and professionals miss out on its greatest contribution to the explanation and prediction of normal personality.

Opposites in Jungian Psychology

We saw earlier that Jung conceived of the psyche as active, vital, and energetic—as a dynamic system. This system draws vitality from sets of opposite mental processes whose interaction provides the system's energy. Jung's typological theory focuses on three pairs of opposites: opposite functions of perception, which are sensing and intuition; opposite judging functions, which are thinking and feeling; and opposite attitudes or orientations in which perception and judgment are used, which are extraversion and introversion. Myers and Briggs found a fourth pair of opposites implicit in Jung's type theory, a judging versus perceiving attitude toward the outer world.

The Character of Opposites

Opposite mental processes cannot be used at the same time because they are diametrically different. If we tried to use two opposing processes at the same time, a blockage would prevent either process from being effective. According to both Jung and Myers, adequate **differentiation** of the opposites is necessary for effective functioning and good **type development.** In order for a person to function effectively, the opposites must be clearly distinguishable from each other. For example, if both sensing and intuitive perception carry equal amounts of mental energy, they are *undifferentiated*—that is, the person cannot focus on either kind of information long enough to arrive at any kind of judgment about it.

This was the case for a nurse whose first job was employment in a hospital pediatric unit. While in nursing school, this woman had prided herself on the level of accuracy she demonstrated with the many details required of her work, and she enjoyed tasks involving details. She had also received positive evaluations on her ability to establish a rapport with patients and anticipate their needs and concerns. However, in her current job, these two areas seemed to conflict. She would be preparing a medication for one of her young patients, carefully and systematically following the prescribed dosages, when suddenly, she would find herself thinking about an impending meeting with the parents of a patient, imagining what she would say and how they might respond. Returning to her task of preparing the medication, she would find that she had lost count. She would begin again, only to find herself imagining what would happen if she gave a patient the wrong dose of medication. Once again, she would begin her task, only to have yet another intrusive thought about an anticipated future task. As time went on, she found herself habitually unable to focus on either the present or the future or the concrete or the abstract long enough to successfully perform her work. She was unable to gather adequate data (perception) on which to make decisions regarding what needed to be accomplished and when. The distress, anxiety, and confusion she experienced finally led her to give up her career.

A clear distinction between each pair of opposites and the development of one preference over its opposite is not the only differentiation Jung identified. Vital to type dynamics is the notion of different levels of consciousness characterizing the functions, with one of the four functions for the most part completely conscious, and one for the most part completely unconscious.

For Myers (1980), the dynamic nature of these mental processes provided a model for the development of individual differences over the life span, causing her to conclude the following:

Good type development, therefore, demands two conditions: first, adequate but by no means equal development of a judging process and a perceptive process, one of which predominates, and, second, adequate but by no means equal facility in using both the extraverted and introverted attitudes, with one predominating.

When both conditions are met, the person's type development is well balanced. In type theory, balance does not refer to equality of two processes or of two attitudes; instead, it means superior skill in one, supplemented by a helpful but not competitive skill in the other.

The need for such supplementing is obvious. Perception without judgment is spineless; judgment with no perception is blind. Introversion lacking any extraversion is impractical; extraversion with no introversion is superficial.

Less obvious is the principle that for every person one skill must be subordinate to the other and that significant skill in any direction will not be developed until a choice between opposites is made. (p. 182)

Some people object to this aspect of type theory because it proposes a hierarchy of differentiation or development, and thus possibly different levels of capability in using four very important mental processes. Some see it as placing limits on human potential, even as contradicting our democratic notion of equal opportunity. "Why can't I be equally good at everything?" is a question frequently asked. People who misunderstand type theory may believe that equal development of all four functions is an appropriate and desirable goal—and they may hope that reading a book about the inferior function will show them how to develop it fully and therefore control it.

As we will see, even if equal development were possible, it would diminish our capacity for positive growth and our ability to relate effectively to our environment. The dynamic character of our personalities would be eliminated, and with it the critical role of the inferior function as a link to that vital source of growth and renewal, our unconscious. Jung's rationale for the hierarchy of differentiation that characterizes our mental processes is discussed below.

A Model for Type Dynamics

The dynamic character of psychological type theory is consistent with Jung's overall approach to psychic functioning. The following discussion highlights key features of Jung's approach that are useful for understanding the dynamics of his typological system.

Primitive Unconsciousness

Civilization's advancement has been marked by increasing specialization in the knowledge and skills required for human survival and progress. Primitive people responded largely instinctually to their environment, with relatively little ability to control and direct it. Yet given these limitations, each person in a primitive civilization possessed much of what was necessary for basic survival.

The ability of primitive civilizations to control and change the world, however, was severely limited because the skills needed for survival pretty much required an equal share of attention. Because the available time and energy were evenly divided among so many arenas, the development of a special skill in any one area was unlikely. Without devoting a fair amount of energy to something, people do not become adept at it. Without being better at some things than others, one person is largely indistinguishable from another, is likely to act and react in automatic, instinctual ways, and is, as a result, likely to lack what we recognize as individuality.

This describes the state of unconsciousness that Jung ascribed to primitive people, in that their psychological functions were still operating in their unconscious and were not differentiated. A primitive might therefore be unable to differentiate between an intuition and an actual event. What occurred inside a primitive's head and outside his or her body would be indistinguishable. A tribe member might say, "A spirit came to me and told me the tribe must move to the other side of the valley in order to survive." The tribe members might very well trust the importance of the spirit's message and thus follow a leader's "instinct" for survival.

In contrast, people in modern civilizations are ill-equipped to exist on their own in an increasingly complex world. As individuals, we have become highly specialized or differentiated in our knowledge and skills and therefore require a large and complex society to meet our survival needs. But our increasing differentiation as individuals has led to our ability to significantly affect our environment (with both good and bad results), and thus to shape our individual and collective lives. If a person in a modern civilization said, "My intuition is that the company should invest in electronic stocks," the company's board of directors would evaluate this insight from a number of perspectives, accepting the intuition as one piece of data worth considering. They would not typically act on the advice unquestioningly.

Modern Consciousness

For Jung, the increased specialization associated with civilization parallels the development of human consciousness.[6] Control and influence over the environment requires differentiation between such things as verifiable external events and inner psychic events like dreams and visions. The largely unconscious primitive psyche did not make these kinds of critical discriminations, without which neither causal connections nor effective control over the environment can occur. For the primitives, a dream message was just as real and valid as a concrete event.

Jung saw the *differentiation of opposites* as critical to consciousness. Distinguishing male from female, darkness from light, good from evil, outer from inner, real from imagined, and cause from effect are necessary for people to govern their lives. Similarly, the sets of opposites described by psychological type theory require differentiation in order for people to function effectively. The modern person's intuition about the company's stock investment is clearly identified as just that—an intuition—and not as a message from the gods.

Consciousness increases as we successfully differentiate opposites: The more differentiated preference of a pair receives the greater quantity of energy. **Differentiated functions** and attitudes focus a person's intentions and direction. Psychological type theory assumes a hierarchy of consciousness among the functions, with a superior, more differentiated function capable of conscious direction at the top of the ladder (dominant), and a largely unconscious function at the bottom end (inferior). In between are a function somewhat less differentiated than the dominant (auxiliary) and a function somewhat more differentiated than the unconscious inferior (tertiary). As Jung (1959) put it:

> Only one function becomes more or less successfully differentiated, which on that account is known as the superior or main function, and together with extraversion or introversion constitutes the type of conscious attitude. This function has associated with it one or two partially differentiated auxiliary functions which hardly ever attain the same degree of differentiation as the main function....The fourth, inferior function proves...to be inaccessible to our will. (p. 238)

Within typology's system of opposites, it is the flow of psychic energy between and among the functions that provides its dynamic character. Table 2 depicts the hierarchical structure of the Jungian functions.

TABLE 2 Hierarchy of Jungian Functions

Dominant
[Conscious]

Auxiliary
[Somewhat conscious]

Tertiary
[Somewhat unconscious]

Inferior
[Unconscious]

Because type theory describes each personality type as normal, adaptive, and of equal inherent value, type descriptions emphasize the positive attributes of each type.[7] In fact, a significant asset of this approach as compared to pathology-focused systems is its validating and affirming nature.

Adaptive Access to All Mental Processes

It is important to remember that all four processes and all four attitudes identified by psychological type theory can be used effectively by everyone. So even though a person's dominant function may be feeling, for instance, that person can and will follow rules of logical analysis. Suppose that person were a writer. The act of writing requires the application of logical rules of grammar and language. The person can use his or her thinking abilities comfortably and willingly because they can help them organize and communicate their ideas (intuition) about something that is very important to them (their dominant feeling function). This is an example of what is referred to as *using a less preferred function or attitude in the service of a preferred one.*

Thus, a manager whose dominant function is intuition may develop skill in devising and implementing detailed plans and structures that require his inferior function, sensing, because the increased efficiency will help him develop future strategies that engage his dominant intuition. A manager whose dominant function is sensing might lend her support to a brainstorming session for her many intuitive employees, knowing that ultimately many practical plans might emerge from the process that will satisfy her preference for sensing.

The dynamic approach of Jung and Myers permits the fullest opportunities for individual development of personality and personal effectiveness. Taking things perhaps a step further, psychological typology may constitute the basic structure of personality, serving as a template that guides and colors other aspects of our lives. If this is true, both genetic endowments and environmental influences affect and are affected by our underlying typological character structure.

CHAPTER 3

The Effects of Type Dynamics

FOR THE MOST PART, Jung's writings on type dynamics are powerful but sketchy, insightful but unsystematic. It is therefore difficult to fully understand the complex interactions of functions and attitudes implicit in the theory. Briggs and Myers faced this problem when they developed the MBTI personality inventory as a self-report questionnaire designed to elicit an individual's preferences regarding pairs of equally valuable mental processes. The construction of the paper-and-pencil instrument allows a person to indicate his or her preference for the opposites of extraversion versus introversion, sensing versus intuition, thinking versus feeling, and judging versus perceiving. A critical additional requirement for the MBTI personality inventory, however, was a method for determining the dynamic relationships among those preferences, as specified by Jung's theory.

Myers and Briggs' careful reading and interpretation of Jung's theory enabled them to devise a clever and accessible method for identifying dynamics based on an individual's responses to the instrument. Their method is reflected in the content and order of the four letters of any one type formula. As with any attempt to identify something as complex as a human personality, the MBTI personality inventory may not accurately identify a particular person's type and associated dynamics. Within such limits, however, it seems to provide the best available indicator of a person's dynamic personality type. And people whose MBTI results don't seem to fit them are given the opportunity to identify for themselves what they feel is a "better-fitting" type.

Many people take the MBTI personality inventory in situations that provide limited information about the dynamic character of the theory underlying the instrument. As a result, such people may know the four letters of their type but not appreciate the depth of information that type can provide them. The first section of this chapter is designed with such people in mind. It describes the rationale and method for identifying the dynamics of any four-letter MBTI type. Those already familiar with the theory and method for identifying dominant, auxiliary, tertiary, and inferior functions in any MBTI type may choose to skip the next section and move on to the second section of this chapter, "Differing Dynamics and Their Effects," beginning on page 37. This section describes the effects of type dynamics on the character and behavior of people who have different types and provides examples that demonstrate these dynamic differences. If you skip the first section of this chapter, however, you may want to read the endnote for this chapter, which discusses alternative hypotheses about the attitude of the tertiary function.

Identifying Type Dynamics

To understand the dynamic relationships within each of the sixteen four-letter MBTI types, you must first examine the sequence of the letters.

The first letter designates a person's preferred attitude or orientation of energy, which is either E for extraversion or I for introversion. People who prefer extraversion tend to use their energies in the outer world of people, things, and activity, and are in turn energized when they interact with their outer environment. People who prefer introversion tend to orient their energies to the inner world of concepts, ideas, and reflection, and are in turn energized when they interact with their inner environment.

The second letter identifies how a person typically gathers information, their preferred perceiving function, which is either S for sensing or N for intuition. People who prefer sensing tend to trust and use information acquired through their five senses, focusing on the individual facts and details in a present situation. People who prefer intuition tend to trust and use information acquired through a "sixth sense," which focuses on patterns and possibilities that imply a future situation.

The third letter gives a person's preferred judging function, which is either T for thinking or F for feeling. People who prefer thinking tend to make decisions or reach conclusions by focusing on nonpersonal logical analysis and include only information that seems directly and logically relevant to the problem at hand. They are most interested in the logical consequences of a decision. People who prefer to make their decisions through feeling tend to focus on people-centered values relevant to the problem at hand and include in the decision-making process factors that may not be logically relevant to the problem. They are most interested in the feeling or value consequences of a decision. Remember that feeling in Jung's system does not refer to emotions. However, people with a preference for feeling are more likely than those who prefer thinking to include their own and others' emotional reactions in the decision-making process.

The fourth letter in a person's type is the judging/perceiving index or attitude toward the outer world, which is either J for a judging attitude or P for a perceiving attitude. People who prefer a judging attitude when they are extraverting enjoy making decisions and reaching conclusions when they are dealing with the outer world; they tend to function best when they can be systematic, methodical, and scheduled. People who prefer a perceiving attitude when they are extraverting enjoy gathering as much information about the outer world as is possible; they tend to function best when they can take a flexible, adaptable, and spontaneous approach to the world. Remember that J points to a person's preferred judging function shown in the third letter of a person's type (T or F), while P points to a person's preferred perceiving function shown in the second letter of a type (S or N).

Thus:

- E or I refers to the direction of a person's energy flow
- S or N refers to a person's preferred form of perception
- T or F refers to a person's preferred form of judgment
- J or P refers to a person's preferred function when he or she is extraverting

The Form of Each Function

The dominant function The *dominant function* represents what we want to devote our attention and activity to most of the time. This is either a person's preferred form of judgment (i.e., either thinking or feeling), or his or her preferred form of perception (either sensing or intuition). We tend to use our dominant function primarily in our preferred attitude or orientation of energy, either extraversion or introversion. So if your dominant function is thinking and you prefer the extraverted attitude, you probably enjoy spending much of your time making logical judgments, reaching conclusions, and accomplishing things out in the world.

> Dominant extraverted thinking——▶ Logical judgments,
> conclusions, accomplishments
> *in the world*

If your dominant function is intuition and you prefer the extraverted attitude, then you probably enjoy spending much of your time coming up with new ideas and possibilities for projects out in the world and letting others know about your enthusiasm.

> Dominant extraverted intuition——▶ New ideas, possibilities for
> projects, enthusiasms *in the world*

The auxiliary function A second, or *auxiliary,* function complements the dominant function in two ways. First, it is always from the other pair of functions—that is, if the dominant is a judging function, then the auxiliary will be the preferred perceiving function; if the dominant is a perceiving function, then the auxiliary will be the preferred judging function. Second, it will tend to operate primarily in the less preferred attitude—either extraversion or introversion. Thus, if the dominant function is extraverted, then the auxiliary will be introverted; if the dominant function is introverted, then the auxiliary will be extraverted.

So if your dominant function is extraverted thinking, your auxiliary will be either introverted sensing or introverted intuition, whichever function you prefer. If your auxiliary preference is introverted intuition, the information you gather is likely to emphasize internal ideas, hypotheses, and theories.

> Auxiliary introverted intuition——▶ Internal ideas,
> hypotheses, theories

Your dominant extraverted thinking judgment will focus on that kind of information in order to create models and systems and ways to implement them in the world. Because your dominant, driving function, extraverted thinking, attracts you to accomplishing things in the world, implementing your ideas will be more appealing to you than the ideas themselves.

Dominant extraverted thinking
+   = *Implementation* of ideas
Auxiliary introverted intuition

If your dominant function is extraverted intuition, your auxiliary will be either introverted thinking or introverted feeling, whichever you prefer. If your auxiliary preference is introverted feeling, the conclusions you reach about which ideas to pursue will probably be oriented to your values, the things that are most important to you.

Auxiliary introverted feeling——▶ Value, things of importance

Your dominant extraverted intuition will therefore generate ideas and possibilities about your important values. And because your dominant, driving force, extraverted intuition, attracts you to exploring ideas in the world, coming up with the ideas will be more appealing to you than implementing them.

Dominant extraverted intuition
+   = *Exploration* of ideas
Auxiliary introverted feeling

The dominant and auxiliary functions complement each other by providing balance between perception and judgment and introversion and extraversion. Myers believed that this kind of balance was necessary for good type development.

The judging versus perceiving attitude   Myers used the fourth pair of opposites, implied but not made explicit in Jung's writings, to enable us to determine type dynamics. This judging versus perceiving dimension indicates one's attitude toward the outer world, that is, whether the preferred perceiving function (either sensing or intuition) or the preferred judging function (either thinking or feeling) is used when a person is extraverting, regardless of whether extraversion is the person's preferred attitude. In the examples of dominant and auxiliary functions that were just discussed, the person whose dominant function is extraverted thinking has a judging attitude toward the outer world (J); she extraverts her thinking. The person whose dominant function is extraverted intuition has a perceiving attitude toward the outer world (P); he extraverts his intuition.

Here is an example to show how Myers used the JP concept to identify type dynamics. We begin with ISTJ—a type that prefers introversion, sensing, thinking, and a judging attitude.

Looking at the type ISTJ, we see the following:

- The preferred attitude or orientation of energy is introverted.
- The preferred way of perceiving is sensing.
- The preferred way of judging is thinking.
- The preferred function to use while extraverting is the judging function, in this case, thinking.

Here is a procedure to help identify type dynamics. First, look at the last letter of the type formula. For ISTJ, the formula tells us that this person extraverts the preferred judging function. The third letter of the formula tells us that it is thinking. This is illustrated in Figure 4.

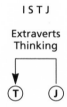

I S T J

Extraverts
Thinking

Figure 4   Identifying the Extraverted Function of ISTJ

We now need to know whether the person prefers extraversion or introversion as an attitude. So our second step is to look at the first letter of the type. It identifies introversion as the attitude preference. This is shown in Figure 5.

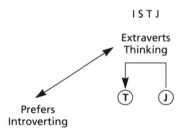

I S T J

Extraverts
Thinking

Prefers
Introverting

Figure 5   Identifying the Preferred Attitude of ISTJ

Since we know that people reserve their dominant function for use in the preferred attitude, the function being extraverted cannot be the dominant one and therefore must be the auxiliary. So for ISTJ, the auxiliary function is extraverted thinking, as Figure 6 illustrates.

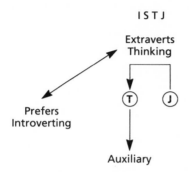

Figure 6   Identifying the Auxiliary Function of ISTJ

Remember that if the auxiliary is the preferred judging function, the dominant must be the preferred perceiving function. The second letter of the type formula identifies sensing as the preferred perceiving function, and therefore the one used predominantly in the preferred introverted attitude. So for ISTJ, introverted sensing is the dominant function, as Figure 7 illustrates.

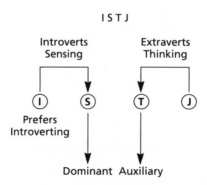

Figure 7   Identifying the Dominant Function of ISTJ

The two letters that don't appear in the type are N for intuition and F for feeling. In any type formula, the two missing letters designate the tertiary and inferior functions. By definition, the *inferior function* is the polar opposite of the dominant function, that is, it is opposite in both function and attitude. So for the dominant introverted sensing ISTJ, the inferior function is extraverted intuition, as Figure 8 illustrates.

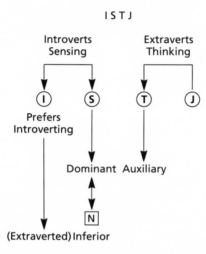

Figure 8   Identifying the Inferior Function of ISTJ

The tertiary function is always the function opposite the auxiliary. For ISTJ, whose auxiliary function is thinking, it is feeling, as Figure 9 illustrates. There is some disagreement about the attitude associated with the tertiary function. The view taken by Myers and McCaulley (1985) is that the tertiary shares the same attitude as the auxiliary and inferior functions, that is, the dominant takes the preferred attitude, with the auxiliary, tertiary, and inferior all taking the less preferred attitude. However, two alternative views have been suggested.[8] Because of these differences of opinion, the attitude of the tertiary function will not be specified in this book.

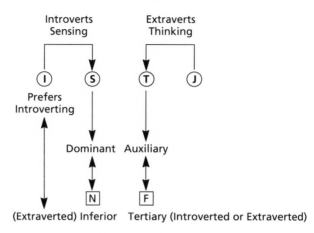

Figure 9 **Identifying the Tertiary Function of ISTJ**

Now let's look at the dynamics of a type that prefers extraversion. For an easy comparison, we'll look at ESTJ. Once again, we determine what function the person uses when extraverting by looking at the last letter of the type formula, which for ESTJ is J for judging function. And, once again, we find that the person prefers thinking, as Figure 10 illustrates.

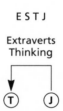

Figure 10 **Identifying the Extraverted Function of ESTJ**

The first letter in the type formula tells us that this person prefers the extraverted attitude. Since the preferred attitude is the one in which the dominant function is used, thinking must be the dominant function for ESTJ, as Figure 11 illustrates.

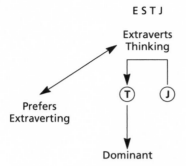

Figure 11 Identifying the Dominant Function of ESTJ

Now, since the dominant function came from the judging pair, we know that the auxiliary function must be from the perceiving pair, in this case, sensing. Since the auxiliary takes the less preferred attitude, introverted sensing is the auxiliary for ESTJ, as Figure 12 illustrates.

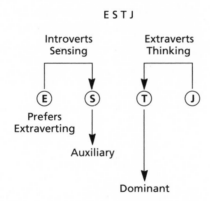

Figure 12 Identifying the Auxiliary Function of ESTJ

To complete the picture, we identify the inferior function as the polar opposite of the dominant, that is, introverted feeling, and the tertiary as introverted or extraverted intuition, as Figure 13 illustrates.

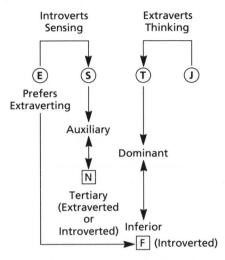

Figure 13   Identifying the Tertiary and Inferior Functions of ESTJ

Differing Dynamics and Their Effects

Now that I've illustrated the underlying theory of type dynamics and a system for identifying the dynamics in any one type formula, we can explore what difference these dynamics make in people's personalities. For example, how are ISTJs and ESTJs different?

Based on their shared preferences for sensing and thinking, we might safely assume that an ISTJ and an ESTJ would prefer the same kinds of information-gathering approaches and decision-making methods. We would also expect both to be comfortable with structure and closure. Both have the same two letters missing from their formulas, F and N. So we should not expect the two types to pay a great deal of attention to feeling values and future possibilities.

However, the degree of differentiation of the sensing and thinking functions of these two types should produce different effects. Jung and Myers specified that the dominant function is the most highly differenti-ated and under the most conscious control. The auxiliary, tertiary, and inferior functions are, respectively, less developed.

Thus, for the ISTJ, dominant introverted sensing would be most differentiated and therefore the most consciously directed. We would expect an ISTJ to first process information internally and to be quite confident about the accuracy of her perceptions. Auxiliary extraverted thinking would be less developed, but quite accessible. We would expect her to be somewhat less confident about communicating logical conclusions. Tertiary feeling is less developed than auxiliary thinking, so she might not have ready access to her feeling values. Inferior extraverted intuition would be virtually undifferentiated and unconscious. We would expect her to pay little attention to outside possibilities.

For the ESTJ, extraverted thinking is most differentiated. We would expect an ESTJ to make judgments about the outside world quickly and with great certainty. Introverted sensing is next in line; the ESTJ's second concern would be with processing the data relevant to his decisions. Tertiary intuition might be expressed through reluctant or occasional attention to possibilities. Inferior introverted feeling—undifferentiated and unconscious—would result in little or no attention to the feeling values in a situation.

This is true for other types who share the same functions and attitudes, but for whom the dominant and auxiliary differ. Research by Mitchell (1992b) suggests that the following model may form the basis for differences in dominant versus auxiliary differentiation.

If introverted feeling is my dominant and your auxiliary, I should use introverted feeling more often and with greater confidence and facility. Most likely, I would also have developed all or most of the personality characteristics associated with habitual use of the preference and have a fair amount of expertise in using them. In contrast, your auxiliary form of introverted feeling would be expressed less often and with less confidence and facility. And you might have developed only some of the attributes associated with a preference for introverted feeling and have somewhat less expertise in using them.

The remainder of this chapter describes some of the important effects of type dynamics. These include differences related to things such as which function is used first; whether the dominant is a judging or a perceiving function; whether the dominant is extraverted or introverted; using the dominant in the less preferred attitude; and an alternative way of looking at the JP dimension.

Which Function Is Used First?

An ENFP (dominant extraverted intuition, auxiliary introverted feeling) and an INFP (auxiliary extraverted intuition, dominant introverted feeling) were the co-leaders of a seminar. During the afternoon session, both noted and commented to each other that there was something amiss in a particular segment of the lesson. They agreed to review it later. As soon as the seminar ended, the ENFP said, "Okay, we need to talk about that now and figure it out." The INFP said, "But I'm not ready yet. I need some time to evaluate it by myself before I'll be ready to talk about it."

The ENFP wanted to explore the possibilities first and then reach a conclusion. The INFP needed to get a feel for (make a judgment about) what happened before being ready to consider possibilities that could confirm or negate her conclusions. Thus, the dominant function of each tends to be engaged first. It serves as a kind of default mechanism in the psyche, much like the default settings in a computer program.

Is the Dominant a Judging or Perceiving Function?

An ISTJ (dominant introverted sensing, auxiliary extraverted thinking) and an ESTJ (dominant extraverted thinking, auxiliary introverted sensing) were business partners. After investigating alternative computers, they agreed on one. But just before they were about to purchase it, one of their customers told them about another machine that had additional features that might be useful in their business. The ISTJ was ready to buy this other computer; the ESTJ gave many reasons for sticking with the original decision and played down the alleged assets of the alternative machine. It took several days to convince him to alter his decision.

Dominant judging types, regardless of whether their preference is for thinking or feeling, tend to be more reluctant to change a decision in the face of contradictory evidence than dominant perceiving types. For the latter, the data (perceptions) are primary; conclusions (judgments) are less important. So when new information alters a previously held conclusion, dominant perceivers find it fairly easy to change a decision, even if they were comfortable with it. For dominant judgers, the conclusion is primary, and much energy is invested in it. In the face of contradictory evidence, they find it more difficult to give up their initial conclusion. They may doggedly question the new data before reluctantly altering their decision.

Is the Function Extraverted or Introverted?

A common area of difficulty for people learning about type is the difference between extraverting versus introverting a particular function. Here are some examples that highlight such differences.

Is sensing extraverted or introverted? Myra, an ESFP (extraverted sensing), and Bonnie, an ISFJ (introverted sensing), went to the Bahamas together. Neither had been there before. Bonnie came prepared with an itinerary of specific things to see and do and time estimates for doing them. Myra objected to this imposed structure. She wanted to have the fullest possible range of experiences and to remain open to any sensory exploration that came her way. They succeeded in compromising by alternating days of doing it "Myra's way" with days of "Bonnie's way." But neither was quite comfortable with the other's preferred mode of operation.

Extraverted sensing types take in the widest range of available sensory messages from the environment, receiving pleasure from their intensity and breadth with little or no restrictions on what are acceptable data. Introverted sensing types, in contrast, seem to operate with an inner structure within which incoming sensory information is classified and ordered. The data are then readily available in all their detail for the appreciation of and use by the introverted sensing type.

Is intuition extraverted or introverted? Yolanda, an ENFP, feels that she is frequently criticized and put down for her ideas. As an extraverted intuitive, she talks about her ideas as they are being formed, before she subjects them to her own critical judgment. In contrast, Hal, an INFJ (introverted intuitive), keeps his ideas to himself for a long time before sharing them. He wants to ensure that his ideas are seen as only ideas, and not as finalized, worked-out systems. When he does talk about his ideas, he uses disclaimers, emphasizing their tentative nature.

The dominant introverted intuitive tends to focus primarily on ideas and possibilities at a conceptual level and focuses down to the essence of those inner ideas that are certain. Introverted intuition is tuned in to inner interconnected possibilities that may take the form of complex theories, models, and the like. Their relevance to the outer world is usually secondary, so only well-thought-out and important ideas are shared with others.

The dominant extraverted intuitive tends to be more attracted to a wide range of possibilities in the outer environment, readily sharing them with others as ideas to be explored, and applying those ideas in the outer world. So Yolanda, in sharing her ideas before she has critiqued them herself, risks being misunderstood by others. Hal, in initially keeping his ideas to himself, misses out on feedback that could possibly help him further shape his ideas.

Is thinking extraverted or introverted?   Two INTP (dominant intro-verted thinking) researchers were discussing possibilities and plans for continuing their research. They explored many wide-ranging possibilities, discussing each with great enthusiasm. At one point in their discussion, their ENTJ (dominant extraverted thinking) project manager came in briefly and listened with great interest as they discussed their ideas. Two months later, the two INTPs were surprised and rather vexed when they discovered that their project manager had applied for a grant to do the research project he had listened in on!

For the INTPs, their discussion was "just tossing around ideas." The particular idea that their project manager overheard them discussing was no more important than ten others they talked about that day. To the ENTJ, their enthusiasm about it (and the fact that it also appealed to him) were sufficient motives for taking action. Extraverted thinkers use their judgment in the arena of the outer world, critically evaluating what is happening (with a sensing auxiliary) or the potential for effective outcomes (with an intuitive auxiliary) with a goal of logic and coherence in the outer world. They are oriented to acting on their conclusions. Introverted thinkers' critical judgment operates internally, figuring out what is going on or what is possible with a goal of inner logic and coherence. Actualizing their conclusions is secondary.

Is feeling extraverted or introverted?   George, an ENFJ (dominant extraverted feeling), hired Ellen, an INFP (dominant introverted feeling), to edit his book manuscript. Ellen was gratified to learn that the edited manuscript had been accepted for publication by a prestigious university press. This news confirmed her feeling that she had done a good job. She was embarrassed, however, when George, who had already paid her for her work, took her out to dinner and presented her with an expensive gift to show his appreciation. Rather than increasing her confidence in her work, this seemingly excessive display of gratitude made Ellen distrust George's judgment of her. His unbounded enthusiasm seemed to indicate to her his lack of discrimination.

This is a good example of how introverted feeling types focus on inner harmony and being at peace within themselves. Extraverted feeling types devote their energy to maintaining harmony in the outer world. George was merely sharing his delight in his success with the person whom he felt had contributed greatly to it. He would have been puzzled and shocked had he known about Ellen's reaction, which she did not reveal to him.

What Happens When the Dominant Is Used in the Less Preferred Attitude?

The examples above show that much misunderstanding can arise between people whose dominant functions operate in opposite attitudes. Von Franz (1971) reiterates Jung's observation that we have more difficulty with people who use their dominant in the "other" attitude than we do with people whose types are the complete opposite of our own. We may become impatient with others on whom we project our own discomfort with using a less preferred attitude.

Thus, introverted thinkers may find their extraverted thinking colleagues to be lacking in depth and conceptual clarity, as too quick to reveal their thinking process to others, and as not thinking things through well enough. Extraverted thinkers may see their introverted thinking counterparts as obtuse, obscure, esoteric in their interests, as unnecessarily complex, and perhaps as withholding and unwilling to share their thoughts with others.

Introverted feeling types may see their extraverted feeling associates as insincere and nondiscriminating in their expression of feeling values, as intrusive and overbearing in their focus on establishing and maintaining harmony for the people in their environment, and as choosing breadth rather than depth of feeling. Extraverted feeling types may feel unsure about the values of their introverted feeling friends and colleagues. They may experience doubts about whether they are appreciated, may feel criticized, and may perceive (often accurately) the introverted feeling type's judgment that they lack depth.

By the same token, when someone actually uses a function in their own less preferred attitude, they experience a sense of "wrongness" or discomfort with themselves. Because attitude determines the sphere in which a function operates—the outer world or the inner world—when we use a function in the less preferred attitude we find ourselves in a foreign land, full of uncertainty and lacking in confidence. We feel and behave differently and may appear different to others. This is especially true when the function in question is the dominant one.

The perceiving function in the less preferred attitude   Introverts who typically introvert sensing or intuition may feel overwhelmed or unfocused when they extravert that function. Exposing their perceiving process to others may interfere with their confidence in their ability to concentrate and direct their train of thought. Their ideas may appear disjointed to both themselves and others, as their inner processing is likely to be much faster than their speech. As a result, much of the detail and complexity of their inner perceptions will not be communicated.

The effects of introverting sensing or intuition in people who normally extravert these functions are less apparent. Extraverted sensing types and extraverted intuitive types describe having great difficulty staying focused on inner perception. Their attention wanders and they become confused and somewhat disoriented. They may feel lost in internal complexity and be unable to communicate what is going on inside them.

The judging function in the less preferred attitude   Introverts who typically introvert feeling or thinking may feel they are overdoing it, telling too much or providing too much detail when they extravert that function. Other people may confirm the introvert's fear that he or she has revealed too much. Because that function is usually used internally, introverts may have difficulty knowing just how much of their inner processes to reveal to others.

The effects of introverting a normally extraverted function are less readily apparent to observers. But extraverts report that when they introvert their typically extraverted feeling or thinking, they can become quite confused and circular in their reasoning. They need to talk out their process and receive feedback from others in order to feel comfortable with their decisions.

Another Way of Looking at the JP Dimension

When people discuss the JP dimension, they usually talk about the attitudinal and behavioral differences that result from extraverting one's preferred judging process versus extraverting one's preferred perceiving process. In this section we will examine another aspect of the JP dimension by comparing the function that is extraverted with the corresponding function that is introverted. We will look at what attitudinal and behavioral differences result from Js introverting their preferred perceiving process and Ps introverting their preferred judging process.

Extraverting versus introverting the perceiving process Bill (INTJ, dominant introverted intuition) and his wife Arlene (INFP, auxiliary extraverted intuition) spent a week at an artist colony in New England. Later, Arlene remarked that she enjoyed participating, at least peripherally, in some of the more unconventional activities at the colony and thought she could get caught up in it for a while if she spent more time there. Bill saw his wife's statement as evidence of a possible character flaw, suggesting a failure on her part to maintain strong, unalterable values. He indicated that he had no such urges and was immune to any dubious attraction to what he termed "immoral" behaviors.

How can we account for the different reactions of Bill and Arlene? Remember that the types who extravert the perceiving function are those whose type ends with the letter P. These are ENTP, ENFP, ESTP, ESFP, INTP, INFP, ISTP, and ISFP. Of course, all of these types introvert their judging function. But the external focus of their perception makes it likely that they will easily change and adapt to a changing outer environment, even having a "chameleonlike" tendency to take on the behaviors and values of people in different contexts.

Those who introvert their perceiving function are types whose type ends with the letter J. These are ENTJ, ENFJ, ESTJ, ESFJ, INTJ, INFJ, ISTJ, and ISFJ. Because their perceptive focus is internal, they tend to be relatively unaffected by a changing environment. Their inner perceptions have a constancy and predictability from one circumstance to the next. All of these types extravert their judging process.

Bill seemed to confuse Arlene's openness to new data with a readiness to change her basic moral standards (as embodied in her dominant introverted feeling). He did not experience the "pull" of the outer environment himself, for his own perceptive focus is internal and relatively unamenable to outside influences.

The fact that Js, who extravert their judging function, like to control and regulate and are more comfortable in a predictable environment is reinforced by the introversion of their perceiving function. This makes the outer environment less salient than it is for those whose perception is extraverted. For the extraverted perceivers, who introvert their judging function, the basic decision-making structure (thinking or feeling) remains constant and secure. But in their efforts to fully observe or experience their environment, they may appear to have shifting and unreliable judgments.

Extraverting versus introverting the judging functions   The phone rang. It was Carla, Rosa's ENFP daughter. Rosa is an INTP (introverted thinking type). Carla was attending college in another state. "Mom, I've got this chance to move out of the dorm and into a six-bedroom house with four girls and a guy," she said excitedly. "It's a great house, right next to campus, and it will even be cheaper than the dorm! It's okay with you, isn't it?"

Rosa quickly thought to herself, She's too young to live off campus. It seems to me it's against the rules for freshmen anyway. She probably doesn't know the prospective roommates very well, and her judgment about people can be really off. It sounds like a bad idea to me. She said to Carla, "Tell me some more about the house and your friends. How did you hear about it? Are the others freshmen, too?"

Just then, her INTJ husband, Mario (introverted intuitive with extraverted thinking), came into the room. "It's Carla," said Rosa. Mario picked up the phone. Carla repeated her exciting news. Mario immediately said, "That's a terrible idea. You're too young to live off campus. Isn't it against the rules for freshmen? And who are these people anyway? You know you're not a very good judge of people!"

Carla burst into tears, accused her parents of treating her like a child, and angrily hung up the phone. The next day, after everyone had calmed down, Carla gave her parents information about the house, the roommates, and the college rules. Both parents were satisfied and relieved, and Carla was ecstatic when they agreed to her request.

This story demonstrates an interesting consequence of opposite attitudes of the judging process. Remember that people whose type ends with the letter "J" extravert their judging function. People whose type ends with

P extravert their perceiving function, so their judging function is introverted. In the example above, whether the judging function was dominant or auxiliary didn't matter.

Later, in discussing what had happened, Mario and Rosa noted that both of them had had very similar judgments about their daughter's plans. But Rosa's introversion of her judgment made her keep her concerns to herself, while her extraversion of her perception encouraged her to ask for more information. Mario's extraversion of his judgment encouraged him to state his concerns up front. He acknowledged that after Carla hung up, he realized he was missing a lot of information about her plans.

There are many more dramatic as well as subtle effects of differing type dynamics, and we can use them to make specific behavioral predictions. The dynamic character of typology teems with possibilities for observing individual similarities and differences. This is a far more fruitful approach than a concept of type that stays at the simplistic level of "I'm an INTP, so I like mathematical models. You're an ENFJ, so you like people to get along!"

CHAPTER 4

The Dynamics of the
Hidden Personality

THIS CHAPTER PROVIDES THE context for recognizing and understanding how the hidden part of personality, the inferior function, is manifested. It will discuss the following:

- Purposeful use of the fourth function
- The conditions for the eruption of the inferior
- The form and character of the inferior
- The role of the inferior in **self-regulation**
- The influence of the tertiary function
- The contribution of the inferior to personal development or individuation
- The role of the auxiliary function
- The importance of the inferior in **midlife**

Purposeful Use of
the Less Preferred Functions

We are all capable of using our tertiary and inferior functions when a particular task requires them. When our least preferred process is being used consciously, we might best think of it as our *fourth* or *least preferred function*. When this process is engaged unconsciously and operates outside of our control, it serves as our *inferior* function. As we discussed in Chapter 3, the tertiary is the function that is opposite our auxiliary. When it is under conscious control, however, we may consider it to be our *third function*. We may even have developed tactics that help us use it more easily and effectively, or we may have learned to ask for expert input from friends or colleagues whose dominant or auxiliary is our third or fourth function. As we will see, however, this deliberate use of the least preferred functions is quite different from the involuntary occurrence, or "attack," that we describe as being in the grip of one's inferior function.

Many people become quite comfortable and skillful in using their less preferred functions. The more our life situations call for it, the easier this is and the more effective we become at using them, especially if less preferred functions serve the goals of our preferred ones. As an INFP researcher, I had to use sensing and thinking a good deal of the time. And although it was difficult and fatiguing at first, it became easier and I became better at those aspects of my work. I was very motivated to use my third and fourth functions well because they provided the sensing data and logical data analysis that permitted me to use my dominant feeling and auxiliary intuition. The research topics were important to me, and I very much enjoyed developing hypotheses and extracting meaning from the results of the research.

However, no matter how experienced, skilled, and comfortable we may be in the *conscious* use of our third and fourth functions, this *does not seem to alter its eruption as an inferior function.* So given the right preconditions that make us vulnerable to being "taken over by the other side," we will likely fall into our inferior modes. Conscious skill and experience with a function does not prevent us from falling into the grip. Given sufficient fatigue or stress, our inferior function will take over, quite beyond our control. And even with considerable skill and familiarity with our less preferred functions, excessive use of them can serve as a trigger for a full-blown "grip" experience.

Conditions for Eruption of the Inferior

The general precondition for eruption of the inferior function is a lowering of our general level of consciousness. Jung referred to this as an *abaissment du niveau mental* (Samuels et al., 1986). It permits a transfer of energy from the more conscious and developed functions to the relatively unconscious tertiary and inferior functions. Several circumstances encourage this transfer of energy; the most common ones are fatigue, illness, and stress.

Alcohol or other mind-altering drugs also lower one's level of consciousness. Therefore, people under the influence of such substances are likely to exhibit personality changes consistent with their particular inferior functions.

The process that occurs when one or more of these preconditions is in effect seems to be the following: The tired, ill, stressed, or drug-altered person becomes careless and ineffective in using his or her usually reliable functions. Perhaps her perception is dulled or his usual good judgment is faulty. So people's normal comfortable orientation to themselves (i.e., their security in their dominant and auxiliary functions) is threatened. It is as if the psyche then says, "This isn't working the way it's supposed to. Let me try a different approach—the most different approach possible. Maybe that will work."

The most different approach possible is likely to be the least familiar, most undeveloped, and unused aspects of personality, which we now recognize as the inferior function (and often the tertiary function as well). For example, if a weary ENFJ supervisor's typical positive and harmonious style is greeted with indifference or negativity from his staff, he may respond harshly and punitively.

Although the conditions for eruption of the inferior include stress, illness, fatigue, and the like, the presence of these conditions does not always activate the inferior. Sometimes the nature of the stress or illness, the degree of fatigue, or the particular context involved, will not immediately produce an inferior function experience. Instead, the response may be an exaggeration of the person's typical problem-solving behavior. But sometimes such exaggeration, especially if the moderating effects of the auxiliary function are absent, may presage an inferior function episode. An ENTP who is becoming stressed may show exaggerated extraverted intuition by frenetically tossing out many ideas while making no attempt to select among them with her auxiliary thinking. As her efforts are met with inevitable frustration, her inferior introverted sensing will take over her personality.

Much of the time, however, people engage in positive and adaptive behavior in response to fatigue and stress. They may do such things as take a break, seek advice, or get a good night's sleep as an effective way of dealing with difficult times. These ways of handling difficult situations seem to be general human responses and cut across all types.

It is difficult to predict just how much stress, fatigue, or illness is enough to stimulate a full-blown inferior function experience. This appears to be highly individual and most likely related to other personality and personal history factors. Type preference itself, however, may influence the frequency and intensity of these experiences. Some types are simply more curious about and tolerant of the mysteries and peculiarities of their psyches, and are more likely to dwell on strange reactions and attempt to figure them out. Often, but by no means always, this occurs with people who prefer intuition. Some sensing types develop an effective way of ignoring their puzzling reactions, as they tend to reject excessive psychological rumination as tiresome and boring. This kind of difference in preference is generally consistent with intuitives' greater attraction to long-term individual psychotherapy; sensing types more often prefer short-term, focused psychotherapeutic approaches.

We may also hypothesize that a person with a well-differentiated dominant function may be less vulnerable to the kind of mild or moderate stress inducers that hook those with poorly differentiated dominants. Insufficient differentiation can put the person in the unfortunate position of switching back and forth between two opposite dominant functions, and therefore between two inferior functions, one or both of which may be activated easily and frequently.

Remember, however, that scores on the MBTI personality inventory do not signify degree of differentiation, nor is such an assumption justified merely because a person habitually experiences more than one form of inferior function. The complexity of type dynamics as played out in different personalities permits a number of possible reasons for a variety of inferior function experiences.

The Nature of the Inferior

The inferior function phenomenon has a number of distinctive feature that are generally associated with the form in which it appears and certain telltale characteristics associated with its activated state. Jung (1976b) described the nature of the inferior in this way:

> The inferior function is always associated with an archaic personality in ourselves; in the inferior function we are all primitives. In our differentiated functions we are civilized and we are supposed to have free will; but there is no such thing as free will

when it comes to the inferior function. There we have an open wound, or at least an open door through which anything might enter. (p. 20)

Clues to the Form

You can get a pretty good idea of what your inferior looks like by reading the description of your opposite type. However, in the grip of your inferior, you don't become a mature, well-functioning opposite type, since your experience and facility with your least preferred functions is relatively limited. So you turn into a rather sorry example of your opposite. Instead of the positive, adaptive character of those qualities when they are developed, there is a negative cast to your "hidden personality." Of course, this is typically not the case when you are purposefully engaging your third and fourth functions or using them in a playful or relaxed fashion.

There are other methods of identifying the form of an individual's inferior function. I often ask people, "What are you like when you are at your worst, when you don't feel like your usual self?" Typically people describe their experience of their inferior function. Another way to identify the inferior is to think about which function fatigues you most when you use it, or which one you are most sensitive about.

Since in Jung's psychology the inferior function is a process rather than a structure, we can describe its form but we cannot specify a content for a particular person. Often, however, the content that accompanies an inferior function episode comes from the person's unconscious, more specifically, from his or her **shadow.**

The inferior and the shadow   Many people confuse the inferior function with the concept of the shadow and use the terms interchangeably (Quenk, 1982). In Jung's system, the shadow is an archetype, one of our innate modes of responding to important universal psychological realities. The shadow personifies those things people would rather not acknowledge about themselves, such as undesirable character traits, weaknesses, fears, or lapses in morality. The shadow is a major component of a person's **personal unconscious,** a layer of the psyche that is more accessible than its much larger counterpart, the collective unconscious.

Although they are not the same concept, the relationship between the inferior function and the shadow is very important. In effect, one's shadow supplies the personal contents that appear when the inferior function is

constellated or evoked. Metaphorically, the inferior function is the skeletal form and the shadow is the flesh that gives it substance and life.

As Jung said in a quotation cited earlier, the inferior function serves as a doorway through which the contents of both the personal and collective unconscious may enter. This can be recognized in the repetitive content "themes" that we experience when we are in the grip of the inferior or when we observe others in this state.

Projection of the inferior   Often the first sign of an activated inferior function is its appearance in the form of a projection. When we project our inferior function onto someone else, we are in effect saying, "I don't have this childish, untrustworthy, and unreliable characteristic. You have it!"

Perhaps to "prepare" for times when we need to project to maintain our psychological balance, people become skilled at identifying their opposite type. Or they may devote much time and energy to pointing out annoying, unacceptable characteristics in a particular person or in a particular "type of person." Often, when a person says, "I can't stand the kind of person who...," the description that follows comes remarkably close to the form of their own inferior function. Even more important, projection is the mechanism underlying our biases about people who have opposite type preferences. For example, it accounts for the arrogance many intuitives direct at sensing types and the disdain many sensing types express toward intuitives. "See how obsessed that guy is with controlling every detail of his business; what a waste of time!" scoffs the intuitive, who, when in the grip, becomes obsessed with irrelevant details. "What a lot of hair-brained, crazy notions she has about what might happen; what a waste of energy!" proclaims the sensing type, who, when in the grip, is overwhelmed by ungrounded possibilities.

Character of the Inferior

There are certain predictable features of the inferior function, regardless of which function it is or the personal history of the individual possessing it. Although the following characteristics may also accompany other psychic manifestations, such as unconscious **complexes**, they often characterize a person's expression of his or her inferior function.

Tunnel vision   An important characteristic of all inferior functions is *tunnel vision*. This is what makes whatever is being experienced real and believable. We can compare this with how we would react to the same thing when we are not in the grip. We think, "How could I have believed that?" or "I must have been blind not to have seen that!" When we focus on a limited piece of reality, what we perceive or conclude may certainly be true, valid, logical, and real. But its import and impact are likely to be out of proportion because all the information that lies outside the tunnel is not available to us. This larger body of data or thought usually tempers the perception or judgment made within the tunnel. The issue on which we focus when in the grip may appropriately be seen as trivial or without substance when viewed in a broader context.

Loss of sense of humor All types generally report losing their sense of humor when in the grip of their inferior. To see anything humorous in our exaggerated, atypical behavior, we would have to be standing outside of it. This is possible when it is a minor episode, but not when it is in its full form. Even if we are aware that we are in the grip, we are usually unable to appreciate the extremity of it. It is therefore generally not a good idea to try to tease people, make light of their reactions, or dismiss their concerns with observations such as, "You're just in the grip of your inferior function."

All-or-none statements The unconscious has a black-and-white notion of the world. It is nondiscriminating; the shades of gray characteristic of conscious and differentiated psychological functioning are absent. When someone starts making categorical, all-or-none statements, chances are the statements come from the person's unconscious. When a person with a feeling preference says, "You always forget to balance the checkbook," or a person with a thinking preference says, "You never say you're sorry!" you are probably hearing from the inferior function or some other aspect of the person's unconscious.

Role of the Inferior in Self-regulation

We know that three of the four functions of consciousness can become differentiated, i.e., conscious, while the other remains connected with the matrix, the unconscious, and is known as the "inferior" function. It is the Achilles' heel of even the most heroic consciousness....(Jung, 1959, p. 237)

Jung believed that the auxiliary and tertiary functions could achieve some degree of differentiation, but was quite clear that it was necessary that the inferior remain outside conscious control. In this form it is able to provide access to the vital contents of the unconscious, the source of growth and development of the personality. Thus, for Jung (1976b) the inferior was a powerful tool of self-regulation, the necessary element that makes our completion possible:

> I do not believe it is humanly possible to differentiate all four functions alike, otherwise we would be perfect like God, and that surely will not happen...we would lose the most precious connection with the unconscious through the inferior function, which is invariably the weakest; only through our feebleness and incapacity are we linked up with the unconscious, with the lower world of the instincts and with our fellow beings. (pp. 97, 98)

Myers was more sanguine than Jung regarding development of the less preferred functions. With her primary focus on conscious adaptation through type development, she seemed to describe the possibility of increasing the degree of conscious control over one's functions and of learning to call them into play at will. Where Jung stressed the compensatory role of the inferior, Myers (1980) gave it a more complementary position in her typological system. She paid considerably less attention than Jung to the inferior as the link to unconscious knowledge and thus to its transformative capability, choosing instead to focus on its ability to offer a new and sometimes useful perspective:

> Because [the less preferred functions] were necessarily neglected while the preferred processes were developed, they are immature and cannot be expected to offer great wisdom....A person can, however, profitably accept them as younger members of the family, who are entitled to speak up in family councils before decisions are made If they are given assignments that use their respective gifts and if their help is appreciated and their contributions seriously considered, they will, like children, grow steadily wiser, and the quality of their contributions will steadily improve. (p. 202)

The compensatory process   If it were possible to make the unconscious inferior conscious, its compensatory role as a safety valve for the psyche would be eliminated. When we are too comfortable and secure in our conscious approach, when we believe that we are fully defined by our dominant and auxiliary processes, or when we are excessive or one sided in any way, we risk overconfidence, rigidity, and stagnation. We need to uncover new information about ourselves or find a different perspective.

This valuable knowledge or perspective may be awaiting access through the inferior function.

The inferior serves as a signaling device in the psyche, warning that something important is out of alignment, in need of attention, or is being misperceived or miscalculated. Sometimes the message is merely that we need to stop doing whatever we are doing, rest, and take a look around. Whatever its impetus, it helps reorient us and provides alternative perspectives and points of view. And it does so in such a forceful and dramatic manner that it cannot be ignored, dismissed, or permanently transferred to someone else (by projection).

Looking at alternative perspectives and new information is often what a psychotherapist does for a client who is locked into a particular way of perceiving or judging and cannot see other options. So we can imagine the inferior as a person's "resident therapist," available to share the broader vision that is possible when unconscious information is accessible to consciousness.

A major consequence of being in the grip of the inferior function is a loss of confidence in what is familiar, valued, or taken for granted. The "flip" into the opposite has shock value—it makes us take a different look at ourselves and acknowledge things we previously ignored or rejected. We sometimes integrate the necessary information into our conscious approach by being chastened: We become more cautious, more self-doubting, and so on. The inferior function experience thus expands consciousness in an adaptive manner.

Avoiding the grip   There are times when we are able to recognize that we are out of sorts or that our perspective is off and we can avoid falling into the grip of our inferior by ignoring or denying it, or by labeling it as just a reaction to stress and fatigue. Do we then miss the opportunity to get new information by avoiding the experience? Or do we simply recognize that we are overreacting because of an altered state and, in a healthy manner, refuse to take the distorted information seriously? Both explanations are possible, but the second probably becomes more prevalent as we grow older and have ample experience of ourselves. We learn to recognize our reactions and develop adaptive ways of dealing with them. If the psyche is truly self-regulating, we can count on any needed new information getting to us sooner or later. Inappropriately avoiding it will serve only as a temporary solution.

The Role of the Tertiary Function

Because the inferior and tertiary are both relatively unconscious, engagement of either one may constellate the other. If an INFP is in the grip of inferior thinking, accusing himself of all manner of incompetencies, his weak tertiary sensing can easily "prove" that even the most minor and routine activity or the simplest directions are beyond his ability. Alternatively (assuming the necessary preconditions), failure or difficulty in performing a sensing task may quickly lead him to generalize his incompetence to all arenas, not just the present task.

Similarly, an ENFP's inferior sensing may emerge as obsessiveness about something someone said to her at work, but if combined with her tertiary thinking, might cause her to reach the illogical conclusion that she will therefore not receive a desired promotion.

The tertiary function influences the expression of the inferior and thus provides additional predictive and explanatory information. This is apparent in comparing manifestations of the inferior in people who have opposite auxiliary (and therefore tertiary) functions. Although there is a fair amount of similarity between ENFPs and ENTPs, or between ISTPs and INTPs, the differences between each pair are very consistently related to their different tertiary functions.

Contribution to Personal
Development and Individuation

Jung (1970a) said that "the 'other' in us always seems alien and unacceptable; but if we let ourselves be aggrieved, the feeling sinks in, and we are the richer for this little bit of self-knowledge" (p. 486).

Von Franz (1971) described the inferior function as slow, touchy, tyrannical, and childish. But she saw the tremendous charge of emotion that accompanies the inferior as providing us with a new potential for life, noting that

> the behavior of the Inferior Function is wonderfully mirrored in those fairy tales where there is the following structure. A king has three sons. He likes the elder sons but the youngest is regarded as a fool. The king then sets a task in which the sons may have to find the water of life, or the most beautiful bride....(p. 8)

What then occurs in this fairy tale scenario is familiar. The king (dominant function) assumes that the two competent older sons (auxiliary and tertiary) will succeed at the task. They try but fail miserably. The youngest son begs to be given a chance. In his foolishness and naïveté, he comes up with an unorthodox but effective solution and thus succeeds where his "betters" have failed. He wins the prize, is recognized as valuable, and takes on a significant role in ruling the kingdom wisely.

Thus, the inexperience and innocence of an inferior function can hold the key to the new awareness necessary for an innovative solution to a work or life problem. Solving the problem—winning the prize—leads to acknowledging the value of one's neglected and unappreciated inferior. As a result, it can take its rightful place in one's life—help to rule the kingdom wisely.

The inferior also appears during important transitional periods in our lives. People report that memorable encounters with their inferiors have often preceded or accompanied significant developmental changes. Moving out of one's childhood home, graduating from college, getting married or divorced, or experiencing the death of a loved one are the kinds of transitional events that people mention.

Sometimes an intense inferior function experience results in a renewed appreciation of parts of ourselves that we have taken for granted. Familiarity with our strengths may lead us to minimize them, thereby not developing them to their fullest potential. We may then start to overvalue our less preferred characteristics and people in whom those qualities are well developed. Ultimately, becoming aware of an unrecognized or unappreciated aspect of oneself releases energy that is then available for constructive growth.

Another way that the inferior broadens our knowledge of ourselves results from its attachment to the less preferred attitude, be it extraversion or introversion. Not only is the opposite, inexperienced function activated; the less preferred attitude is as well. The combination of the two introduces two "alien" factors.

When an extravert is forced to introvert while in the inferior, an uncomfortable situation results, regardless of which function is being introverted. The extravert's typical and natural way of dealing with things—talking to people, asking for advice, taking action, and engaging in some energetic activity—become inaccessible because energy has been transferred from the outer world to the inner world. Perhaps this accounts for the observation that depression is harder on extraverts than it is on introverts in that depression involves turning inward to the intro-verted mode of being. This turning inward is a comfortable arena for introverts, while it is a more alien, uncomfortable one for many extraverts.

Though painful and somewhat alien, new and welcome awareness often results when extraverts seek out or find themselves in an introverted mode. In fact, it is likely that formal meditation techniques are much more helpful to extraverts because they encourage entering and remaining in an intro-verted mode.

For the introvert forced to extravert while in the inferior, the discomfort and sense of losing one's bearings can be equally disruptive. The introvert is less able to keep things inside or reflect in the privacy of his or her own mind. Rather, what would ordinarily stay inside and safe from external scrutiny is inevitably blurted out, acted on, or shared (often with inappro-priate people). This can lead to fear of public humiliation. Operating in the extraverted world for any length of time can feel alien and disconcert-ing to many introverts. On the other hand, extraverting can stimulate many satisfying and positive experiences for introverts, which are similar to those experienced by extraverts when they achieve greater comfort while introverting.

One introvert said that when he becomes stressed, he compulsively seeks people out, engages them in long conversations, or gets involved in various activities with them. Often this leads him to new insights into himself or recognition that things he habitually rejected as irrelevant or unimportant to him were quite the opposite. Similar benefits of being forced into the opposite attitude are reported by extraverts forced into introversion. They are able to recognize their own inner richness and experience an unfamiliar pleasure in solitude.

The Role of the Auxiliary Function

What accounts for the termination of an episode of the inferior function and the subsequent return of equilibrium? Does it require actual restora-tion of balance and correction of one-sidedness, that is, does some message have to be received? People report that the length of time they may spend in the grip of their inferior varies a great deal—from minutes to weeks.

Remember that an inferior function experience creates something like chaos in a personality, altering the prominence of each typological element, energizing aspects that usually have little energy, putting aside usually reliable and trustworthy parts of ourselves. When such an episode has run its course or served its purpose, we somehow return to "normal" and no longer feel and seem "beside ourselves."

Exactly how this happens is difficult to observe precisely, but the process or mechanism whereby equilibrium is achieved seems to occur through constellation or activation of the tertiary and, more directly, the auxiliary function. This process enables the gradual reestablishment of trust and confidence in oneself. The grip of the inferior diminishes through activation first of the tertiary function, then increased energy and attention to the auxiliary function, and finally to reexperiencing the confidence, competence, and centeredness of one's dominant function.

Sometimes we can be astute and observant enough to see this kind of progression from tertiary to auxiliary and, finally, to dominant. More often, however, we notice the auxiliary coming back into play and forming a helpful bridge or link to the dominant form of our personalities. With the dominant and auxiliary functions restored to their former ascendance, our essential character structure is back in control and able to function effectively.

Importance of Midlife

Victor Hugo (1988) wrote that "forty is the old age of youth; fifty the youth of old age." Hugo's observation underscores the importance of our forties as a transitional decade often aptly distinguished by a "midlife crisis." As a decade of transformation, it can be both enhancing and destructive in causing people to come to terms with the neglected aspects of their psyche. The often frequent eruptions of the inferior that occur during midlife can provide the crucial awareness necessary for our transition from the follies of youth to the wise acceptance of old age.

We spend the first half of our lives establishing our identity in two important areas—love and work. We appropriately need awareness, control, and consciousness to succeed in these two worlds. Thus, competence at this point in our lives is best achieved by using our most conscious and developed processes, our dominant and auxiliary functions.

Assuming adequate success in the tasks of the first half of life, the goal of midlife and beyond is completion of one's personality. We strive to become the best and most complete version of ourselves possible. So in the natural scheme of things and without conscious effort, we find the neglected, undeveloped sides of ourselves increasingly compelling. Previously unimportant and uninteresting things become appealing in ways unimagined during the first half of life.

In typological terms, those things that were unimportant, uninteresting, or unvalued in the first half of life are embodied in the inferior and tertiary functions. Accordingly, people consistently report that beginning around middle age, they find themselves attracted to pursuits requiring their least preferred processes. Previously unappealing things become a source of excitement, renewal, and relaxation. Sometimes older or retiring people develop a new career based on a former hobby that may have involved less preferred processes.

Von Franz (1971) described incorporation of the inferior as follows:

> To the general outline of the inferior function belongs the fact that it is generally slow, in contrast to the superior function....If you think of the turning point of life and the problems of aging and of turning within, then this slowing down of the whole life process by bringing in the inferior function is just the thing which is needed. So the slowness should not be treated with impatience;...one should rather accept the fact that in this realm one has to waste time. (p. 8)

However, some older people do not appear to follow this path. They do not mellow as they get older by gradually integrating their tertiary and inferior functions. Rather, this second group of older people become more rigidly committed to their dominant and auxiliary processes, which they use in an exaggerated and extreme manner.

Slowly integrating previously neglected functions furthers the task of wholeness and individuation. Stubborn adherence to the consciously developed processes appropriate to the tasks of early adulthood seems to impede progress toward that goal. Older people in this position may look like caricatures of their type. Even well-developed perception and judgment can be maladaptive when applied compulsively and exclusively.

People with different personality types show consistent patterns of development within their type. Careful study reveals the influence of their tertiary and inferior functions as they contribute to completion of personality and the individuation process. However, as is true in so many arenas, the ways in which different types approach the task of integrating formerly ignored aspects of themselves can differ greatly. Some, most notably those who prefer intuition and a perceiving attitude (NP types), enjoy the natural unfolding of their midlife development. They have little desire to actively direct it, preferring instead to experience the surprise associated with discovering yet another new aspect of themselves. Others, often (but by no means always) those who prefer sensing and a judging attitude (SJ types), may take an active part in developing previously neglected parts of themselves. Their tendency to seek out information and methods for stimulating their own midlife development is characteristic of their predominantly experiential and pragmatic approach to life tasks.

PART 2

The Hidden Personality in Action

•

CHAPTER 5

Approaching the Hidden Personality
of the Sixteen Types

THIS CHAPTER PROVIDES A brief description of the areas covered in Chapters 6 through 13, which are devoted to each dominant type. These eight chapters each present a dominant function with its preferred attitude and two opposite auxiliary functions. Because this orientation gives the rationale for the subsections in the type chapters, it is important that you read it before reading any one of the next eight chapters.

The chapters on each dominant function cover six topics relevant to the inferior function. The brief discussions of these areas in this chapter, which are described below, summarize and expand on the discussions in Chapter 4.

The Dominant Function
Versus the Inferior Function

This section contrasts effective use of the dominant function of the type in question with effective use of the dominant function of the opposite type (e.g., extraverted thinking types will be compared with introverted feeling types). This information is divided into two subsections: "Important Features of the Dominant Function" and "Important Features of the Opposite Type's Dominant."

Important Features of the Dominant Function

A brief type description will highlight qualities of the dominant function that will be important to our understanding of its inferior manifestations.

It will also help us contrast the typical behavior of people who have a particular type with their behavior when in the grip of the inferior function.

Important Features of the Opposite Type's Dominant

I list three qualities associated with the dominant of the opposite type that are relevant to a prediction of its form as an inferior function. They will alert you to my later descriptions of these same features in their inferior form. For example, the three qualities of dominant introverted feeling are listed in the chapter that presents extraverted thinking types. I include suggestions for reviewing the characteristics of people with the dominant of the opposite type, referring the reader to other relevant discussions in this book. The review will provide the background needed to explore the various ways in which the inferior function is expressed for the types in question.

Everyday Manifestations of the Inferior Function

The influence of the inferior can be seen in two areas of everyday behavior. They are: (a) typical sensitivities and (b) projections.

Typical Sensitivities and Projections

Our least preferred, inferior process influences us even when we are not in its grip. This section centers on the two ways that the inferior affects our everyday lives.

Typical sensitivities   We tend to lack confidence in areas where we are inexperienced. When we are forced to use our least developed function or other neglected parts of ourselves, we are uncomfortable, insecure, nervous, and vulnerable. Von Franz (1971) made the observation that

> people are very easily influenced when it is a question of their inferior function. Since it is in the unconscious, they can easily be made uncertain of their position, whereas in the realm of their superior function they generally know how to act when attacked....As soon as you feel strong you are quite willing to discuss things or to change your attitude, but where you feel inferior you get fanatical and touchy and are easily influenced. The expression on a friend's face can affect the feeling of a

thinking type because his feeling is unconscious and therefore open to influence. (p. 53)

The particular sensitivities of each type are consistent and predictable. Clues to these sensitivities are presented in each of the next eight chapters.

Typical projections Each type projects the inferior function in characteristic ways. Remember that projection involves attributing to others our own unacknowledged and unconscious qualities. Because inferior function episodes often involve projection, this information is helpful in becoming aware of one's own and others' impending "altered states." This section identifies typical projections of the type being described.

Expressions Through Interests and Hobbies

Exercising an unfamiliar process can be relaxing and enjoyable, especially when one's competence is not an issue of concern. If we need a break from using our dominant and auxiliary functions, a hobby using our inferior or tertiary may be just the right thing.

This section identifies some of the ways people of each type engage their inferior and tertiary functions for rest, relaxation, and recreation.

Eruptions of the Inferior

The two subsections included here introduce the type-related circumstances that tend to provoke inferior function reactions and the form in which the inferior function of the type is manifested.

Typical Provocations or Triggers

Chapter 4 described the general conditions for eruption of the inferior function for all types. This section deals with some typical type-related situations, events, or contexts that provoke or trigger the experience. As we might expect, these often involve having to use one's less preferred processes or being around people or in situations where those processes predominate. Keep in mind, however, that what provokes the experience may be highly individual and the effectiveness of the triggers described depends on the person's vulnerability at the time.

The Form of the Inferior

In Chapter 3, I mentioned that each inferior function has a predictable form. The form of the inferior roughly corresponds to the particular qualities associated with that function when it is a dominant function— but with a negative, primitive, and undifferentiated cast to it. The three salient qualities listed under "Important Features of the Opposite Type" are listed again but in their negative, inferior form. A table then compares the three features in their dominant and inferior forms. This table is followed by descriptions and brief examples of each of the three forms of the inferior.

Grip Experiences

This section consists of stories about people's experiences of their inferior function. In addition to striking variations in their essential nature, the examples provided by the eight dominant types reveal some basic type differences. These influence the style, length, and number of different elements that appear in their stories. For this reason, the number of stories needed to illustrate various aspects of the inferior varies from chapter to chapter. Some chapter stories are brief and focus primarily on one expression of the inferior. Others are more complex, illustrating the interactions of all three salient features in one experience.

Where the information was available, I have included the individual's assessment of the importance of the experience in their awareness of themselves and how they conduct their lives. Often, however, the value of inferior function episodes is not immediately apparent. For some people, the experiences are too unpleasant and painful to think about. For others, such awareness comes later, sometimes in conjunction with other similar episodes.

Return of Equilibrium

An inferior function experience cannot fulfill its self-regulating purpose if we deny it, reject it, or try to get rid of it. Yet we often resort to such "solutions" because we feel uncomfortable, anxious, embarrassed, or perplexed by our out-of-character behavior. However, the dynamics of the inferior function suggest that most episodes come to an end naturally, regardless of whether we profit from them. Once constellated, a natural progression occurs that ends in a return to our natural equilibrium. This progression seems to move from the inferior to the tertiary to the auxiliary and, finally, back to the dominant function.

People who have the same inferior function report consistencies in how their return to equilibrium occurs. This section describes typical ways people extricate from their out-of-character selves, as well as the helpful or detrimental things others may do to contribute to their return to equilibrium.

Expressions in Midlife

Jung put a heavy emphasis on the developmental tasks associated with the second half of life. Remember that the chief task of adulthood is to establish oneself in work or career and in significant relationships. We therefore rely heavily on our dominant and auxiliary during our young adult years. Our later years are accompanied by a natural movement toward completion or wholeness, which occurs through attention to and gradual integration of our tertiary and inferior functions.

Whether the ideal and the real are congruent, however, varies widely among older people. As described in Chapter 4, some aging individuals appear to become stuck in their type, with increasing exaggeration and rigidity of their dominant and auxiliary functions accompanied by strong resistance to even minimum inclusion of their tertiary and inferior functions.

Older people whose natural development permits incorporation of previously neglected functions seem to mellow in the expression of their personalities. Previously ignored aspects of life are added; formerly crucial goals and behaviors become less compelling. The subordinate tertiary and inferior processes are thus added to the personality; they do not replace or in any way supersede the developed dominant and auxiliary processes.

This section describes ways of responding to the aging period as it is manifested in individuals of that type.

Summary

The last section of each chapter gives a brief summary of the form of the inferior, how equilibrium is regained, and the kinds of new information typically acquired through the experience. A table summarizing the major features of that type's inferior function experience lists the typical triggers, forms, and new knowledge gained.

Some Cautions and Caveats

Here are a few cautions and caveats to keep in mind when reading the next eight chapters, especially the ones that discuss your own type and the types of people closest to you.

"I Don't Relate to Any of These!"

Some people don't find themselves in the description of their inferior, or for that matter in any of the eight inferiors. Sometimes these are well-functioning people for whom psychological type is not the most helpful or salient set of personality descriptors. Sometimes they are individuals with psychological difficulties that inhibit recognition and expression of their type. For such people, type is but one aspect of personality that remains unclear and undifferentiated. For a discussion of this and related issues, see N. L. Quenk, (1984, 1985b) and A. T. Quenk (1985).

Other people clearly identify with one of the sixteen types but don't experience any of the inferior functions with notable frequency or intensity. Again, their particular mode of adaptation or developmental path may be outside of this system of explanation. Still other individuals may experience the identified inferior but in an unusual manner. They may not recognize their expression of the inferior in the descriptions provided. All of these variations on the theme add to the already rich diversity of individual differences.

"I Experience All of Them!"

Other people find themselves well described by two or more inferiors that are manifested either together or equally frequently. There are several possible explanations for this. For one thing, it is fairly common to experience negative expressions of one's tertiary as well as one's inferior, often at the same time. And those people who have a conflict between their dominant and inferior functions (i.e., where both use an equal share of the available energy) may concurrently or alternately experience both as inferior functions. (For a discussion of the latter, see N. L. Quenk, 1985a.)

Bear in mind also that the inferior function is the doorway to the unconscious and all its contents. Once opened, a wide variety of unpleasant and undesirable "stuff" may emerge. This is one major source of the confusion, distress, and distraction we experience when we are not ourselves. We are faced with all kinds of repressed, neglected, and otherwise unfamiliar parts of ourselves.

You may also find in reading about your own type that some things are very true for you, while others simply don't apply. This is to be expected when we are describing individuality. It is the same with general type descriptions. Some aspects of our type are simply more salient than others.

Reality and the Inferior

There is no necessary relationship between being in the grip of your inferior function and the reality of your perceptions or judgments at the time. The two are often independent of each other. So if you are in the grip of an inferior whose form focuses on incompetence, the particular incompetence you notice may actually be there! You or some other person might in fact have made a mistake or performed some task in an inadequate manner.

It is in the reaction to the error that the operation of the inferior can be identified. We will see an overreaction, a single-minded focus, a high level of emotion, and a readiness to generalize and expand single incidents into global or eternal "truths." When these kinds of responses occur, we are likely to be experiencing or witnessing the state of being "beside oneself."

The reality of other kinds of responses may be somewhat different, however. An example is a situation where a headache triggers obsessive concern that one has a brain tumor. The headache is real; the conclusion regarding the brain tumor is likely to be unfounded. However, there may be a different "truth" embodied in this kind of inferior function manifestation. Perhaps the person's readiness to imagine a life-threatening illness portends an underlying distress or despair with some current life situation.

An astute person might examine the possible roots of the overreaction and then reassess important relationships, career goals, or the like.

Reading the Next Eight Chapters

Many readers will start with the chapter about their own type. Others may read the chapters in the order they appear, beginning with extraverted thinking types and ending with extraverted intuitives. Whichever method you choose, I hope your reading will be as satisfying and enlightening as writing the chapters was for me in my understanding of myself and others.

CHAPTER 6
Extraverted Thinking Types
ESTJ and ENTJ

BASIC TYPE DYNAMICS
....

Dominant extraverted thinking

Auxiliary introverted sensing or intuition

Tertiary intuition or sensing

Inferior introverted feeling
....

Extraverted Thinking
Versus Introverted Feeling

THIS CHAPTER EXAMINES THE way effective extraverted thinking types experience their inferior function, and the temporary transformation they make into ineffective, inferior introverted feeling types when they are "in the grip." The following review of the characteristics of extraverted thinking and introverted feeling will be helpful to our discussion.

Important Features of Dominant Extraverted Thinking

Extraverted thinkers enjoy making decisions. They like to be in control of things and value efficient and effective decision making. They are comfortable in leadership positions and readily accept responsibility for making things happen. They want things to be logical, so they require rationality in most situations. They expect goals to be reached in a competent manner and they want to be recognized for their own accomplishments. Being respected is therefore of greater importance to them than being liked.

Critiquing comes naturally to them, and they often solicit constructive criticism of their own work from trusted colleagues. However, they do not appreciate critical comments about their personal qualities, critiques that are personal attacks on their competence or integrity, or unsolicited criticism by people they don't know or respect. They are seen by others and see themselves as having rigorous standards that typically take precedence over both their own and others' personal needs. Their communication style is honest, direct, and to the point, and they prefer others to be similarly candid with them.

With their dominant focus on truth, accuracy, and productivity, extraverted thinkers can be seen as one-sided in their commitment to work. The high value ESTJs and ENTJs place on critical analysis, competence, and forthright communication may foster a perception that they don't care about people. Others are therefore often surprised to discover that extraverted thinkers are typically quite devoted to family and friends. They energetically strive to ensure the well-being and happiness of their loved ones.

ESTJs and ENTJs are adept at dealing with crisis situations that don't engage their inferior function. They readily take charge, organize people for effective action, and communicate a sense of calm, security, and confidence.

Important Features of Dominant Introverted Feeling

The qualities associated with introverted feeling that are relevant to our discussion of its form as an inferior function are an emphasis on:

- Inner harmony
- Economy of emotional expression
- Acceptance of feeling as nonlogical

For a detailed description of dominant introverted feeling, read the beginning of Chapter 7, "Introverted Feeling Types: ISFP and INFP," and the type descriptions for ISFP and INFP that appear in Appendix A. This will provide you with the background needed to explore the various ways in which inferior introverted feeling is expressed in ESTJs and ENTJs.

The Everyday Introverted Feeling of Extraverted Thinking Types

The inferior function affects extraverted thinkers in several different ways. These include everyday sensitivities, projections, and ways of relaxing, as well as the dramatic manifestations that can be seen when the inferior erupts and a full-blown episode occurs.

Typical Sensitivities and Projections

When feeling types talk about things they care about—their feeling values—they may feel and express an emotion. For introverted feeling types, the emotion may be somewhat muted, but it is still clearly important in their decision making. Extraverted thinkers may not differentiate between feeling as a judging process and a feeling type's use of emotion. They may therefore confuse the use of feeling for rational decision making with sentimentality and emotionality. They thus reveal and illustrate their experience of their own inferior feeling.

With the all-or-none quality of a largely unconscious process, ESTJs and ENTJs may express seemingly excessive emotion in response to sad movies or true stories about pain and suffering. "I get all choked up by those really sentimental greeting cards," said one ENTJ, "and it feels out of control, overly sentimental, and illogical. I want sad stories to have a happy ending, even if it isn't true to life."

Extraverted thinkers may see feeling types as overly sensitive to criticism and as needing frequent reassurance about themselves. They may be dubious about the actual effectiveness of these people, fearing that their judgment may be faulty or that their emotions will inappropriately influence their decisions. Since they distrust their own judgment when emotion rules them, they assume the same unreliability is true for dominant feeling types.

ESTJs and ENTJs report being quite uncomfortable with their own and others' feeling judgment. "It seems mushy and chaotic and scary; not crisp and precise like thinking," said one ENTJ. An ESTJ described her uneasiness about expressing appreciation or complimenting others verbally: "I never know how much is appropriate. It always feels gushy." She found writing thank you notes to be much more satisfying to her as well as to the recipients, who recognized the genuine depth of her feelings.

Because their complete opposites, introverted feeling types, are so hard to "read," extraverted thinkers may react more to extraverted feeling types who readily express their dominant feeling. They tend to see people who readily express feeling as excessive, phony, and manipulative. When they are around introverted feeling types, they may feel off balance, needing to "walk on eggshells," and afraid of being misunderstood or of unintentionally offending the person. But more often they may ignore introverted feeling types because they don't express themselves directly. As we will see, the sensitivities of extraverted thinking types toward both of the dominant feeling types are reflected in the expression of their own inferior feeling.

Expressions Through Interests and Hobbies

The introverted feeling values of extraverted thinking types may be seen in their intense passion for a particular cause. This may take the form of tireless devotion to a civic cause such as prevention of child abuse, aid to the homeless, or some church or community activity. The extraverted thinker is likely to contribute to the chosen arena by doing what he or she loves most, that is, providing effective leadership and constructive critical judgment.

A similar expression may occur in the religious and spiritual realm, or in the kind of music, art, and literature they prefer. These areas may play to their more romantic, dramatic, and emotive sensibilities, giving free reign to their other, typically unexpressed side. Here again, ESTJs and ENTJs may not only gain aesthetic pleasure but often also contribute time and energy to the organizations that are affiliated with the music, art, and literature. They may chair a philanthropic board, manage fund-raising projects, and the like. Sometimes their contribution makes use of the special talents of their dominant function as well as engages their inferior feeling function in a gratifying way. Often the most meaningful hobbies serve this kind of dual purpose. As one ESTJ explained, "The volunteer work itself is very enjoyable. I like being able to contribute what I know. But the sense of community, the connectedness with others on something larger than any one of us, is even more important."

Like other extraverted types, extraverted thinkers can find excessive solitary time unpleasant. One ENTJ reported that she tends to feel sad and lonely when she spends too much time alone. Her hobbies of sewing, quilting, and other craft activities alleviate her negative reactions to being alone. For her, tertiary sensing may moderate the negativity of inferior introverted feeling.

Many extraverted thinking types report that they don't have outside interests and hobbies, that their work is their passion, and that working provides them with their greatest pleasure. The husband of one ESTJ worried that his wife might never retire. The only way he could get her to go on vacation was by planning such exciting trips that she couldn't possibly refuse to participate in them.

In spite of this, however, some extraverted thinkers identify specific activities or times when things other than work hold a special appeal. One ENTJ reported that she sometimes gives herself permission to be entirely unrestrained, often when she is dancing. She plans to be spontaneous when she dances and does so with great expression and abandon.

Eruptions of Inferior Introverted Feeling

When one or more of the preconditions for an eruption of the inferior function are present, introverted feeling appears in its more exaggerated and disruptive form. In addition to the general conditions described in Chapter 4, extraverted thinkers are vulnerable to the type-specific factors described below.

Typical Provocations or Triggers

Like their dominant introverted thinking counterparts, extraverted thinking types tend to be quite selective in the choice of areas in which they invest their feeling. They are intensely passionate about only a few things. So when one of their cherished values is disregarded, ignored, or unappreciated, their inferior feeling is likely to be constellated.

One ESTJ who felt type was very useful in understanding people purposely omitted his type on his evaluation of a type conference, only to be told that his evaluation would not be counted without his type on it. He had not indicated his type on the evaluation because he had felt in the past that his opinions were ignored because of the reputation ESTJs have for being "critical." He lashed out at the evaluator and was immediately embarrassed. Later, in recounting the incident to friends, he explained that he felt discounted, dismissed, and ignored: "It's as if they were telling me that my strong commitments were worthless simply because of my type."

Accusations of coldness and lack of concern for others can serve as a trigger for the inferior function, as can fears of having been excessively harsh with someone. A spouse bursting into tears, or other expressions of strong emotion from people they care about, can also set the stage for an eruption of inferior introverted feeling.

The Form of the Inferior

One of the manifestations of any inferior function is diminished effectiveness in the use of the developed dominant function. For extraverted thinkers, there may be a loss of ability to think logically and take effective action, or an inability to recognize the relevance of logic in a situation. One ESTJ said, "I bounce from task to task with no results. I have internal arguments with myself, but I can't come to any conclusion." And an ENTJ observed, "The feeling that I am unappreciated becomes the central thing, and I can't consider anything else."

Others report being unable to think, having tunnel vision, and being easily fatigued at work. What they normally do very easily requires great effort. An ESTJ described being unable to organize the structure for a work assignment. An ENTJ felt powerless to influence future events significantly. Another reported that when under great stress, he would lose the capacity for verbal expression and would have difficulty getting his words out. In general, there is an uncharacteristic reduction in productive work accompanied by a feeling of failure.

In the initial stages of the process, ESTJs may lose access to their auxiliary sensing, while ENTJs may lose access to their auxiliary intuition. They seem to function only "from the neck up," operating entirely out of their heads. This results in an exaggeration of their thinking, which they and others experience as the excesses of their natural approach. It is an example of how a dominant process operates without the balancing effects of the auxiliary.

As dominant and auxiliary functions continue to recede into the background, the qualities of inferior introverted feeling become manifested in hypersensitivity to inner states, outbursts of emotion, and a fear

TABLE 3 **Dominant Versus Inferior Introverted Feeling**

	Qualities Associated With Introverted Feeling
As Dominant Function	Inner harmony
	Economy of emotional expression
	Acceptance of feeling as nonlogical
As Inferior Function	Hypersensitivity to inner states
	Outbursts of emotion
	Fear of feeling

of feeling. The comparison between dominant and inferior introverted feeling is shown above in Table 3.

Von Franz (1971) captures all three aspects of inferior introverted feeling in the following statement:

> The hidden introverted feeling of the extraverted thinking type establishes strong invisible loyalties. Such people are among the most faithful of all friends, even though they may only write at Christmas. They are absolutely faithful in their feelings, but one has to move towards it to get to know of its existence....[But] unconscious and undeveloped feeling is barbaric and absolute, and therefore sometimes hidden destructive fanaticism suddenly bursts out of the extraverted thinking type. (p. 40)

Hypersensitivity to inner states Effective dominant introverted feeling types use a finely developed awareness of their inner values as a reliable guide for judging themselves and others. In the grip of inferior introverted feeling, extraverted thinkers become hypersensitive to their own and others' emotions, often misinterpreting comments from others as personal criticism. In their dominant approach, they typically interpret objectively offered criticism by respected colleagues as an appropriate means to promote excellence. In the grip of their inferior introverted feeling, they may easily take offense and overreact to such criticism. Unaware of the extraverted thinker's vulnerable "altered" condition, however, colleagues, family members, and friends may communicate criticism as directly as usual. Even mild negative comments may provoke hurt feelings when the extraverted thinker is in this state. ESTJs and ENTJs report having difficulty acknowledging that their feelings have been hurt, even to themselves, but particularly to the person who has helped bring about the hurt feelings. They may lash out at others instead, as the examples below illustrate.

"I feel that I am being criticized unfairly," said an ESTJ. "I blame others for my own faults and find fault with others over nothing. I become demanding because I am in a panic about possibly missing deadlines. I watch the clock. I think lots of negative thoughts, put myself down, and feel that others dislike and reject me. My self-esteem about my abilities gets lower and lower." Note the illogical progression of his thoughts.

"I think I'm pretty confident about my abilities as a trainer," said an ENTJ. "But when I've worked very hard preparing for a training session and am especially tired out, I am plagued with the thought that the trainees don't like me, that they like my colleagues better, especially if the colleague I'm teaching with is a feeling type."

Another ENTJ described "feeling like a victim, persecuted, unappreciated, and used. I don't see things clearly and I can't seem to think. I take things personally and am hypersensitive. I will say something without thinking, then become defensive and feel threatened."

An ESTJ made this observation: "I find myself taking a martyr role, alone and unloved, totally unappreciated. Then I shut down." An ENTJ described being "particularly sensitive to any signs of being excluded from important roles. When that happens, I feel that my contributions are not being valued."

In a variation of this theme, some ESTJs and ENTJs describe situations where they effectively apply their usual action-oriented, logical problem solving. But later (perhaps even years later), if they are in a vulnerable state, they will recall a specific incident and beat themselves up for not being conscious of other people's feelings. One ESTJ recalled thinking, "Why did I say that to Ellen at that party five years ago? How stupid and insensitive of me!"

Some extraverted thinkers are painfully aware of the dilemma they face in dealing with relationship issues within a task-oriented setting. Focusing on others' feelings inhibits their ability to take effective thinking action, though it prevents negative feedback from others about their lack of caring concern.

Outbursts of emotion Effective dominant introverted feeling types show an economy of emotional expression. They are typically quite selective and discriminating in revealing their deepest and most cherished values and feelings. Extraverted thinking types in the grip of inferior introverted feeling lack control and discrimination when expressing their inner emotional states. However, their fear of having others witness their rejected, irrational selves strongly motivates them to stay in control if at all possible. They especially worry about losing control in public, particularly at work. Avoiding a public display often results in an even stronger outburst of affect at home, directed at family members, since the emotions have to be released somewhere.

An ENTJ said, "I feel lost and out of control. I know I am not myself, but I can't help it. I don't want company or to be touched. I want to be left alone and I want to escape."

"I will get a headache or shoulder ache and feel really tense. I feel like crying but try to hide it. I hide my feelings inside and push them down, and then become angry, depressed, and withdrawn," recalled an ESTJ.

Both ESTJs and ENTJs report sometimes feeling suddenly tearful for no apparent reason, and crying in private. However, if the worst happens and they lose control, they may explode in public. This may begin as expressions of intense anger about others' incompetence but quickly evolve into tearful recriminations about a lack of appreciation and recognition.

In recalling one such incident, an ESTJ said, "I am normally not an emotional person, at least I don't show my emotions. I am a very steady person externally. My outburst was quite unlike me."

An ENTJ minister worked hard over a period of five years and saw his church grow from a few hundred members to more than a thousand parishioners. Throughout this stressful time he managed all facets of his work calmly and effectively. But one day at a church board meeting, he broke down sobbing, lost all control, and was unable to function in his job. It took him several months to recover completely, during which time his grateful and concerned church officials carried on his work for him.

Extraverted thinkers may be on shaky ground in situations that call for expressions of feeling. One ESTJ described her difficulty with intimate relationships in this way: "I'm normally gregarious and outgoing with people. But if I get into a one-on-one relationship that's significant, especially romantically, I can't express what I feel or what I'm experiencing. Eventually, I blurt out some really exaggerated emotion at exactly the wrong time. I feel childish and silly and don't want to ever do that again."

Fear of feeling Talking about innermost values, feelings, and concerns is quite difficult even for dominant introverted feeling types. Jung (1976a) observed that "the very fact that thoughts can generally be expressed more intelligibly than feelings demands a more than ordinary descriptive or artistic ability before the real wealth of this feeling can be even approximately presented or communicated to the world" (p. 388).

Effective dominant introverted feeling types accept the nuances of feeling they experience as natural and welcome evidence of their own inner complexity. But feelings and emotions intruding into the consciousness of an extraverted thinker who is in the grip of inferior introverted feeling are experienced as so alien and overwhelming that they are inexpressible. From a thinking point of view, the eruption of "illogical," uncontrolled, and disorderly feelings is like being at the mercy of strange and overwhelming forces that threaten a person's equilibrium, if not whole existence. As a result, extraverted thinkers are rarely able to communicate their distress to others, often maintaining their typical controlled demeanor while fearing that they will lose control of their emotions. In extreme instances, they may be terrified that they are going crazy.

To fend off the feared result, initial attempts involve maintaining cool and detached effectiveness and objectivity. Casual observers will not detect the intense inner battle for control. More careful observation, however, may reveal uncharacteristic silence, withdrawal, moodiness, or flat and depressed affect. An ESTJ described feeling "a swirling in the pit of my stomach and a desperate attempt to figure out why and to define my reaction logically."

Because the extraverted thinker has few resources for communicating what is going on inside, potential helpers may remain largely unaware of any distress, even when the person is in serious trouble. The despair, sense of isolation, and feeling of worthlessness may become so extreme that the person may become severely depressed, sometimes requiring medication or hospitalization. Acquaintances and colleagues may be surprised to learn that such an episode has occurred because until final control is lost, the ESTJ or ENTJ may appear fairly "normal." This manifestation of the inferior is an exaggeration of the dominant introverted feeling type's "economy of emotional expression."

Two extraverted thinkers described their experiences with their inferior functions in these ways after their episodes had run their course:

"I became overly sensitive and tried to cover it with biting sarcasm. My energy was focused inside and I felt shaky. I wanted to be alone. I put on a front of being a strong soldier, but it was really only a protective shell to hide my vulnerability."

"I was different in being very negative. Everything appeared bleak. I was disoriented and aggressive. I talked to myself more. I got emotional—angry or sad, tearful or despondent. In very bad cases, I even contemplated suicide."

Grip Experiences

The stories included in this section illustrate one or more forms of inferior introverted feeling as experienced by ESTJs and ENTJs. These types report that significant or long-lasting experiences of the inferior are rare. They tend to be reluctant to recognize and acknowledge them unless they appear in an extreme form, and they prefer to interpret them within a logical framework.

"You Won't Have Me to Kick Around Anymore!"

Dr. Wong, an ENTJ university professor, had once again obligated himself to too many professional and civic projects. One of them was conducting an evening seminar for graduate students. Throughout the semester, the students often complained to him about his overbearing and officious lecture style. They requested a more collegial, participative approach. Dr. Wong listened dispassionately to these requests but did little to accommodate the students.

Finally, in protest, the students boycotted the seminar and for two weeks in a row no student showed up. Incensed and hurt, Dr. Wong wrote a memo to each student berating each personally for a lack of gratitude for his hard work, what he was giving up to teach, and gross insensitivity to his needs. He further informed them that he was resigning his faculty position because of their vicious attack on him and would no longer be available as a victim of their immature and petty nastiness.

After a week of fuming, during which time he discussed the incident with colleagues, he realized that he had overreacted, wrote a brief note of apology to the students, and reconvened the seminar for the next week. "I learned a lot about the logic of emotion from that episode," he said. "I was really able to understand how the students experienced my style. I realized that they wanted a more collegial relationship *because* they respected me. We were able to talk directly and honestly to each other at the next seminar, which was probably the best we'd ever had."

"How Do I Love Thee..."

The loss of important relationships often triggers an inferior function response, as the next story illustrates. After thirty years of marriage, Mike's wife Alicia, an ISFP, insisted they get a divorce. She told Mike, an ESTJ, that although she loved and admired him, she had also put up with too many years of emotional coldness from him.

Mike became flooded with strong and disturbing feelings. He wrote gushingly sentimental poetry and love letters to Alicia extolling her virtues and the spiritual nature of their relationship. He frequently cried and begged her to change her mind. She became so concerned about his out-of-character reaction that she made an appointment for both of them with a marital therapist to "help him deal with the divorce."

When he had calmed down from his initial extreme reaction, Mike recognized that his responses were quite out of character. But his experience of intense despair and isolation allowed him to empathize with Alicia's reactions to his habitual coldness. The couple reached a mutual decision to divorce, but afterwards were able to enjoy each other's company and their shared memories for the first time in many years.

"A Time to Weep"

Jenny's company was in great upheaval; they were undergoing a major reorganization and had had several takeover threats from other companies. Employees were worried, demoralized, and increasingly ineffective. As an ESTJ high-level manager, Jenny was responsible for holding everything together, making efficient management decisions, and confronting the fears of everyone who worked under her.

To anyone observing her, Jenny dealt with this difficult situation with cool detachment and efficient determination. She was able to calm others down, suggest practical alternatives to people who felt stuck in negativity, and provide support for her management colleagues as they too took on the stress of the situation.

But when Jenny left work every afternoon and entered her car to drive home, she would burst into tears and weep for the entire half-hour drive. She was unable to control her reaction no matter how hard she tried. After several months with no hope of significant improvement in her work stress, she acknowledged to herself just how devastated she was by the distress around her. After careful investigation of alternatives, she sought and accepted a position with another company.

Her decision turned out well for her. Reflecting on her reaction to stress at her other job, she said, "I'm being more careful to acknowledge my feelings, at least to myself. Though this job can become pretty stressful, too, I think I can avoid getting into the extreme state I was in before."

"But the Audience Never Knew It"

Frank, an ENTJ, related the following incident:

> My boss asked me to do a presentation about volunteerism for his church congregation. I would be the guest speaker they often scheduled between the two church services. I was under great time pressure on a number of work tasks and was somewhat uneasy because I perceived this church audience as quite judgmental. But I was secure in my knowledge of my material and wished to accommodate my boss, so I agreed to do it.

> About three minutes into my talk, I noticed a man in the third row, who many years ago had been extremely critical of me, causing me great distress at a particularly difficult period of my life. I immediately felt out of control internally and feared that I would be unable to go on. But the audience never knew it. I was on automatic pilot for the rest of the time.

> A friend who was sitting in the front row later told me that my only indication of discomfort was that I turned beet red for a few minutes, but my voice did not waver at all.

Frank reported being so shaken by his exaggerated emotional reaction that he had to think about the meaning of the man's criticism of him. He discovered a connection between that incident and one that occurred during his grade school years. This awareness helped Frank understand other puzzling feelings he had experienced over the years. In the end, he was pleased and energized by his insight.

"It Was a Lovely Wedding..."

Margo's son Andy, an INFP, was getting married. Andy and his fiancée, Sue, an ESFP, wanted their large wedding to be very special and meaningful. The couple took great care in selecting invitations, music, decorations, food, guests, and entertainment. Every aspect of their celebration was to have significance. Margo knew that it was especially important to Andy and Sue that their families, and especially their mothers, be fully involved in the event. Sue's family was delighted and readily threw themselves into the spirit of things. But Margo, an ENTJ, was rather beside herself.

"I felt like I was in a foreign country," she said later. "I felt inept, awkward, unable to tell what was important and what I was supposed to do. It was so alien. Most everyone else seemed excited and in tune with all the preparations, and that made me feel even more out of touch. Yet I very much wanted to please Andy, knowing how important it was to him. Now I understand why I eloped when I got married. It let me avoid dealing with this kind of thing!"

In spite of her discomfort, Margo persevered and the wedding came off beautifully. At the actual event, she was able to relax and enjoy herself and the fruits of everyone's labors. "I'd rather not have to go through this again," she said, "but if I do at least I will have learned from this experience that I'm not as bad at it as I first thought, and it can be fun once you get into it!"

"A Peaceful End to a Long Life"

Most of the time, the beneficial effects of the inferior function come after a painful grip experience, but here is an example of how one ESTJ drew on her positive feeling and intuition in a crisis situation.

Lorna's grandmother was a strong and determined woman who had almost single-handedly raised her large family, brought them from poverty to security, and gained the admiration and respect of her community. As family matriarch, however, she was also critical, domineering, and controlling. Lorna, an ESTJ, had always had a difficult relationship with her and disliked many things about her.

At the age of ninety-five, Lorna's grandmother had a stroke and was hospitalized. One day the family was told that she had taken a turn for the worse, so they all gathered at her bedside. No one knew whether she was conscious or could understand anything that was said to her. Lorna recalled: "Suddenly, I knew I should reach out, take her hand, and tell her what she had meant to me thoughout her life—the good things. I told her all my positive memories of her, not knowing whether she heard or understood. When I stopped, she began to cry. During the days that followed, everyone in the family talked to her in the same way. We were all able to feel good in saying goodbye to her. She had a peaceful end to her long life."

Return to Equilibrium

Some of the ways people regain the comfort and security of dominant and auxiliary functioning are common to all types, such as a change of scene or engaging in a physical activity. As described in Chapter 5, however, the auxiliary function and, less obviously, the tertiary function, seem to serve as a bridge in the natural process of regaining equilibrium.

Extraverted thinkers report needing to be left alone for a period of time both during and after an incident occurs. ESTJs say that solitary physical activity and attending to their own needs and comfort is helpful, as is a change of scene and a focus on things outside themselves (sensing). An ENTJ reported that what helps her most is retreating to her bed with snacks and some light reading. The next morning, after a good night's sleep, she has many new ideas (intuition), which permit her to reconnect with important projects and plans.

Some extraverted thinkers need to experience the depths of their feeling side and talk about it to trusted people. If others intrude too aggressively, however, they will be rebuffed and almost snubbed by the extraverted thinker. But a more gentle approach can encourage the expression of difficult feelings. Silent support, a nonjudgmental approach, and avoidance of direct attacks on the problems at hand, are most appreciated. One extraverted thinker acknowledged that "others should not be logical, but take care of the logical needs in my situation. Be there to listen and understand my feelings, if I am able to express them."

Perhaps more than any other type, many ESTJs and ENTJs report very few or quite minor eruptions of their inferior, and these tend to last minutes or hours rather than the days and weeks reported by other types. Some explain that their dislike of such experiences encourages them to develop methods of avoidance, since it becomes just one more problem or interference to be dealt with. They therefore use practiced techniques for recognizing and diverting an impending "loss of self." The meaning of the experience, however, may not be lost for them. Early signs of an impending episode remind them of their humanity and vulnerability, and they respond to this by tempering a perhaps overly task-oriented approach to life.

One ENTJ was described by his wife as rarely staying in a bad place for very long. His only inferior function manifestation was an occasional irrational emotional outburst that appeared extremely out of character for him. The episodes didn't last long, however. She reported that he took them in stride and did not seem to dwell on them.

At times, the distraction of new input—even something like a phone call from a friend or an interesting article or TV program—is enough to stimulate a return of equilibrium. However, in more extreme episodes of the inferior, simple distractors are likely to be ineffective.

Expressions in Midlife

As described in Chapters 4 and 5, midlife can take two alternative tracks for people of each type. Some extraverted thinkers become "stuck" in their type, perhaps having failed to satisfactorily accomplish the tasks of adulthood. Other ESTJs and ENTJs, however, temper their type through gradual integration of inferior feeling and tertiary intuition or sensing.

Like other extraverted people, ESTJs and ENTJs report a previously unfamiliar pleasure in solitude and silence. However, those who substitute rigidity for growth become inflexible in their insistence on private time. They may organize their lives around invariable routines, becoming irritable and accusatory when unaccustomed events or unexpected people intervene.

Adult children of rigid extraverted thinkers get a message that the grandchildren are tolerated but not enjoyed, and that family visits are necessary but unwelcome burdens. The ESTJ grandfather of a newborn showed no interest in the child, reluctantly holding him briefly only when cajoled by his daughter. A 65-year-old ENTJ insisted that her five children and twelve grandchildren spend Christmas morning at her home, but complained for weeks before and after the event about how much trouble it was.

TABLE 4   Major Features of Inferior Introverted Feeling

Triggers	Forms	New Knowledge
Disregard of values	Hypersensitivity	Recognizing limits
Others' emotional expressions	Emotional outbursts	An acceptance of the irrational
Regret of one's own harshness	Fear of feeling	The importance of close companions

Older extraverted thinkers who add feeling to their lives, however, often delight in the newfound pleasures of warm and close relationships with their children and grandchildren. Friendships with peers may also become increasingly important and enjoyable. Unlike their less developed counterparts, who often become depressed if forced to retire from work or home activities, they welcome new relationships and the challenge of new activities. This is a marked contrast to their earlier disinterest in hobbies and nonwork activities.

Having good role models who have opposite preferences seems particularly helpful to extraverted thinking types, although this is generally true for all types. The converse is also true: If an opposite preference comes to be associated with a negative role model, it is less likely to be welcomed and developed during our middle and advanced years.

Summary

In the grip of inferior introverted feeling, extraverted thinking types become sensitive to relationship issues, have outbursts of extreme emotion, and experience a loss of self-worth or a sense of inner incompetence. They typically have difficulty expressing their internal distress directly and try to hide their inner turmoil from others. Auxiliary sensing or intuition serve as buffers against the inferior function experience as well as aiding them in reestablishing equilibrium. ESTJs use factual reality to maintain or regain control of their inner state; ENTJs address hypotheses and possibilities that take them beyond and outside of their distress.

Important inferior function experiences remind extraverted thinking types of their own limitations, their basic connection with the more "irrational" ways of being human, and the importance of close companions and intimate relationships to their sense of competence and well-being. A brief overview of the major features of their inferior function experience appears in Table 4.

CHAPTER 7

Introverted Feeling Types

ISFP and INFP

BASIC TYPE DYNAMICS

Dominant introverted feeling

Auxiliary extraverted sensing or intuition

Tertiary intuition or sensing

Inferior extraverted thinking

Introverted Feeling
Versus Extraverted Thinking

THIS CHAPTER EXAMINES THE way effective introverted feeling types experience their inferior function, and the temporary transformation they make into ineffective, inferior extraverted thinking types when they are "in the grip." The following review of the characteristics of introverted feeling and extraverted thinking will be helpful for our discussion.

Important Features of Dominant Introverted Feeling

Introverted feeling types are flexible, open, complicated, mild, modest, and often self-effacing. Though hard to get to know, they are seen as trustworthy confidants who are tolerant of a wide range of differences. Their habitual approach to people is nonjudgmental, understanding, and forgiving. They place a high value on affirming both their own and others' individuality and uniqueness. They seek to affirm all parties in a controversy and thus readily see the validity of contradictory points of view. Underlying their characteristic tolerance is an overarching natural curiosity. They find the diversity in the world immensely appealing. ISFPs want to experience as much of the environment, especially the natural environment, as possible; INFPs' desire for broad experience, especially human experience, may be secondary to their need to understand it.

Both introverted feeling types may find it difficult to take a firm stance on issues that are not centrally important to them. As a result, they may see themselves and be seen by others as indecisive and lacking in conviction. In matters where they hold strong values, however, they are firm and uncompromising in expressing and enacting their beliefs.

Introverted feeling types focus on what is good in others, so they tend to downplay others' faults, often forgiving them for slights or minor hurtful behavior. At their best, they accept their own mistakes and imperfections as well, achieving some success in maintaining the inner harmony that is so important to them.

In crisis situations, they will typically hold back to see if others will solve the problem competently. They are then content to follow someone else's lead. But if adequate leadership is absent, ISFPs and INFPs may assume a dominant role, acting swiftly, confidently, and competently to handle the difficult situation.

Important Features of Dominant Extraverted Thinking

The qualities associated with extraverted thinking that are relevant to our discussion of its form as an inferior function are an emphasis on:

- Competence
- Truth and accuracy
- Decisive action

For a detailed description of dominant extraverted thinking, read the beginning of Chapter 6, "Extraverted Thinking Types: ESTJ and ENTJ," and the type descriptions for ESTJ and ENTJ that appear in Appendix A.

This will provide you with the background needed to explore the various ways in which inferior extraverted thinking is expressed in ISFPs and INFPs.

The Everyday Extraverted Thinking of Introverted Feeling Types

Introverted feeling types are affected by their inferior function in several different ways. These include everyday sensitivities, projections, and ways of relaxing, as well as the dramatic manifestations that can be seen when the inferior erupts and a full-blown episode occurs.

Typical Sensitivities and Projections

Like their extraverted feeling counterparts, introverted feeling types may be concerned about their intellectual abilities, viewing others, particularly thinking types, as smarter and more knowledgeable than themselves. Their hypersensitivity to truth and accuracy makes them quick to detect insincerity or phoniness in others. They readily take offense when faced with the kind of hyperbole so typical of television commercials and candidates running for political office. One INFP who hated magic shows and card tricks gave as her reason for this her dislike for "being fooled."

Introverted feeling types may also be somewhat disdainful of others who act quickly and with insufficient information, seeing the advantages of their own careful, reflective, and restrained approach to problem solving. They may be quick to point out the errors made or opportunities missed by people who hastily reach conclusions.

Projection of the inferior is revealed in a readiness to notice and comment on mistakes made by other people. "I start noticing that there are an unusual number of rude and incompetent drivers on the highway," said one INFP. An ISFP notices that she becomes "very aware that people at work are not following procedures and are making the same mistakes over and over again. But when I think about it later, I have to admit there are no more mistakes than usual."

An extreme, even passionate focus on the evil and wrongdoing in the world may also indicate an introverted feeling type's hypersensitivity to the "thinking" issues of truth and justice. Their often-noted idealism about the perfectibility of humanity may also relate to the unconscious, black-and-white character of their inferior function.

Expressions Through Interests and Hobbies

Introverted feeling types may select hobbies that engage their thinking function. One INFP thoroughly enjoys computer games that require logic and strategy; an ISFP spends many hours developing software programs to automate the computer entry of his pharmaceutical data. An INFP is a skilled equestrian, devoting much of her spare time to learning precise and intricate riding techniques. An ISFP who is prone to intense headaches finds that grooming her cats and dogs invariably alleviates her pain.

As an INFP, I often find cleaning the house, organizing drawers, or alphabetizing spices particularly relaxing and a welcome break from seeing clients, theorizing, doing research, and writing. This gives my dominant feeling and auxiliary intuition a rest when they have been used particularly intensively. Another INFP engages her tertiary sensing in her detailed, photo-realistic drawings of objects and people. An ISFP relaxes most successfully while doing the Sunday *New York Times* crossword puzzle. He enjoys being able to put the many facts he knows into the logical order of the English language and giving his tertiary intuition free rein to fill in the gaps in the puzzle.

People whose daily work requires them to use less preferred functions may use their preferred processes in their leisure time. An ISFP business manager described suppressing her dominant feeling and auxiliary sensing at work, where thinking and intuition were more highly valued. She then spent as much of her free time as possible enjoying the outdoors. This came naturally to her and was the most comfortable and relaxing place for her to be. There is a similar tendency for extraverted feeling types to engage their preferred functions in leisure activities.

Eruptions of Inferior Extraverted Thinking

When one or more of the preconditions for an eruption of the inferior function are present, extraverted thinking can appear in quite an exaggerated and disruptive form. In addition to the general conditions described in Chapter 4, introverted feeling types are vulnerable to the type-related factors described below.

Typical Provocations or Triggers

Introverted feeling types frequently mention that an atmosphere of negativity and excessive criticism provides a fertile context for an eruption of their inferior. Even if the criticism is not directed at them, it brings out their own extraverted thinking in a black-and-white form. They harshly attack the people who are being negative and critical—for being negative and critical!

As an important part of her job, an INFP nursing supervisor critiqued the records and charts of the nurses who worked under her. One nurse, also an INFP, invariably became furious when his charts were reviewed. He accused his supervisor of gross insensitivity and pettiness and of being unfit for her job. And though she tried valiantly to view his attacks in context, they would often "send her into a tailspin," wherein she was filled with self-doubt, guilt, and a sense of incompetence about her performance. In the context of each having to use less preferred processes, these two INFPs constellated their own and each others' inferiors.

Fears of impending loss and separation from important relationships can serve as a trigger for ISFPs and INFPs. One INFP said that he is most likely to fall into his inferior function "when something very dear to me is threatened and I'm afraid I'll lose my most valued connections with life." An ISFP said that for her it is "when my attachments to people are demeaned and invalidated."

Introverted feeling types quickly fall into their inferior mode when an important value has been violated. One INFP said:

> I put my feelers out to detect more and even unrelated violations. Once when reviewing my manuscript, which had been typed by a new typist, I found he had made all kinds of really stupid errors. Just after that, I called a colleague at a hotel where I was to meet her. The operator connected me with a wrong room three times. I concluded that the hotel was badly managed and all the staff were incompetent. I went back to the manuscript and found more mistakes and blamed the typist. But this time they were *my* mistakes!

Another trigger for the inferior of introverted feeling types occurs when they project their own unrealistic standard of competence onto others and feel they have not lived up to other people's expectations. "I know I should have been better prepared for that one scene in the play," said an INFP. "It ruined the whole thing." Obsessing on this one perceived inadequacy could quickly lead to a full-fledged experience of inferior extraverted thinking.

A highly regarded ISFP office manager persistently berated himself for his imperfect filing system. "Even though I do everything else adequately, I know my boss is disappointed in my overall performance," he said. As a chronic focus for his imagined inadequacy, he was hypersensitive to any reference to the files, readily seeing criticism in the most innocent comments, and quickly generalizing it to be a negative assessment of his overall performance and his acceptability as a person.

The Form of the Inferior

The characteristic tolerance, flexibility, and quiet caring of introverted feeling types diminishes as the energy available to their dominant introverted feeling dwindles. Initially, INFPs and ISFPs may control their urge to blurt out hostile thoughts by engaging in destructive fantasies directed at just about anyone available. Alternatively, they might employ biting sarcasm and cynicism. As these tactics fail, the negative extraverted thinking of their inferior function becomes manifested in judgments of incompetence, aggressive criticism, and precipitous action.

The comparison between dominant and inferior extraverted thinking is shown in Table 5.

Jung (1976a) alludes to these inferior manifestations in the following statement:

> Just as introverted thinking is counterbalanced by a primitive feeling, to which objects attach themselves with magical force, introverted feeling is counterbalanced by a primitive thinking, whose concretism and slavery to facts surpass all bounds. (p. 388)

Incompetence   In the early stages of their inferior function, introverted feeling types often project their unconscious fears of their own incompetence. They become hypersensitive to others' mistakes. Because of the extraverted attitude of their inferior, the projections often extend to large segments of the outer world, encompassing much of humanity. Once

TABLE 5 **Dominant Versus Inferior Extraverted Thinking**

	Qualities Associated With Extraverted Thinking
As Dominant Function	Competence
	Truth and accuracy
	Decisive action
As Inferior Function	Judgments of incompetence
	Aggressive criticism
	Precipitous action

caught up in this state, incompetence is seen in employees, bosses, colleagues, strangers on the street, the person on the other end of the telephone, drivers on the highway, local and national institutions, and major world figures.

Introverted feeling types in this state may complain loudly about others' gross ineptitude. ISFPs and INFPs seem to turn into the very opposite of their accepting, nonjudgmental, and flexible selves, coming across as harsh critics and judges whose standards of competence are too extreme to be met.

Inferior thinking often comes out in an unrelenting search for accuracy—in a precise, nit-picking logic and focus, and an almost legalistic standard of validity.

One INFP said, "I get honed in on precise logic and truth and am very critical, detailed, picky, frustrated, and irritable. I'm nit-picky and see only what is in front of me."

An ISFP said, "I'm in a bad mood and show it. I cut myself off, am critical, judgmental, bitchy; I am not accepting, happy, optimistic, nice, or understanding. Usually, I am friendly and always have time for people. When I'm tired and vulnerable, I can get into this state by remembering some incredibly dumb thing I did—an embarrassing moment. Or somebody else's incompetence that reflects on my own will set me off."

When projecting their sense of incompetence fails to take care of whatever has triggered their unconscious projections, the negative energy of the inferior takes the form of critical self-judgments. Introverted feelers become focused on their own incompetence, extending it both back and forward in time and including the world at large in their conclusion. In the words of one INFP:

I become overwhelmed by an awareness that I am totally incompetent at everything that I do, that I always have been and always will be—and that the whole world knows it! The truth of this is beyond doubt. I am mortified at not recognizing this before, and of compounding the offense by acting as if I were competent. I am unable to verbalize my despair to others for fear I will make a fool of myself by acknowledging my former ignorance of my true lack of ability. I view my advanced degrees and other achievements as the result of people feeling sorry for me—I was too emotionally fragile to be told the truth.

"Everything seems impossible," said an ISFP. "I begin to lose faith in my ability to do even the simplest task, and I especially distrust my ability to make competent decisions about my life."

When feeling vulnerable, another INFP would worry about whether his teachers had paid sufficient attention to his work to properly evaluate it. "Maybe they were so wrapped up in their own work that I slipped through undetected," he said.

An ISFP said, "I review all the mistakes I ever made in my life and then conclude that I am a bona fide failure at everything I attempt to do, despite any evidence to the contrary."

Aggressive criticism We know that effective dominant extraverted thinkers make useful critical judgments about the world. In the grip of inferior extraverted thinking, introverted feeling types make judgments that are overly categorical, harsh, exaggerated, hypercritical and often unfounded. In marked contrast to their typical gentle, self-effacing manner, they become so aggressively judgmental that they come across as caricatures of their opposite types, the extraverted thinkers. Depending on the nature and intensity of the precipitating circumstances, the excessive criticism may be immediately directed at themselves or may focus first on the objectionable qualities of others, only later culminating in severe self-criticism.

One ISFP described becoming extremely critical of others: "My humor becomes biting and cynical and I take an "army-navy" dictatorial approach to communicating with others. I am very negative."

An INFP becomes "more intense. I tend to lash out at people with great anger. I am blaming and accusatory. I get vicious 'Ben Hur'-type images with a lot of violent action. I feel cold, intolerant, uncaring, rigid, straitjacketed, focused, and terrier-like."

Another INFP said, "I become self-critical, doubting, irritable, inflexible, and more picky. I focus on details. Usually, I am flexible and quiet, and like new challenges, new ideas, and working with people."

When one ISFP becomes especially irritated with her husband's chronic indecision, she provides him with lengthy, logical accounts of his available choices, adopting a combative, lawyerlike tone.

One INFP makes almost vicious attacks on people who fail to live up to his ethical standards. "One winter I found out the gas company had turned off service to my disabled neighbor, who couldn't pay her bill. I flew into a rage, called the president of the company, and threatened to expose him to the newspapers. Even I was surprised at the language I used," he said.

Precipitous action   Introverted feeling types in the grip are often overwhelmed by the urge to take some action, usually to correct some imagined mistake or incompetence of their own. But where the dominant extraverted thinker uses differentiated judgment in deciding on what action to take, if any, the introverted feeling type's actions often exacerbate the problem. A difficult situation may be created in cases where there initially wasn't one.

At her engagement party, Sylvia, an INFP, was kissed playfully by a former boyfriend while both were alone in the kitchen. Later that night, she remembered that a friend of hers had passed by the kitchen door and might have seen the kiss. She called her friend and begged her not to tell anyone. She interpreted her friend's puzzled response as evidence that she had already told several other people. She then called four more close friends to warn them not to tell. By this time, the innocent kiss was known by virtually everyone who was at the party. Of course, her fiancé found out about the kissing incident and was hurt and angry. Her precipitous "fixing" created an unnecessary issue that required a great deal of real correction.

The urge to action can also be seen in attempts by introverted feelers to take control. One INFP reported that when things seem out of control, he attempts to put things in order, organize them, and piece data together in an orderly, logical, linear fashion. An ISFP responds to such episodes by taking charge of people and ordering them around. Others make lists, organize the list contents logically, and methodically check items off once they are accomplished.

Undertaking large household cleaning projects, reorganizing, and moving furniture are also ways of responding to increasing stress. They are usually accompanied by concerns about one's abilities—perhaps indicative of attempts to ward off inferior thinking by acting in a decisive, controlled way.

Grip Experiences

The stories included in this section illustrate one or more forms of inferior extraverted thinking as experienced by ISFPs or INFPs. Characteristics of dominant introverted feeling types come through in the telling of these episodes—their deeply held values and unassuming approach and their readiness to take responsibility for themselves and others.

Out of the Depths Comes Appreciation

Jack, an INFP, related the following story:

> As part of a professional training program I was enrolled in, I had to complete a take-home exam that required me to integrate the complex information in the course. I had never written a take-home exam before, and I looked forward to it, as the questions were challenging and I enjoy writing. But I had great trouble answering the questions. I thought everything I wrote was either wrong, trivial, or irrelevant. I was in the depths of despair, seriously questioning my competence and professional skills. I kept thinking it would get better if I kept at it, but over the six weeks I worked on the exam, it only got worse.
>
> Several days before I had to bring in my examination, I somehow realized that I had unwittingly defined the take-home exam as a requirement to cite chapter and verse, and provide carefully substantiated facts leading to logical conclusions. This was not my comfortable approach to problem solving. I depended largely on my ideas and insight to guide my work. I then realized that in writing the exam, I had been treating my ideas as if they had to be facts, and I was expecting my conclusions to have the status of truth. No wonder I couldn't tell if my ideas were any good: I was evaluating them from an inappropriate perspective.
>
> I was able to easily redefine the task, set aside the books I was consulting, and answer the questions with confidence and satisfaction. I got an A+ on the exam.

Attacking Without Premeditation

"I would say that I'm normally sarcastic about idiotic TV commercials, politicians, university presidents, and the like," said an INFP college professor. He went on to explain how he expresses this

> on a daily basis without any predisposing stress. But when I'm caught under the influence of my hidden and mysterious other side, I lash out at people close to me—my family and colleagues. I attack suddenly and without premeditation. This ruptures the relationship until we work it out.

Recently, I challenged the dean of my department in a very biting and sarcastic way because he insisted that I follow standard procedures for conducting an upcoming program review. Actually, I approved of the procedures, but I was feeling over-whelmed and uncertain as to whether the reviewers would appreciate my hard work and recognize my expertise. I feared they would give me a bad review and I would be found inadequate. Unfortunately, I barked out my criticism at my dean, who was actually very supportive of me. I recovered my demeanor and made amends the next day by assuring him that I agreed with his procedure.

"But There Have to Be Rules and Procedures!"

Mona, an ISFP owner and operator of a fabric store, had a relaxed, easygoing management style. Her five full- and part-time employees enjoyed a friendly, cooperative relationship with her. Mona's style of recordkeeping, ordering stock, accounting, and other business activities were equally casual. Eventually, everything would be taken care of, though perhaps not in the most efficient fashion.

During a time of particular financial stress when business appeared to be waning, Mona decided that she needed to put her business activities in order. She spent two evenings writing out detailed and elaborate "rules of law," specifying how her employees must conduct business affairs and interpersonal relationships with each other and with customers. She called an early morning meeting to convey the new requirements.

"They all listened quietly and attentively," Mona remembered. "Each said something like, 'Uh, huh,' 'Sure, Mona,' or 'Fine, that's okay.' But then they totally ignored my rules and conducted themselves and the business as usual!

"Later, several of them told me they figured I was stressed and wasn't acting normally, so they figured the best thing to do was to humor me until I came out of it. They were right. When I did come out of it, I looked at my two evenings' worth of rules and regulations and was flabbergasted. I couldn't understand how I could have possibly thought any of it was appropriate!"

Embarrassing Error or Earache?

An INFP philosophy professor related the following experience that had occurred years earlier while he was a graduate student.

"I was invited to deliver a lecture on my area of specialization in philosophy at an annual philosophical society meeting. Although somewhat anxious, as this would be my first major presentation, I was excited about it and quite pleased with my professors' high opinion of me.

"I was told that several philosophers who were experts in my area might be attending my presentation. The lecture was attended by over 100 people. I introduced my talk with a brief overview of the philosophical system underlying my approach. I had been speaking for about ten minutes when a man at the back of the room began shaking his head vigorously.

"In that instant I *knew* that he was one of the 'experts'—that I must have made some egregious error, was making a fool of myself, and was in danger of continuing to do so. All my thoughts flew from my head! My choice was either to persevere and forge ahead with a high risk of making further stupid statements or mortify myself by being unable to continue. Under the circumstances, the first option was the lesser of the two evils. I recovered and continued, though with quite a bit of uneasiness.

"At the end of my lecture, the man came up to me and said, 'I'm sorry to ask you to repeat something you said during your lecture, but I have a terrible ear infection and I couldn't clear my ears enough to be able to hear you.'

"I now recognize that his headshaking was due to his attempts to unclog his ears—that I had not said something wrong, but that my readiness to distrust my knowledge was clearly a sign that I was insecure and thus basically incompetent. I interpreted my quickness to 'lose it' as a way of unconsciously chastising myself for my arrogance in thinking too well of myself.

"Years later, I recognized that my expectations of myself had been unrealistic. I had wanted to explain my philosophical approach perfectly and was afraid of making any kind of error. Thinking about this made me reflect on the realistic consequences of making a mistake in public. Would one error really be so terrible? Wasn't an important aspect of competence the ability to accept one's errors and learn from them?

"As a result of this experience, I am better able to accept my mistakes as natural consequences of being human. They do not interrupt my train of thought, nor do I overreact to them as I once did."

"I Wasn't Good at That Anyway"

Ben, an ISFP, had majored in physical education in college and planned to teach at the high school level. But because he was unable to find a position in his field, he took a job in the drafting department of a large manufacturing firm. His minor in college had been art, and he had always enjoyed the creative outlet his artwork provided him. He liked designing teaching materials for the company's training department and was particularly good at improving on other people's designs, putting to good use his fine sense of color, shape, and texture.

As a result of his excellent work, Ben was promoted to a project manager position. His job now required him to read and evaluate reports and decide what kinds of training materials were appropriate. After two weeks in this new position, Ben developed stomach problems, back pain, and headaches. He was unable to concentrate at work and responded to requests by saying, "I can't do that," or "I don't know how."

"I feel really stupid, incompetent, and worthless," he told a career counselor. "My boss agrees. He says I am totally uncreative because I can't come up with original training designs. He's right. Before, I was good at improving on other people's designs—not coming up with my own. Now I don't think I can even do that. I don't think I was ever really good at that anyway. The rest of the team made up for my lack of talent."

Promoted to a position beyond his level of expertise, Ben lost contact with his real sources of competence, which, abetted by his boss, he now devalued. When he eventually moved into a position that again made use of his particular talents, his sense of self gradually returned. "I realize now that I don't have to accept other people's idea of creativity. I can be happy with my own definition," he said.

"Go Ahead, Make My Day!"

After thinking about it for a long time, Suzanne, an INFP, decided on a career change that required an advanced degree. She applied to a graduate program at a university in a nearby state, and because the deadline for admission to the fall program had passed, hoped she would be admitted for the spring semester.

Early one morning during the last week of August, Suzanne received a phone call from the head of the graduate department informing her that because her qualifications for the program were so outstanding, the department was offering her a complete tuition scholarship as well as a sizable fellowship to help defray her living expenses. And even though the semester had already started, they wanted her to enroll for the fall semester rather than wait until spring. How soon could she come?

Suzanne was overwhelmed. Though she had been planning to complete various projects in the next few months, they would have to wait. The offer was too good to turn down. She felt pleased and affirmed by the university's recognition of her past accomplishments. After considering how much time she needed to fulfill current commitments, she informed the department head that she could start in ten days.

By the following day, however, the stress of the move to another state, the prospect of having to find a place to live that would accept her three cats, the concern about needing to supplement her fellowship money, and the countless other details that came into her mind utterly changed her initial happy mood. Her thoughts raced:

> What if they just had this fellowship left over and had to get rid of it and I was the only person available? What if it's not that I'm so great, but that everybody else in the program is mediocre? What if I get there and can't catch up with the work I've missed? I shouldn't be making a precipitous decision like this. The last time I decided on a move quickly, it turned out to be a big mistake. And there won't be any good places to live because the semester has started. And what if I just don't like it and I quit and disappoint these people who are going out of their way for me? And what if I don't live up to their expectations? And what if....

Suzanne disregarded reassurance from others, descending further into negative judgments of herself, her competence, and her decision-making abilities. Finally, she gained sufficient perspective to recall that her current negativity was "standard operating procedure" when she felt uprooted and disconcerted by all the practical details facing her. She was then able to accept putting up with her discomfort until she moved and her life situation became more settled.

Return of Equilibrium

As Suzanne's story illustrates, inferior function experiences for all types usually require time for things to play out before equilibrium is restored.

The following comments were made by some introverted feeling types about how they typically disengage from an inferior function experience.

"It has to expire on its own. If someone else says something about it, it can make it worse—unless I am already coming out of it. If someone I respect but am not emotionally close to says something, I may check it out. It depends on how it is said."

"I need to go with the flow and allow myself time to experience it. Others need to be patient and empathic. They need to allow me time to reflect."

"Exercise helps and so does talking to someone. But others need to listen and not try to reason with me or be logical. Having my feelings validated is important."

A consistent theme that seems to signal that the experience is unwinding is an often painful awareness of the effect their inferior is having on people. "We become aware of the damage to relationships caused by the episode and are thankful it's over," reported a group of introverted feeling types.

Auxiliary sensing or intuition aid the winding-down process. For ISFPs, starting a craft project that uses established skills may signal the diminishing effects of an inferior episode. INFPs also find new energy and motivation by coming up with an intriguing thought or a new approach to an ongoing project.

INFPs report that the process of emerging from their inferior experience happens simultaneously with the new learning or awareness that occurs. This happens for other types as well, but seems to be more noticeable for those who have intuition as their auxiliary. Often the new knowledge comes in the form of a previously unrecognized idea or new insight. This is what occurred for the person who realized he had approached the take-home exam from the wrong perspective.

Expressions in Midlife

Midlife is not always accompanied by a positive and progressive integration of inferior extraverted thinking. Nor do we see evidence of the inclusion of tertiary sensing or intuition in the personality of all aging introverted feeling types.

The aging process finds some introverted feeling types becoming stuck in their type rather than broadening their perspective. They may appear to others as perpetually searching for self-fulfillment, changing jobs or careers, assuring others and themselves that this next time will be the last and "right" choice. This may also take the form of repetitive searching for a "soul mate" of the opposite sex, resulting in failed marriages and dissatisfying romantic affairs.

Others may incorporate inferior thinking and tertiary sensing or intuition into their personalities, but in a somewhat rigid, extreme, and stereotypical way. They seem hypercritical of others, obsess about minor details, and lose their former facility with ideas and possibilities. Rather than simply adding appropriate thinking to their repertoire, they seem to merely delete feeling. Aging finds them frequently in the grip of inferior thinking and tertiary sensing or intuition.

Introverted feeling types whose course of development is more fortunate reveal an increased sense of confidence in their own values, a new interest in activities that involve their tertiary sensing or intuition, and an attraction to analytic approaches. They report more comfort in logical decision making, less concern about hurting others' feelings, and greater impatience with sentimental expressions of feeling. They may enjoy doing things in an orderly, logical sequence and appreciate the beauty of the universe as expressed in the laws of physics and chemistry. This may emerge in as common an activity as cooking. An INFP cook, who had habitually deviated from recipes as a young adult, discovered in his fifties that following the order and precision of a detailed recipe was quite appealing. He was intrigued with the particular mix of ingredients and the logic of their proportions. This INFP cook's midlife change contrasts with that of an ISTJ cook described in Chapter 12, who, having adhered strictly to recipes in her youth, dispensed with them entirely in midlife.

Positive incorporation of inferior and tertiary functions can appear in the career area. One 47-year-old INFP said:

> I think that in the last ten years or so I have gained psychological reassurance that I am competent at some things. It needed to come first in my chosen professional arena—through gaining confidence as a professional, as a faculty member training students, and then as a bit of an authority in certain theoretical areas. Then I could play with areas where I had never sought competence before. I recently took a night course in electrical rewiring and practiced it in my own home. But the secure base of my preferred world (teaching and writing) needed to be there, as well as in my personal life (as a partner and a parent), before I could have energy to devote to such things as mastering electrical circuits. It had to happen at the right time also. I could never have done it in my twenties or younger.

TABLE 6 Major Features of Inferior Extraverted Thinking

Triggers	Forms	New Knowledge
Negativity	Incompetence	An acceptance of power needs
Fear of loss	Aggressive criticism	Acknowledged competence
Violation of values	Precipitous action	Moderated idealism

Summary

In the grip of inferior extraverted thinking, ISFPs and INFPs focus on their own and others' incompetence, are hypersensitive to signs of dishonesty, and take precipitous action, often aimed at correcting an imagined error. The new awareness that occurs is often in conjunction with the process of regaining their introverted feeling equilibrium and tends to engage their auxiliary extraverted sensing or intuition. Discovery of facts that explain puzzling reactions occurs for ISFPs; significant insights that stimulate a new point of view are helpful to INFPs. As a result of important inferior function experiences, introverted feeling types are able to accept and value their own competitiveness, need for achievement, or desire for power and control—motives that their conscious introverted feeling values tend to reject and deny. They are also better able to accept and acknowledge their own competencies, as well as their insecurities and failings. They are thus able to temper their sometimes excessive idealism with more realistic goals. A brief overview of the major features of their inferior function experience appears above in Table 6.

CHAPTER 8

Introverted Thinking Types

ISTP and INTP

BASIC TYPE DYNAMICS

Dominant introverted thinking

Auxiliary extraverted sensing or intuition

Tertiary intuition or sensing

Inferior extraverted feeling

Introverted Thinking
Versus Extraverted Feeling

THIS CHAPTER EXAMINES THE way effective introverted thinking types experience their inferior function, and the temporary transformation they make into ineffective, inferior extraverted feeling types when they are "in the grip." The following review of the characteristics of introverted thinking and extraverted feeling will be helpful to our discussion.

Important Features of Dominant Introverted Thinking

Introverted thinkers maintain the utmost objectivity. They approach people and events as dispassionate observers, with the main goal of arriving at the most comprehensive possible truth. The process of objective analysis is a source of great enjoyment to the introverted thinker, with its outcome often of much lesser importance. Introverted thinkers typically do not take constructive criticism and disagreement personally. They often welcome tough, unrelenting critiques as helpful in achieving the highest levels of accuracy and objectivity.

Because they themselves do not take criticism personally, introverted thinkers are often surprised when they discover that others may be hurt or offended by the constructive criticism they offer. They may be seen as distant, unfeeling, disinterested in people, and often arrogant—character-istics that they disavow. The fact that they may appear to have these qualities, however, is a function of their basic typological approach, which applies objective analysis to most things, including people.

In a crisis that does not provoke their inferior function, introverted thinkers take the same detached, objective approach typical of their nonstressful problem solving. They don't tend to report the internal (and undetectable) turmoil described by the introverted sensing types, and thus experience little or no emotional response to objectively experienced crises.

Important Features of Dominant Extraverted Feeling

The qualities associated with extraverted feeling that are relevant to our discussion of its form as an inferior function are an emphasis on:

- Harmony over logic
- Sensitivity to others' welfare
- Sharing of emotions

For a detailed description of dominant extraverted feeling, read the beginning of Chapter 9, "Extraverted Feeling Types: ESFJ and ENFJ," and the type descriptions for ESFJ and ENFJ that appear in Appendix A. This will provide you with the background needed to explore the various ways in which inferior extraverted feeling is expressed in ISTPs and INTPs.

The Everyday Extraverted Feeling of Introverted Thinking Types

The inferior function affects introverted thinkers in several different ways. These include everyday sensitivities, projections, and ways of relaxing, as well as the dramatic manifestations that can be seen when the inferior erupts and a full-blown episode occurs.

Typical Sensitivities and Projections

Introverted thinkers may frequently notice and comment on what they consider to be inappropriate, irrelevant, even histrionic communication styles and behavior of others. These qualities are often attributed to extraverted feeling types or extraverted intuitives with auxiliary feeling. They may treat such people with disdain, and in turn be seen as hypercritical, dismissive, and lacking in social graces.

An INTP father was chastised by his wife and children—all of whom had a preference for feeling—because his first question when his son came to him and told him he had crashed his bike into a wall was, "Is the bike badly damaged?" They all agreed he should have first asked his son if he were hurt. The father replied that he had already determined by seeing him that his son was not hurt, and therefore chose the condition of the bike as the next logical priority. This father was quite puzzled at his family's perception that he cared more for a bike than his son. He assumed his love for his family was self-evident.

Introverted thinkers may assess behavior based on subjective values as "noise in the system" that interferes with accurate appraisal of situations and is therefore a waste of time. Extraverted feeling types can seem out of control to them. The value ESFJs and ENFJs place on harmony over logically determined truth arouses distrust in the introverted thinker, who then doubts these types' intellectual abilities. They may therefore interpret other peoples' need for frequent personal validation as weakness and insecurity.

As to expressing their own feeling side, Von Franz (1971) states that

> the feeling of the introverted thinking type is extraverted. He has the same kind of strong, loyal and warm feeling described as typical for the extraverted thinking type, but with the difference that the feeling of the introverted thinking type flows toward definite objects. (p. 41)

Those definite objects may be people, causes, spiritual arenas, and so on. In their raw, inexperienced form, these feeling expressions come out as clichés and sound sentimental and excessive. Sensing this, introverted thinking types hesitate to express them.

Expressions Through Interests and Hobbies

Many ISTPs and INTPs have a passion for challenging but primarily solitary physical activities. They may be avid mountain or rock climbers and serious hikers or backpackers. They describe having a deep emotional and spiritual reaction to wilderness experiences and their oneness with the universe. The mountain, trail, or rock can become the "other" in their experience of intense feeling.

One INTP mountain climber writes emotionally evocative poetry describing his reactions to his climbing experiences. An ISTP police lieutenant loves listening to music of the Romantic era, especially Wagner.

Eruptions of Inferior Extraverted Feeling

When one or more of the preconditions for an eruption of the inferior function are present, extraverted feeling appears in its more exaggerated, disruptive form. In addition to the general conditions described in Chapter 4, introverted thinking types are vulnerable to the type-specific factors described below.

Typical Provocations or Triggers

Being around people who are expressing strong emotions can serve as a trigger for introverted thinkers, especially if others are criticizing their personal characteristics. And as is the case for extraverted thinkers, ISTPs and INTPs can be pushed into the grip when their own strong values and feelings are not recognized or affirmed.

Others' insensitivity to an introverted thinker's need for silence and solitude can also provoke the experience, as can the short-term, intense stress of a crisis situation. Introverted thinkers may react with an uncharacteristic display of emotion or readily take offense at such times.

Other triggers are feeling controlled by arbitrary situations that limit freedom of choice and action or feeling that others are intruding on the introverted thinker's space.

The Form of the Inferior

As the introverted thinker's conscious control of differentiated thinking starts to diminish, use of that dominant function along with auxiliary

TABLE 7   **Dominant Versus Inferior Extraverted Feeling**

	Qualities Associated With Extraverted Feeling
As Dominant Function	Comfortable inattention to logic Sensitivity to the welfare of others Sharing of emotions
As Inferior Function	Logic emphasized to an extreme Hypersensitivity to relationships Emotionalism

sensing or intuition becomes increasingly difficult. The internal struggle for control, however, may be largely unobserved by others. But as time goes on, others may notice a certain slowness, vagueness, and distractibility replacing the sharp acuity that they generally see in the introverted thinker.

As inferior extraverted feeling becomes more and more prominent in the demeanor of the introverted thinker, it comes out in the form of logic being emphasized to an extreme, hypersensitivity to relationships, and emotionalism. The comparison between dominant and inferior extraverted feeling is shown above in Table 7.

Jung (1976a) touched on a combination of these characteristics as they can be seen in their inferior form:

> Because of the highly impersonal character of the conscious attitude, the unconscious feelings are extremely personal and oversensitive, giving rise to secret prejudices—a readiness, for instance, to misconstrue any opposition to his formula as personal ill-will, or a constant tendency to make negative assumptions about other people in order to invalidate their arguments in advance—in defense, naturally, of his own touchiness. (p. 350)

Logic emphasized to an extreme   Effective dominant extraverted feeling types are quite comfortable making decisions that are nonlogical. Introverted thinking types in the grip of inferior extraverted feeling may become passionately insistent on the application of logic, becoming quite emotional about their approach. As an extension of the loss of control over the thinking function, the introverted thinker begins to engage in excessively logical, unproductive thinking. There may be an obsessive quality to this thinking. One ISTP feels compelled to "prove" the accuracy of his perception of things. An INTP said, "If a problem comes up that I'm unable to resolve, I work at it anyway and can't let go of it, even if I know I can't solve it."

Other introverted thinkers report becoming less articulate, speaking rapidly and disjointedly, obsessively trying to solve the insoluble, using sharp, clear, but "paranoid" logic. They may find that they forget things, misplace objects, and engage in futile projects that don't accomplish anything and are marked by disorganization.

One INTP described becoming rigidly stuck on a false belief that at the time seemed totally supported by logic. Later, he was able to reassess his conviction as an inferior "feeling judgment masquerading as logic."

Hypersensitivity to relationships   Effective dominant extraverted feeling types value their relationships with others. They carefully consider the well-being of others in making decisions and devote energy and enthusiasm to personal and social interactions. In the grip of inferior extraverted feeling, the introverted thinker experiences increasing hypersensitivity to "feeling" areas. And just as extraverted thinkers struggle to maintain controlled efficiency and competency when in the initial grip of the inferior, so introverted thinkers valiantly try to hide their formerly alien concerns with being liked and appreciated. In this unfamiliar state, they overinterpret or misinterpret others' innocent comments or body language. However, to the introverted thinker, the perceived slights are accurate and authentic. Something as innocuous as someone failing to say hello upon entering a room, or briefly interrupting a conversation to greet a passerby, may be interpreted as indicators of dislike and disapproval. ISTPs and INTPs tend to feel discounted when others do not listen to them attentively.

Others are usually slow to catch on to the altered state of the introverted thinker, as was noted earlier for extraverted thinkers. Distress, anxiety, and annoyance are typically expressed with minimal cues—a raised eyebrow, a distant look, or other subtle body language may be the only signal. Further, family, friends, and colleagues, who are in the habit of trusting the person's careful, objective analysis of people and events, are likely to take the introverted thinker's conclusions as objectively true. They have little reason to doubt, for example, that the boss doesn't appreciate the introverted thinker and therefore won't let him do a particular project. They are therefore unlikely to inquire about the evidence used to reach this definitive-sounding judgment.

In its extreme form, the introverted thinker in the grip may experience a profound and infinite separateness from the whole of humanity, convinced that he or she is unloved and ultimately unlovable. Some relive their childhood feeling of being extremely different from other children, marching to a different and unacceptable drummer, often with no clue about how others see things. The memory of childhood misery and helplessness may intensify the adult's inferior function experience.

Emotionalism Effective dominant extraverted feeling types readily share their values with others and are comfortable expressing their emotions. In the grip of inferior extraverted feeling, introverted thinking types may not differentiate between the expression of feeling values and the expression of emotion. We may witness a confusion between feeling as a judging function and emotion as a state of physiological arousal. Jung (1976b) was explicit in his differentiation of the two:

> What I mean by feeling in contrast to thinking is a *judgment of value;* agreeable or disagreeable, good or bad, and so on. Feeling so defined is not an emotion or affect, which is, as the words convey, an involuntary manifestation. Feeling as I mean it is a judgment without any of the obvious bodily reactions that characterize an emotion. Like thinking, it is a *rational* function. (p. 219)

Nevertheless, it appears true that dominant thinking types, especially introverted thinkers, do not have ready access to their emotions when they are operating in their habitual, dominant mode. Often they report not knowing or being able to describe a feeling at the time it is occurring. Some INTPs, however, report being able to infer the presence of a feeling by attending to intuitive cues. It may be recounted later in thinking, analytical terms. They fear that once in the realm of intense emotion, they may become possessed by it and never be able to come out. That is why descending into "the depths" is rare, and entered into against the will of the introverted thinker.

Lack of familiarity with felt emotion is probably due to the fact that thinking judgment typically excludes subjective values and affective data from the decision-making process. How they or others feel about things may be judged irrelevant to the problem at hand and therefore as interfering with logical decision making. In contrast, feeling types consider such data as entirely relevant to their decisions. Their primary decision-making criteria include personal values, feelings, and consequences for important people and things.

Due to limited experience, therefore, thinking types' emotional expression lacks the differentiation and subtlety of feeling seen in well-differentiated feeling types. When positive feelings are involved, they may seem maudlin and sentimental. With greater intensity, inferior feeling comes out as raw, extreme emotion. Feeling judgment seems to become increasingly exaggerated and obsessional, reaching a point where it no longer serves a judging purpose, but becomes unbridled emotionalism.

When the contents of this normally unconscious, primitive function rise to the surface, they appear as a loss of control over emotional expression. There are reports of irritability and difficulty in holding back frustration and anger. In early phases, the introverted thinker may become fidgety, trembling, and sarcastic, stomping around and making verbal attacks, exaggerating and accusing others. In more extreme cases, there may be physical outbursts that include breaking things and attacking people.

An INTP college student was deeply involved in a research paper when some of his friends asked him to go to a carnival with them. He refused, but they persisted anyway. When one grabbed his pen and paper and teasingly refused to return it, he began yelling at her and grabbed her arm. Both he and his friends were surprised and frightened by the swiftness and intensity of his reaction.

Although expression of anger is common, often there is increasing self-pity and a sense of feeling neglected, unappreciated, and even victimized. With greater loss of control, introverted thinkers can burst into tears with no warning. One wrong word can trigger an emotional outburst accompanied by rage, crying, and rising emotionality. Some describe feeling as if all their emotions are all mixed up, released with uncharacteristic spontaneity. "I start to notice my own feelings and become moody and impatient; I deny to others that anything is wrong, but all the while I feel like I am drowning in emotions," said one ISTP.

Not only are their own emotions problematic, but so are the emotional reactions of others. Introverted thinkers report that when in the grip of their inferior, emotions from others are upsetting and only intensify the magnitude of the situation.

The three manifestations of the inferior typically appear together. One INTP woman feels martyred and cannot help snapping, whining, and complaining to people. She reports becoming very emotional and a little on the irrational side, unable to organize or problem solve with her usual efficiency and competence. Another INTP describes feeling numb, frozen, or enraged, accompanied by extreme exhaustion and an inability to concentrate.

Some describe an inability to keep their emotions to themselves, even though they wish to reveal little of their internal processes. In this state, said an ISTP, "I act out my displeasure rather than keeping it to myself as I am more inclined to do. The actual acting out is usually brief, but feeling stressed out about it may last longer." An INTP described the shame she associates with experiencing extreme feelings; she also described blaming others for not appreciating or loving her enough. Paramount is a sense of being misunderstood, with no way to correct the misunderstanding. Other ISTPs and INTPs report similar reactions.

Grip Experiences

The stories included in this section illustrate one or more forms of inferior extraverted feeling as experienced by ISTPs or INTPs. Note the nature of introverted thinking that comes through in relating the episodes. They tend to be presented as a detailed, logical progression of events that are analyzed objectively. For this reason, some of the stories are longer than those for other types. Like their extraverted thinking counterparts, introverted thinkers report the inferior function experience as rare but powerful.

"Who Was Sitting Beside Me?"

Andrea reported that her ISTP husband, Jim, was normally cool and controlled, rarely showing anger. But he was becoming increasingly frustrated over his failure to reach a compromise with his ex-wife over the education of their son. One afternoon, after a frustrating visit with his ex-wife, Jim and Andrea were driving home on a busy city street. Jim was driving. At a stop light, the driver in the car beside them shouted at Jim that he was driving too closely. Jim said nothing, but got out of his car, reached into the other car, and punched the driver in the nose. Still silent, he returned to his own car and drove on. Andrea was shocked. She did not recognize the man beside her.

Jim made no mention of the incident and acted as though it had never happened. Days later, when Andrea asked him about it, he explained that his reaction in the car was unpremeditated. He recalled that just before the incident occurred he was feeling intense frustration and helplessness about the disagreement with his ex-wife. "That jerk in the car gave me a quick way to get rid of my anger," Jim said. "I felt better immediately. I stopped obsessing about that lousy visit right after that."

Unknown Depth of Feeling

Martha, an INTP, is divorced and has two sons. She had never had a close relationship with her older son, who was typically undemonstrative and independent. But she was quite close to her younger son, whom she described as a feeling type. When the older son went to live with his father, she was not upset and felt comfortable with the decision. However, several years later, the younger son decided to live with his father, too. Even though she thought the move would be good for her son, she found herself increasingly distraught as his departure approached. She felt rejected and discounted.

When her older son came to pick up his younger brother to take him to their father's house, Martha broke down sobbing. Her older son held and comforted her. From that moment on, their relationship changed dramatically. They became close and intimate and were no longer distant and aloof. Apparently, neither Martha nor her son were aware of the depth of feeling in their relationship. This moment of intense vulnerability that occurred when Martha's dominant function could not solve the problem permitted the welling up of genuine emotion stimulated by her normally unconscious feeling function. By experiencing a part of herself she rarely acknowledged, Martha was able to make an important and lasting connection with her son.

"I Can't Do My Job Because Nobody Likes Me!"

Eleanor, a CPA and professor of accounting at a small college, recalled a puzzling episode that happened to her. She had recently undergone major surgery and had been very apprehensive about it. It was early March, the height of tax preparation time, when she typically works 15-hour days, seven days a week. Her children were involved in a lot of activities at school, and she was also responsible for running several training programs at her college. On the weekend preceding the "event," she had driven sixteen hours to get to a training session she was to run.

Orville, an administrator at her college, was fired on a Friday morning. Eleanor was aware of how upset everyone was as a result of the events precipitating the firing. On Monday, she was asked to replace Orville and to reorganize his department. Orville's second-in-command, Ted—an ISTP who was also his best friend—thought he would be the one appointed to the position. He thereupon verbally attacked Eleanor in an abusive, violent manner. Eleanor did not react emotionally. "I figured it was reasonable and logical that he would be upset, so I didn't take it personally."

She felt fine on Tuesday, but on Wednesday, Ted repeated his abuse. She reminded herself of her logical analysis of the situation and thought he was being really stupid. In fact, she phoned him that night and told him she was angry at him for his childish behavior.

On Thursday, she felt disconnected, couldn't concentrate, and was plagued with doubts about her judgment. On Friday, Ted resumed his attack on her, leaving Eleanor feeling confused and disliked:

> I then began asking everyone in the organization whether they liked me. I made an appointment with the president of the college and told him I was resigning because no one liked me. I told a colleague I couldn't work in the department because no one liked me. I told my dean the same thing. I kind of took a survey of everyone to find out how they felt about me.

One colleague, knowing Eleanor's typical INTP values, told her it didn't matter if people didn't like her, as long as they respected her. "I just couldn't see the logic in that," said Eleanor.

She felt she had to resign everything administrative and resume her teaching. This conviction lasted all day.

Eleanor went to bed very early that night, woke up the next day and thought, "My God, what have I done?"

In analyzing what happened, Eleanor described herself as at first denying her own upset, excusing the behavior of her colleague, and disavowing her own humanness and vulnerability to being hurt. This new awareness led her to "try to recognize when I'm hurt and call people on it. But I have to give myself permission to need time to get to my feelings."

Solving the Puzzle

Carl, an ISTP businessman, had for years kept an earlier life episode locked away as puzzling, unsettling, and unexplainable. Hearing a brief description of the effects of the inferior function provided him with instant understanding and relief from the unresolved but still disturbing memory of the event.

He had been divorced for several years when the incident occurred, some ten years before. It was close to Christmas, and he had just broken up with a woman he had been seeing for some time. He found that though he apparently functioned adequately at work, he could not remember what he had actually worked on at the end of the day. His work life was a blank. At night when he was alone, however, he was hypersensitive to any kind of stimulation, such as the sound of dogs barking or cars driving by.

He started reading various self-help and inspirational books. He recorded his feelings in the form of poetic yearnings for love, attention, and a need to be cared for. He became so immersed in this side of himself that he ate and slept little. When he discovered that he had lost thirty pounds in as many days, he visited the doctor who recognized his need for a psychologist and referred him accordingly.

The doctor's confirmation that something was out of joint psychologically for Carl apparently pushed him out of his inferior extraverted feeling and back to himself. By the time he appeared for his appointment with the psychologist, he was handling things normally and was back to equilibrium again.

In one of his late night musings, Carl had written a lengthy essay that began with the words, "Am I a lost little boy in a grown-up world?" It went on to speak of his pain, loneliness, and desire for love and intimacy. He signed the essay, "By Author Unknown."

After his insight into his grip experience, he revisited this earlier two-month episode, reread his essay, and wrote a new conclusion: "Author Understands…ISTP," and signed it Carl Smith.

Descending Into the Painful Depths

Elizabeth, an INTP, discovered that understanding her own inferior function and that of her son led her to valuable insights. She described "descending into the murky, confusing, painful depths and learning an important lesson." She wrote the following account of her experience:

> It had been a difficult year and a half. My 14-year-old INFP son, a handsome, loving, and smart child, had turned into an angry, surly teenager. I knew he was using drugs, shoplifting, even staying out all night. I was having my own problems—unemployed and dealing with a serious family illness. With the help of some wonderful people in social services, I found help for my son, which eventually resulted in his spending more than a year in a mental hospital treatment program.
>
> Now things were vastly better. I was working, the family illness problem had receded, and my son was able to come home from the hospital. Through family

therapy, we had learned to deal with each other in a much more positive and cooperative way. I was cautiously optimistic.

Almost immediately, a serious disagreement arose about what my son was to do in the long afternoons after he got out of school, before I returned home. My perspective was totally reasonable: He had been locked up for more than a year with every minute in his life structured. He needed structure and support as he made this big adjustment to freedom. The high school was full of drugs and the kind of people he had hung out with before his hospitalization. We needed to agree on a plan for his free time. But he was beginning to sound like he did before the hospitalization— it's my life, I'm old enough to decide for myself, I can take care of myself, it's none of your business!

This discussion was repeated nightly for several days. I used my best calm and reasonable thinking approach, while my son became more and more nasty and angry. Our new relationship seemed pretty fragile.

After one of these evening discussions, I was suddenly swept by a feeling of total inability to deal effectively with my son and the fact that everything we had done had not worked—my daily visits to the hospital, the weekly meetings with his therapist, the agonizing learning I had done in the weekly family therapy, the thousands of dollars I'd spent—all for nothing. We were right back where we started. Worst of all, my son, my beautiful, intelligent son whom I loved and had tried to save, was back to his self-destructive behavior and completely lost to me.

I burst into tears and, fortunately, instead of recounting all the sacrifices we had made for him, what came out of my mouth was my deepest anguish—my love for my son. I sobbed, "Jim, I can't tell you how awful this is for me. At work, I can't concentrate, I'm distracted all the time. When I know it's almost time for you to get out of school, I start getting sick to my stomach. I can't eat lunch, I become ill. I'm so worried about what might be happening to you, that you might be hurt, might be in trouble, and I wouldn't even know."

My disrespectful son was transformed into a loving boy again: "Oh, Mom, I'm so sorry, I didn't know you felt like that. I'm sorry, Mom, I'm so sorry!" By now, he was sobbing, too. "I don't want you to feel like that. Look, as soon as I'm out of school, I'll call you and tell you what I'm going to do. If I'm going to somebody's house, I'll give you their name and phone number. I'll call you when I'm going to leave. I'll call you every hour if you want," and on and on with restrictions I would have never thought of suggesting to a 15-year-old boy. After a time of hugging and patting and wiping away tears, we were able to agree to an arrangement that worked for both of us.

What I now see is that my long, careful appeals to his reason—his inferior function—had not worked. They hadn't all his life; I don't know why I thought they would then! In despair and helplessness, I fell into the grip of my inferior function and expressed spontaneous feeling, something he had rarely, if ever, seen me do.

This spoke to his dominant function and brought out his truest judgment—that he loved me and wanted me to be happy. Every other consideration fell by the wayside; all he wanted to do was to relieve the genuine anguish he sensed in me.

The lesson I learned is that if I am willing and able to go into this alien part of me—to experience and express what I spontaneously feel—I can make real contact with my son. It is so difficult to do, so uncomfortable for me, though, that I seldom do it. Only once can I remember doing it voluntarily. But it's good to know that when all my reason and logic and imagination and humor have failed that this other part of me is there.

Return of Equilibrium

Introverted thinkers find that changing activities aids the normalization process. They need to be alone and physically separated from others, doing something they enjoy. Light problem solving that engages but doesn't strain their thinking, such as reading a mystery novel, can be helpful.

ISTP's auxiliary sensing can be helpful in encouraging them to do a reality check on the stressful situation. This occurred when Carl, the ISTP businessman, discovered that his doctor recognized his distress. This made his situation real and forced him to deal with it. INTPs can calm themselves down by playing unusual games of solitaire that don't depend on luck for success. Such games engage their auxiliary intuition. The repetitive handling of the cards (tertiary sensing) also has a calming effect.

Being excused from usual responsibilities and having someone else deal with the outer world helps introverted thinking types achieve equilibrium. Like many other types, ISTPs and INTPs find physical activity of some kind, especially hiking, to be a good way to detach themselves from a grip state.

Others can help by staying out of the way and forgiving the out-of-character behavior. A trusted person's physical presence is not intrusive, but psychological space should be respected. It is also helpful if someone close to the person can gently encourage them to talk about their feelings. However, many introverted thinkers report that the very worst thing that someone can do is to ask them how they feel about things. Often there is little that others can do. Internal acceptance and calm are what is needed most.

Expressions in Midlife

Ideally, midlife is accompanied by a positive and progressive integration of inferior extraverted feeling, and along with it tertiary intuition or sensing. Some introverted thinkers, however, do not achieve such integration.

Older introverted thinkers who may not have succeeded at reaching their full potential in life's developmental stages become increasingly malicious in their criticism, seeming to take pleasure in others' distressed responses. Their sphere of interests and tolerance of others' differences narrow considerably. They may be seen as eccentric recluses to be feared and avoided. Responses by others then serve to confirm the introverted thinker's conviction that he or she is unloved and unlovable. When this conclusion becomes immutable, there is little that can be done to alter beliefs on either side.

Midlife in well-differentiated introverted thinkers is accompanied by increasing sensitivity to the nuances of important relationships. There may be a corresponding decrease in the hypersensitivities that characterized their grip experiences when they were younger. Emotionalism is largely replaced by more readily expressed warmth and affection. An ISTP in his early forties discovered the pleasures of spending "unproductive" time with his wife and family. An INTP decided to marry her partner of twenty years, negating her previous view that "the piece of paper was irrelevant and illogical."

Notwithstanding the degree of adaptation of the individual, the right circumstances can still constellate a full-blown inferior function experience, with all its intensity. A 50-year-old INTP became increasingly depressed and despairing when her only son and his family left the country for three years. She became convinced that she had failed him emotionally and that his leaving was a result of that.

Some introverted thinking types become articulate about their feeling values during the second half of life. A 54-year-old INTP said:

> When I am in the grip, it generally doesn't concern things that I know I am intellectually competent at doing, but rather relationship issues. Investments in relationships are made at the core of who I am. What sends me over the brink are incidents that significantly devalue the meaning I have attached to my part of the relationship. It is almost as if the other person has come along and erased the

TABLE 8   **Major Features of Inferior Extraverted Feeling**

Triggers	Forms	New Knowledge
Strong emotions by others	Overemphasized logic	Acceptance of the illogical
Disconfirmation of feeling values	Hypersensitivity to relationships	Acknowledgment of vulnerability
Insensitivity to introversion needs	Emotionalism	Ability to express depth of feeling

blackboard—first by indicating that the meaning I thought I had communicated no longer exists and second by indicating that the essence of myself that was invested in those meanings has no more significance than chalk marks on a blackboard.

Summary

In the grip of inferior extraverted feeling, introverted thinking types have difficulty functioning at their typical level of cognitive acuity, are hypersensitive to relationship issues, and can be touchy and emotional. Equilibrium is often accomplished via their auxiliary sensing or intuition. ISTPs acknowledge one or more important realities bearing on their situation; INTPs find a new idea or perspective that interrupts and modifies their exaggerated sensitivity or emotionalism.

As a result of important inferior function experiences, introverted thinking types can acknowledge the importance of the "illogical and unexplainable" and accept their vulnerability to their own and others' emotional states. They may then have access to and be able to express the depth of their feelings for others. Table 8 above provides an overview of the major features of their inferior function experience.

CHAPTER 9

Extraverted Feeling Types
ESFJ and ENFJ

BASIC TYPE DYNAMICS

....

Dominant extraverted feeling

Auxiliary introverted sensing or intuition

Tertiary intuition or sensing

Inferior introverted thinking

....

Extraverted Feeling
Versus Introverted Thinking

THIS CHAPTER EXAMINES THE way effective extraverted feeling types experience their inferior function, and the temporary transformation they make into ineffective, inferior introverted thinking types when they are "in the grip." The following review of the characteristics of extraverted feeling and introverted thinking will be helpful to our discussion.

Important Features of Dominant Extraverted Feeling

Extraverted feeling types typically radiate goodwill and enthusiasm. They are optimistic about life in general, and human potential in particular. Their preferred focus is on the positive, harmonious, and uplifting aspects of people and human relations. They correspondingly pay little attention to negative, pessimistic, limiting, and divisive messages, situations, and conclusions. Their major goal is to create and maintain good feeling and harmony among people. Extraverted feeling types may recognize judgments that rely heavily on logical analysis, cause-and-effect relationships, and statistical odds, but they largely ignore such factors in making decisions. Others may therefore see ESFJs and ENFJs as making decisions that "fly in the face of logic." It can be puzzling and frustrating to thinking types in particular when an extraverted feeling type accurately describes the logical conclusions warranted by a situation, but decides in favor of harmony and caring. From a thinking point of view, such a criterion for a decision is inappropriate.

Extraverted feeling types are careful not to hurt others' feelings and try to take the well-being of others into account. If they cannot avoid telling someone an unpleasant truth, they will carefully soften the message by putting it in an affirmative context. Unconditional positive regard is a strongly held value.

As a result of their natural pleasure in pleasing others, extraverted feeling types can mistakenly be seen as overly caring or even codependent. In reality, however, attending to others' needs is usually a satisfying, legitimate way of expressing their dominant preference.

In a crisis that does not activate their inferior function, ESFJs and ENFJs focus on alleviating the concerns and suffering of others. They are comfortable letting others manage the more technical aspects of any crisis so they can devote their full energies to creating a cooperative, comfortable atmosphere for crisis victims. When a situation demands more forceful methods, however, they will take any action necessary for the benefit of others.

Important Features of Dominant Introverted Thinking

The qualities associated with introverted thinking that are relevant to our discussion of its form as an inferior function are an emphasis on:

- Impersonal criticism
- Logical analysis
- Accuracy and truth

For a detailed description of dominant introverted thinking, read the beginning of Chapter 8, "Introverted Thinking Types: ISTP and INTP," and the type descriptions for ISTP and INTP that appear in Appendix A. This will provide you with the background needed to explore the various ways in which inferior introverted thinking is expressed in ESFJs and ENFJs.

The Everyday Introverted Thinking of Extraverted Feeling Types

The inferior function affects extraverted feeling types in their everyday sensitivities, projections, and ways of relaxing, as well as the dramatic manifestations that can be seen when the inferior erupts and a full-blown episode occurs.

Typical Sensitivities and Projections

Extraverted feeling types can be particularly sensitive about others' assessment of their intellectual competence. Though usually not doubtful about their abilities, they are concerned that they might not communicate their knowledge clearly. In comparing themselves to others, they may feel they are slow to learn and lack analytical facility. Though many, especially ENFJs, are high achievers, some feel they are at a disadvantage in highly intellectual and technical endeavors.

Sensitivity about intellectual competence makes extraverted feeling types particularly attuned to comments that can be interpreted as reflecting inadequacy. In the early stages of an inferior function episode, this may come out as a projection onto others. They may notice and comment on the inaccuracies of others and a failure in others to recognize reality and confront the truth.

Such projection may be seen in the intensity with which they criticize others' behavior, particularly in the area of control. An ESFJ became furious every time her INTP supervisor barged into her office and interrupted her to talk about whatever was important to him at the time. In thinking about this, she realized that she herself needs to resist barging in on others and demanding their attention when she has a problem to solve or is upset about something.

Extraverted feeling types may be quick to identify other people's illogical behavior, but they may apply a different set of criteria to their own equally nonlogical actions. An ENFJ complained that his INFP wife's art studio was not set up systematically. "You really should put things into some logical order so they'll be right there when you need them," he told her. She replied that her current system suited her way of working. "But it's just not rational," he responded. When his wife likened the "disorganization" he perceived in her studio to his illogical way of organizing his house-hold chores—his inefficient way of ordering tasks and his tendency to leave tasks half done—he insisted that this was not the same thing. "The cleaning gets done, doesn't it?" he said heatedly. "My artwork gets done, too," she replied. He remained blind to the similarity.

Expressions Through Interests and Hobbies

Perhaps because the demands of their daily work and home lives require them to use their less preferred processes, extraverted feeling types seem to relax and choose recreational activities that engage their dominant and auxiliary functions rather than their tertiary or inferior ones. They enjoy such activities as entertaining, playing bridge, participating in group sports, and socializing in whatever ways that present themselves. Often avid readers, they enjoy discussing books with friends or becoming members of book discussion groups.

Home improvement hobbies are also quite satisfying to them. Sewing, crafts, building, carpentry, decorating, and gardening are often mentioned. They may be great joiners of civic, political, or school-related groups and tend to willingly take on leadership roles. One ESFJ, who enjoys a demanding career, takes pleasure in cooking elaborate meals for others, working in her garden so it will look beautiful, and writing lengthy letters to old friends—all activities that give her special joy because she has so little time for them.

ESFJs and ENFJs may also enthusiastically support the work, interests, and hobbies of their spouses and/or children, gaining great pleasure from developing at least some expertise in the relevant areas. One ENFJ learned all he could about his wife's research area and was as genuinely excited as she was when the results fit her hypotheses.

Eruptions of Inferior Introverted Thinking

When one or more of the preconditions for an eruption of the inferior function are present, inferior introverted thinking appears in its more exaggerated, disruptive form. In addition to the general conditions described in Chapter 4, extraverted feeling types are vulnerable to the type-specific factors described below.

Typical Provocations or Triggers

Extraverted feeling types respond with inferior introverted thinking when they are misunderstood, not trusted, or not taken seriously. A similar response occurs when they feel pressured to conform to some prevailing view they disagree with. In fact, any situation where conflict rather than harmony prevails can effectively activate the inferior for ESFJs and ENFJs.

When asked what provoked being "beside himself," an ENFJ responded, "Too many demands and feeling that I'm not appreciated, that I'm taken for granted, and that what I do doesn't matter to anyone." An ESFJ said, "When people disagree with my point of view and attack me personally." Another replied, "If I can't get my point across no matter how hard I try; when I'm not allowed to talk something out to get it resolved."

The Form of the Inferior

Evidence of inferior introverted thinking is preceded by a diminution or an absence of characteristic extraverted feeling qualities. General optimism, enthusiasm, and interest in people gives way to withdrawal, low energy, pessimism, and depression. Extraverted feeling types have described their loss of equilibrium as follows:

"I'm different in being introverted. I don't make contact, call friends, go to social events, meetings, the theater. I may accept an invitation, but only if someone urges me. I get concerned about my health. I have no plans, no vision, the future is bleak. I am numb, without feeling or zest for life."

"I am quiet and withdrawn and want to be alone and reflect on what is happening."

"I feel phony and uncomfortable, like a fish out of water. I am unable to be my usual spontaneous self."

TABLE 9   Dominant Versus Inferior Introverted Thinking

	Qualities Associated With Introverted Thinking
As Dominant Function	Impersonal criticism Logical analysis Search for accuracy and truth
As Inferior Function	Excessive criticism Convoluted logic Compulsive search for truth

"I don't make eye contact. I can't share what is going on inside me. I feel tight and negative."

As energy continues to be withdrawn from the dominant and auxiliary functions, inferior introverted thinking intrudes in the form of excessive criticism, convoluted logic, and a compulsive search for truth. The comparison between dominant and inferior introverted thinking is shown above in Table 9.

Jung's (1976a) comment on the inferior function of extraverted feeling types touches on all three of these features:

> The unconscious of this type contains first and foremost a peculiar kind of thinking, a thinking that is infantile, archaic, negative....The stronger the conscious feeling is and the more ego-less it becomes, the stronger grows the unconscious opposition.... The unconscious thinking reaches the surface in the form of obsessive ideas which are invariably of a negative and deprecatory character. (p. 359)

Excessive criticism   Effective dominant introverted thinkers critique ideas, products, systems, or methods. The inferior introverted thinking of extraverted feeling types appears in the form of a sweeping condemnation of people. In the grip of inferior thinking, ESFJs and ENFJs may "dump" on other people, slam doors, yell, make biting comments, and say terse, mean, or even cruel things to others. They often become physically tense, grit their teeth, clench their fists, and are visibly agitated. Laying a "guilt trip" on those closest to them is frequently mentioned by both extraverted feeling types.

As their extraverted energy further diminishes, their criticism becomes internalized, resulting in self-deprecatory judgments. Turning the criticism inward encourages depression, low self-worth, and guilty embarrassment at revealing what they view as their alien and unacceptable side.

A hostile, negative atmosphere can bring out sharp, biting, and even vicious comments from extraverted feeling types. They seem to dig in their heels, intractable to either logical or feeling arguments. As one described, "I become cranky, judgmental, and angry. I mistrust myself and others. Normally, I instinctively trust everyone. I am different when I am not acting from trust. Often this occurs when I feel I am not trusted or understood, or when there is conflict and tension around me."

An ESFJ reported becoming steely and caustic; another described herself as coolly objective when her strongly held feelings were violated. One ESFJ was convinced that everyone took advantage of her good-natured, helpful ISFP husband. She persistently berated him for his weakness and loudly condemned his family and friends for their rude behavior.

"I am like Dr. Jekyl and Mr. Hyde," said an ENFJ describing his reaction to extreme stress. "My humor becomes inappropriate, meant to shock people. I've even been known to throw things while in this frame of mind."

Convoluted logic   In the grip of inferior thinking, the extraverted feeling type's attempts at logical analysis take the form of categorical, all-or-none judgments that are often based on irrelevant data. A highly idiosyncratic "logical" model may be developed internally, but the resulting conclusions may violate good logic.

In describing this quality, Von Franz (1971) stated that because their thinking is neglected, "it tends to become negative and coarse. It consists of coarse, primitive thinking judgments, without the slightest differentiation and very often with a negative tinge" (p. 45).

"My thinking becomes rigid and I insist on solving problems alone with none of my typical sharing," said one ENFJ. "I maintain a front, even though I feel unworthy. I become verbally critical, organize more, and become rigid, perfectionistic, and angry. I want the world to go away."

Elaborate, logical "plots" may be developed by the extraverted feeling type in the grip of negative introverted thinking. These take the form of complicated and improbable scenarios to deal with or eliminate the distress or disharmony in question. ESFJs and ENFJs frequently describe making up "stories," the goal of which is to explain some upsetting event or solve some nagging problem.

An ENFJ recalled that at the age of twelve, she was required to participate in a field day of sporting events. Convinced of her lack of skill in this area, she wanted to avoid embarrassing herself in front of her peers. She plotted various ways to break her leg or ankle, such as falling out of a tree or being run over by a car, but she abandoned her plans, reasoning that she would probably suffer more than minor injury. She also recognized that a lot of pain could be involved. Ironically, she was forced to participate and placed third in the broad jump.

Often the source of the problem stimulating the "story" is meanness or criticism directed at the extraverted feeling type or a close associate. An ESFJ with a long commute to work was frequently distressed by other drivers' rude, inconsiderate behavior. He found himself "making up a long and involved story about the rude driver, in which I imagined the kind of work he did, his family relationships, the daily events that impacted on him, and the possible mitigating circumstances that caused his meanness to me." The imaginary explanation served to restore harmony and allowed the ESFJ to retain his positive valuation of people.

Compulsive search for truth Dominant introverted thinking types value truth as the criterion for judgments and decisions. They use logical analysis to arrive at the most objective truth possible. For extraverted feeling types in the grip of inferior introverted thinking, seeking absolute, ultimate truth can become an obsession. Many report turning to experts for advice but requiring them to have the "real truth," or at least the latest knowledge and thinking on the subject. When an expert is not immediately available, they may attempt an internal logical dialogue with themselves, often ending up recognizing that their logic is convoluted. This may make them feel frightened, out of control, and despairing of ever extricating from their negative logical conclusions. An ENFJ said:

> I become stuck on an idea and don't have any perspective about it. The devastating truth of my conclusion is overwhelming. I try to think my way out of this tight box I'm in, but there is no escape from my conclusion. I feel compelled to find someone to tell me what to do.

Instead of searching for a specific person who may provide them with needed answers, many extraverted feeling types report a preference for lectures or books relevant to their current problem, often being avid readers of self-help books. ESFJs and ENFJs agree that when stress in some area of their lives occurs, they search bookstore shelves for answers.

One ENFJ had a wall full of books in his office. His colleague wondered how he could possibly have read all of them. The ENFJ reported that when under pressure to solve a big problem, he virtually devours the books, having many of them open at once, searching for expert advice on the problem at hand.

When a stressful area is chronic or serious, extraverted feeling types tend to be attracted to support groups. In the company of others having similar experiences, they can find validation for their perceptions, as well as the latest expertise and thinking about the problem area.

Grip Experiences

The stories included in this section illustrate one or more forms of inferior introverted thinking as experienced by ESFJs or ENFJs. Their dominant extraverted feeling emerges in their concern and distress about the people they have hurt during their out-of-character episodes. Like their introverted feeling counterparts, they take responsibility for repairing damaged relationships when the episode is over.

The Experts Are in the Bag

Emma, an ESFJ, saw a psychologist because of continuing problems with her marriage, her career, and her adolescent children. The difficulties with her husband were particularly upsetting and, as he was willing to attend a session with her, she arranged that they would go to the next appointment together. Later in the afternoon, the psychologist discovered a large shopping bag in her waiting room filled with self-help books on topics dealing with marriage, family, children, and careers. On top of the pile was a note from Emma that read: "These are the experts I've been reading. I'd like to know what you think of them." Apparently, Emma wanted the newest expert, her psychologist, to evaluate the expertise of her predecessors.

I Can, I Can, I Can, I Can't....

When extraverted feeling types are vulnerable to an inferior function experience, they may decide that they absolutely must learn some new skill or accomplish some unfamiliar thinking task. This was the case for Sam, an ENFJ, who decided one March that he would no longer use an accountant to prepare his tax returns. His taxes that year were rather complicated, but he assured himself that any intelligent person could figure it out. Each time the instructions confused him, he laid the taxes aside, telling himself he could tackle it successfully "tomorrow."

As April 15 approached, he became increasingly agitated and angry at himself, but continued to struggle compulsively with his tax problems. "I did not even consider asking for help. Conquering the tax code had become the essential criterion for my intellectual competence," he recalled.

"I couldn't let go of it. It became the symbol of my incompetence. I had to see it through, or forever acknowledge that I was intellectually inferior," he said several weeks later. He went on to explain:

> It was as if I created a self-fulfilling prophecy. I still don't know why I picked that one thing. I tried to remind myself of all the things I was good at, but none of it counted. When I think about it now, I believe I had been undertaking too many things, both at work and at home, feeling like I had to be perfect at everything. This experience forced me to change my expectations of myself. I think that now I can be more reasonable about what I should be able to do.

"Or I Could Bribe the Doorman?"

Angela, an ENFJ, was told that she would have to wait several weeks before learning whether she was to be hired for a coveted job. She felt anxious during that time, powerless to influence the decision in any way. She found herself developing complicated schemes to surreptitiously discover whether she got the job: "I could put on a disguise and reapply for the job to find out if they'd filled it—or I could bribe the doorman of the building to look at my file!"

As time dragged on, she sought advice from others about which interventions to pursue. She reported feeling ungrounded and uncaring about people. Her single-mindedness about this one issue puzzled her friends, who were used to her sensitivity to others' needs and her wide-ranging interests. Her family accused her of not being herself, of being spacy, and of failing to take responsibility for the rest of the family. These accusations increased her sense of "otherness" and her feeling of being outside of herself.

Receiving word that she would be hired for the job was a relief, but also anticlimactic for Angela. But with the unaccustomed stress and her out-of-character reaction to it over, she recognized that she had allowed this one event to be the criterion for her competence:

> It forced me to think about my abilities and to recognize that I was indeed quite accomplished in my field. Since then I've been better able to deal with ambiguous situations and to put criticisms of my work in a positive perspective.

"What Kind of Father Would Raise Such a Son?"

Harold, an ESFJ single father, was helping his 21-year-old ISFP son, Dave, move into his first apartment. Dave had assured his father that he would have all the packing and organizing done ahead of time and would only need some help putting his things into the truck he was borrowing from a friend.

But on the day of the move, Harold found that Dave's things were in general disarray, that little had been packed, and that he had forgotten to ask his friend for the pickup truck! From Harold's point of view, Dave did not know how to proceed, could not even figure out how to ask for help, or know what kind of help he needed. Worst of all, his son seemed quite unconcerned about the whole thing. Harold then began to see his own fault in the matter:

> At first I felt frustrated and angry at Dave. But as the day went on and we got things under control, I felt more and more tired, depressed, and hopeless. I thought about how incompetent my son is about everyday life, recalled all the other examples of this same kind of inadequacy, how unprepared he was to live as an independent person. As a widower, I was responsible for Dave's upbringing. Clearly, I had failed in that task. It was due to my own incompetence as a parent that my son was unable to succeed in life. I sank deeper and deeper into despair.

But after a good night's sleep, things did not seem quite so bleak to Harold. Dave called to say he had gotten his phone hooked up and his utilities turned on and that he had done some grocery shopping. He seemed delighted with his apartment and was enthusiastic about being on his own.

"I started recalling all of Dave's many successes," remembered Harold, "how he could persevere and overcome situations that were difficult for him. I realized that being superorganized is *my* thing, not his, and that lives don't stand or fall on this one ability. My good humor and optimism about the future reappeared. I relaxed and was able to enjoy shopping with Dave for some household items."

Two Inferior Functions Meet in the Kitchen

Judy, an ENFJ, is married to Luis, an INTP. They were cleaning up the dinner dishes together after what had been an extremely stressful and tiring day at work for both of them. Judy let the dog out and he began to bark. Luis particularly disliked the sound of dogs barking and had previously asked Judy not to let the dog outside in the evening, as he often barked at the neighbor's dog. Without a word, Luis stopped drying the dishes, left the kitchen, entered his study, and slammed the door behind him.

Judy finished cleaning the kitchen, feeling increasingly despairing about her inability to meet Luis' need for silence and solitude. She became angry with his habit of shutting her out and "sucking himself into his study. I knew he could avoid dealing with the hurt between us much longer than I could. But I couldn't imagine any way to alter the overwhelming fact of our incompatibility. Obviously we were unable to meet each other's needs, so our marriage would have to end."

Judy sat down to write Luis a letter describing her conclusions. She wrote that she was incapable of creating a comfortable atmosphere for him, acknowledged his right to prefer being alone rather than being with her, and conveyed the logical conclusion that their relationship was therefore over.

Even while she was writing, Judy recognized that her thinking was off. At one point in the letter, she wrote, "This probably sounds out of bounds, even out of mind." She had some inkling that her logic was amiss, but was unable to marshall the energy to remove herself from the logic-tight tunnel she was in. The larger and more potent issues in her marriage were thus unavailable to temper the relatively minor incident of Luis' irritable behavior.

Luis later described his irritation as brief and the result of his fatigue. It was unrelated to his commitment to their marriage. But in Judy's vulnerable state, the incident took on the importance of a defining event for their marriage and logically implied its termination. "Our discussion of this and other similar misunderstandings led us to a new appreciation and interest in each other," explained Judy. "It brought us even closer and made our relationship more intimate and satisfying."

Return of Equilibrium

Normal access to dominant feeling returns as extraverted feeling types allow new information to enter their consciousness. This may occur through either auxiliary sensing or intuition. Experiencing a change of scene, listening to a friend talk about something interesting or amusing, being outdoors, or exercising can aid the process of return to equilibrium. One ENFJ said that he sometimes needs to take long breaks that allow him to withdraw from his usual hectic schedule to spend time in more solitary study and physical exercise.

Extraverted feeling types appreciate being encouraged to get involved in projects. ENFJs find it helpful to embark on an ambitious new undertaking, even if they have to force themselves at first; ESFJs may prefer to work on a smaller, detailed project that can be accomplished slowly and methodically.

ESFJs and ENFJs frequently mention the need to be taken seriously by friends and be allowed to vent and sound off without being talked out of it. They are being genuine when they say they want to be left alone. Writing in a journal can also help them fulfill this function by allowing them to extravert auxiliary sensing or intuition on paper. They may thus get a handle on the problem without fearing external judgment or interference.

Expressions in Midlife

Many extraverted feeling types turn inward during midlife, pursuing more solitary activities. One ENFJ reported that when she was younger, she never spent her free time reading the way she does now. Often the desire to be alone also reflects an emerging attraction to activities that do not focus on having harmonious relationships with others.

Those ESFJs and ENFJs whose adult years were insufficiently fulfilling may become caricatures of their younger selves. They may indeed satisfy the criteria for codependency, demonstrating an inability to separate themselves from others. One ESFJ insisted on doing full-time babysitting for her three grandchildren. She felt useless and rejected, and needed to be treated for depression when her daughter decided to enroll them in a preschool. In fact, the daughter's decision was in response to her mother's "smothering" care, which she feared was inhibiting her children's exploration of their own independence.

An ENFJ minister in his sixties was advised by his physician to give up some of his many community activities, since the fatigue and stress that resulted were seriously affecting his health. He was unwilling to give them up, fearing criticism for failing to fulfill his commitment to serve others. He became anxious and depressed when he was unable to fully devote himself to taking care of others.

Extraverted feeling types whose adult development is more complete tend to temper the kinds of behaviors that in earlier times might have made them look overly attentive to the needs of others. Said one ENFJ:

> I am not the "ever-flowing breast" I was when I was younger. I don't give of myself indiscriminately as I once did. I can say no when a request doesn't appeal to me and not feel badly about it. I still enjoy being helpful and seeing the people around me happy and fulfilled. But I've become very interested in going birdwatching by myself, and this often is more appealing than being with other people.

An ESFJ acknowledged her difficulty in taking care of herself because of her need to accomplish other necessary tasks first. So she has learned to include time for herself in her schedule. She may spend forty-five minutes reading a good book on a Saturday afternoon. This proves so enjoyable that she no longer resents having to stay up late on Sunday night finishing her ironing.

Another ESFJ said:

> I learned not to live through my children or be so concerned about controlling their happiness. I take one day at a time, enjoying the journey rather than the destination. Being liked is not as important to me as when I was younger. It's most important to be true to myself. I can say no a lot more easily and not try to fix everything.

In paying more attention to their own needs, many extraverted feeling types may also rediscover their earlier career interests that were not actualized. This sometimes results in a midlife career change. A 55-year-old ENFJ attorney gave up his successful law practice to attend divinity school and become a minister in the church he had been devoted to much of his life.

Both ESFJs and ENFJs report paying greater attention to their inner lives at midlife, often aided by formal meditation methods. They may feel and may be seen as more calm and focused in their behavior. An ENFJ

TABLE 10   Major Features of Inferior Introverted Thinking

Triggers	Forms	New Knowledge
Absence of trust	Excessive criticism	Less need for harmony
Pressure to conform	Convoluted logic	Trust in one's own thinking
Interpersonal conflict	Search for truth	Tempered response to adversity

described the older ESFJs and ENFJs she knew as "having a gracious, warm extraversion tempered with a calm wisdom. I experience it as containing a realistic objectivity that allows them to possess an acceptance of life's foibles with sad resignation and optimism."

Summary

In the grip of inferior introverted thinking, extraverted feeling types engage in excessive criticism of others as well as themselves, adopt a distorted and convoluted logic, and compulsively search for exacting truth. Auxiliary sensing or intuition may help them reestablish their equilibrium. ESFJs may work on a task requiring systematic attention to detail; ENFJs' return to equilibrium can be aided by planning new projects.

The new awareness extraverted feeling types gain as a result of an important bout with their inferior often centers on an acceptance of the limitations reality imposes on their desire for peace and harmony. They may become better able to evaluate their own logical analyses and face adversity more dispassionately. Their auxiliary sensing or intuition can aid in this process. ESFJs may acknowledge previously rejected unpleasant facts, while ENFJs may permit their intuition to flow into darker possibilities. Both are then able to increase their effectiveness in accomplishing goals important to their value structure. Table 10 above gives an overview of the major features of the inferior function experience of extraverted feeling types.

CHAPTER 10

Extraverted Sensing Types

ESTP and ESFP

BASIC TYPE DYNAMICS
....
Dominant extraverted sensing

Auxiliary introverted thinking or feeling

Tertiary feeling or thinking

Inferior introverted intuition
....

Extraverted Sensing
Versus Introverted Intuition

THIS CHAPTER EXAMINES THE way effective extraverted sensing types experience their inferior function, and the temporary transformation they make
into ineffective, inferior introverted intuitives when they are "in the grip."
The following review of the characteristics of extraverted sensing and
introverted intuition will be helpful to our discussion.

Important Features of Dominant Extraverted Sensing

Extraverted sensing types are typically out "in the world." They experience
sensory data from the environment purely and directly. At their best, they
can cut to the heart of a situation and implement an effective solution.

They are able to appropriately ignore hidden implications, hypotheses, past traditions, and future possibilities. This may underlie the economy of effort that characterizes their style. They tend not to dwell on problems outside of their control, rarely focus for long on anything negative, and are thus typically optimistic. In trusting the evidence of their senses, they do not attribute unseen motives to others; they take people and situations at face value and accept others as they are.

Unlike introverted sensing types, their sensing data are not organized into preexisting categories or systems. Rather, data are accepted without discrimination and are only later subjected to sorting and selection through their auxiliary thinking or feeling functions. This, in conjunction with the immediacy of their perceptual process, may underlie their natural affinity for sensual and aesthetic experience.

ESTPs and ESFPs are likely to be impatient with people who read between the lines and focus on the unseen and the unverified. They have little interest in theories, pure speculation, and imagination for its own sake. They tend to see intuitives as people who live inside their heads while ignoring the realities and beauty of the world.

Extraverted sensing types may be perceived by others as shallow in their pursuit of sensual pleasure and as lacking the goals and ambitions valued by society at large. However, others may also admire and envy the extraverted sensor's carefree enjoyment of everyday living.

In a crisis that does not engage their inferior function, extraverted sensing types are likely to be calmly efficient and effective. Their knack for quickly identifying and attending to critical variables places them in a good position for emergency situations.

Important Features of Dominant Introverted Intuition

The qualities associated with introverted intuition that are relevant to predicting its form as an inferior function are an emphasis on:

- Intellectual clarity
- Accurate interpretation of perceptions
- Visionary insight

For a detailed description of dominant introverted intuition, read the beginning of Chapter 11, "Introverted Intuitive Types: INTJ and INFJ," and the type descriptions for INTJ and INFJ that appear in Appendix A. This will provide you with the background needed to explore the various ways in which inferior introverted intuition is expressed in ESTPs and ESFPs.

The Everyday Introverted Intuition of Extraverted Sensing Types

The inferior function affects extraverted sensing types in different ways. These include everyday sensitivities, projections, and ways of relaxing, as well as the dramatic manifestations that can be seen when the inferior erupts and a full-blown episode occurs.

Typical Sensitivities and Projections

Extraverted sensing types may experience some uneasiness about their natural affinity for fun in the present moment, often picking up on the disapproval others feel for their carefree approach to life. One 49-year-old ESFP mother of three grown children confessed that she did not feel quite "grown up." Her peers had detailed plans for the future, including retirement, while she rarely planned beyond the next month. The nine-year-old son of another ESFP mother often tells her he would like her to "do more things the same way—like eat meals at the same time and know beforehand what we're going to do on Saturday." His mother's reaction is to feel (at least briefly) inadequate as a parent. "He told me I'm like the mother in that movie *Mermaids*—she was constantly moving the family around, and she fed them only snack food instead of real meals."

An ESTP physician reported a recurrent dream in which his medical degree was revoked because of a failure to keep current on the literature. An ESFP corporate executive felt he had to justify his managerial legitimacy since his function was to entertain important potential clients. He sensed that the other executives devalued his contribution to the firm.

In the early stages of inferior introverted intuition, ESTPs and ESFPs may project their negative intuition by attributing meaning to isolated minor occurrences. A phone call from an old friend may lead to an inference about some impending event; a song popping into an extraverted sensor's head might be taken to mean that her supervisor is angry; a "message" is read into a friend's request to borrow a car. One ESFP described seeking "divine intervention" when having to make decisions, especially about the future. He looks for signs that will tell him what to do (if three green cars pass in the next five minutes, it means yes; three blue cars might mean no). Although he never actually uses this strategy to make decisions, the thoughts come automatically and are quite compelling.

Expressions Through Interests and Hobbies

Extraverted sensing types, like their introverted sensing counterparts, may be attracted to areas that address the mysteries of intuition, especially introverted intuition. Systems that deal with inner forces, mysticism, and various forms of extrasensory perception may hold a particular allure. The pull is toward knowledge that depends on processes beyond the immediacy of the five senses. An ESFP/ESTP couple were active in a theosophical society in their city. Their other major recreational activity was the local ski club.

Extraverted sensing types' ability to temporarily take on the qualities of their environment may contribute to their enjoyment of leisure activities. An ESFP is an avid reader of both nonfiction and fiction. She finds that she easily identifies with the characters in good books, "totally becoming them" while she is reading. An ESTP seeks out the company of happy people because it raises her spirits.

Eruptions of Inferior Introverted Intuition

When one or more of the preconditions for eruption of the inferior function are present, inferior introverted intuition appears in its more exaggerated and disruptive form. In addition to the general conditions described in Chapter 4, extraverted sensing types are vulnerable to the type-specific factors described below.

Typical Provocations or Triggers

Inferior introverted intuition can be triggered when extraverted sensing types spend a lot of time with people who are excessively serious or focused on future plans and goals. In fact, any situation that requires projection into the future and commitment to a distant goal may provoke an inferior function experience. For some, even committing to things in the near future can be unpleasant.

"I feel pinned down by commitments," said an ESFP. "What if I don't feel like seeing a movie tomorrow, or going out to lunch, or going on that vacation? Having to do something feels threatening and gives me a feeling of dread."

Extraverted sensors may experience even greater apprehension when they are forced to make decisions about distant possibilities. For them, the information needed for decision making won't be available until the future becomes the present!

"How can I know now what major I'll want in college three years from now?" asked an ESFP high school senior. "What if I pick the wrong thing and have to stay with it?" An ESTP said, "If I decide to be a dental technician, I won't be able to be anything else." Other extraverted sensing types agree that closing off options by making a choice makes them anxious and gloomy. "I'm filled with panic and dread when I am faced with "have to's," said an ESFP.

Operating within a set structure that requires conformity to someone else's schedule may also prove debilitating to extraverted sensing types. Lengthy periods in such a school or work environment may lead to the inertia and despondence that often presages an inferior function experience.

The Form of the Inferior

Early signs of the inferior function are preceded by a loss of the easygoing, agreeable character of the extraverted sensor. No longer are sensory data accepted indiscriminately at face value. Extraverted sensors may seem to withdraw into themselves, lose contact with their habitual optimism, and appear tired, worried, and withdrawn.

An ESFP remarked, "In the beginning, I gradually take on too much work and too many responsibilities, then I become overpowered with negative thoughts and become very quiet and sad."

An ESTP noted, "I start to feel that things are overwhelming, and then I let them accumulate, and then I lose all motivation."

And another ESFP said, "I become more contemplative, less talkative, and I'm seen by others as a serious, withdrawn person. This is not my usual self."

"I feel like I have to get control of the situation," said an ESTP. "I avoid other people, feel guilty about it, and try to speed up everything I do."

TABLE 11   Dominant Versus Inferior Introverted Intuition

	Qualities Associated With Introverted Intuition
As Dominant Function	Intellectual clarity Accurate interpretation of perceptions Visionary insight
As Inferior Function	Internal confusion Inappropriate attribution of meaning Grandiose visions

As their hold on their dominant and auxiliary functions further diminishes, the qualities of inferior introverted intuition become manifested in internal confusion, inappropriate attribution of meaning, and grandiose visions. The comparison between dominant and inferior introverted intuition is shown above in Table 11.

The negative, inferior forms of all three of these qualities are reflected in Jung's (1976a) description of the inferior introverted intuition of ESTPs and ESFPs:

> Above all, the repressed intuitions begin to assert themselves in the form of projections. The wildest suspicions arise....More acute cases develop every sort of phobia, and, in particular, compulsion symptoms...contents have a markedly unreal character, with a frequent moral or religious streak....The whole structure of thought and feeling seems, in this second personality, to be twisted into a pathological parody: reason turns into hair-splitting pedantry, morality into dreary moralizing... religion into ridiculous superstition, and intuition...into meddlesome officiousness. (p. 365)

Internal confusion   Effective dominant introverted intuitives are noted for their intellectual clarity—their ability to process and integrate complex information. In the grip of inferior introverted intuition, extraverted sensing types become confused by unfamiliar inner processes. Because their negative intuition is internal, fantasies of impending disaster and dire possibilities are typically self-referential or limited to the people closest to them. They may have overwhelming fears about fatal illnesses, forebodings about losing an important relationship, and anxiety about harm coming to a loved one.

Fears of impending psychosis can also haunt extraverted sensors. The unfamiliar internal intuitive information appears fraught with danger and impending doom. They may feel overwhelmed by inner possibilities, disturbing images, unfamiliar self-doubt, and loss of connection to their environment. They question their own abilities and fear subsequent exposure as incompetent in their most important endeavors.

"I feel like I am being enveloped in a whirling, swirling maelstrom," said one ESFP.

"I get into a spiral filled with frightening possibilities," said another.

An ESTP describes feeling as though she is in a dark and endless tunnel. Another explains, "I become confused and paranoid. All possibilities are fearsome—any kind of change, anything in the future." When the trigger for the experience is being forced to think about future plans, the reaction can be devastating, as the following example illustrates:

> I am horrified that I won't be where I want to be. Not that my lack of accomplishment will be disastrous, but that it will be dreary. If I try to project myself to where I should be, it will cut off my ability to react to the moment. Instead of exciting possibilities, I can only think of disastrous ones. The thought of future change makes me feel lonely and gloomy and dreary. It all ends up with misery. So it's safer to stick with what is, but the possibilities in what is are also dreary.

For this ESTP, negative introverted intuition is accompanied by tertiary feeling so that the negative possibilities appear as emotional states— loneliness, dreariness, and gloom.

Inappropriate attribution of meaning   Effective dominant introverted intuitives are adept at interpreting their complex inner perceptions. They are highly selective in the environmental information they process. In the grip of inferior introverted intuition, an extraverted sensing type may, because of lack of experience, internalize random cues from the environment and interpret them as negative possibilities. If an intimate relationship is involved, there may be a foreboding that he or she has done something to cause some negative response in the other person. Or, a simple request may be interpreted as a sign of disapproval or disappointment.

A young and newly married ESTP became overwhelmed with the thought that her husband, who had gone out with his friends, had left her and would never return—despite the fact that he visited his friends frequently and the time that he was expected to return had not yet arrived. She obsessed on the thought that she had been nasty to him earlier and became flooded with anxiety and apprehension. She thereupon drove over to his friend's house, only to find that he was just preparing to leave and return home.

Extraverted sensing types in their vulnerable phase may start reading between the lines and attributing malevolent motives to people. A feeling of unreality or disconnection from others may occur, and this may in turn lead to terror at the alien experience of isolation. One ESFP was pleased to have free time when her children happily spent the weekend with her ex-husband and his new wife. But while they were gone, she became consumed with the idea that her children would prefer her ex-husband's wife to her because she was not a good mother. They won't be my kids when they return, she told herself, so nothing is okay and it will never be again.

Grandiose visions The visionary insight of effective dominant intro-verted intuitives has often been noted. They have an uncanny ability to envision the distant future in an almost prophetic way. In its inferior form, this quality surfaces in extraverted sensing types in grandiose, often nebulous cosmic "visions." We saw hints of this quality in the "magical thinking" that was described earlier. Because dwelling on the past or future is unusual for extraverted sensing types, inferior function episodes tend to be short lived, and magical ruminations are rarely acted on. However, when subjected to extended stress, extraverted sensors may search for mystical meaning in the form of an obsessive interest in unseen forces of cosmic proportions.

The omnipresence of profound meaning may stimulate the extraverted sensor to search for or create a grand cosmology. Events typically given no more than a moment's thought are imbued with deep significance; unrelated chance occurrences are subjected to complex integrations and interpretations; theories about the ultimate purpose of life and humanity's place in nature are formulated. Such ruminations may engage the entire attention of the extraverted sensor, and this interest may be seen by others as out of bounds and out of character.

An ESTP who lost his business during a recession became increasingly morose and distant. He tried to reconnect with the church of his child-hood, but was unable to find comfort there. By chance, he saw a notice in the newspaper advertising a lecture by an East Indian guru. He attended the lecture and felt instantly "transformed by the words of this wise man. I knew what my destiny must be," he explained. He abandoned his existing life and joined the guru's spiritual movement. During his year of spiritual exploration, he wrote lengthy mystical poems extolling the unseen forces that shape people's destinies. When he returned home, he started a new business with great enthusiasm and optimism and felt that he brought greater balance and breadth to his enterprise.

Grip Experiences

The stories included in this section illustrate one or more forms of inferior introverted intuition as experienced by ESTPs or ESFPs. Note that dominant extraverted sensing comes through in the evocative sense impressions and the rich detail described.

The Minister's Ordeal

A pastoral ministry of 37 years ended with the ESFP minister's forced resignation. With only five years until his retirement, he had become burned out with his ministry. He had also been dealing for several years with his wife's debilitating chronic illness. He was seen by parishioners as rigid, controlling, pessimistic, and ineffectual. In retrospect, he recognized that he had been in the grip of inferior introverted intuition for several years prior to his resignation.

The added humiliation and loss of identity associated with his resignation resulted in a profound feeling of isolation from the world and a fear of being overwhelmed by mysterious, malevolent forces: "I felt totally abandoned by the God who had been my protector and guide throughout my life."

In this state of hypersensitivity to signs and portents, he found new meaning in phone calls from colleagues, chance encounters, and books friends sent him. He experienced "flashbacks as clear as videos" and pictures and metaphors that gave meaning to his issues. He began paying close attention to dreams and spontaneous images.

Gradually, he emerged from his state of otherness and alienation, profoundly changed by his lengthy grip experience. He found that this extended period in the throes of abstract meaning gave him an appreciation for his "other side" and thus gave him renewed energy for his work. He learned to value things that had previously been of little interest to him, and people whom he had judged "foolish dreamers."

With the renewal of his relationship to himself, his tertiary thinking and auxiliary feeling helped him recognize that he needed to be gainfully employed. He was then able to use his dominant sensing to search for and get a job.

Later, with his expanded understanding of himself and the value and meaning of abstractions, he sought out and counseled other ministers experiencing burnout in their work and personal lives. Eventually, he established a new ministry that incorporated his 37 years of experience with his newfound expanded consciousness.

The Cloud of Unknown

Christine, an ESTP, recalled a time when she was so out of character that her friends became frightened for her. Knowing that her friends were concerned added to her own fear; it meant that she was out of touch with reality (her dominant sensing function). She related the following story:

> At the end of my first Ph.D. year, I realized that I was not very happy. My specialty area was complex and theoretical, and I was unsure about whether to go on. So I made an appointment with my supervisor and told him my doubts.
>
> I remember that it was a sunny afternoon. I anticipated that he would say, "Of course you should go on. You've come this far!" He in fact said, "Well, perhaps you should reconsider."
>
> This put me into a swirling spiral of doom. Every possibility I came up with ended with me as a bag lady. I saw myself constantly feeling a failure for giving up the program, and I would fail at everything else because I would lack confidence. I had this sinking feeling that I was burning a bridge behind me; where I stepped off was a cloud of unknown.
>
> But then I realized that I had not burned any bridges and didn't have to go into all this unknown because I hadn't left the program. But this wasn't a happy thought. It was dreary. I thus saw that my only choice was between dreariness and terror.

Finally, she decided to stay in the haven of security of school, and subsequently completed the Ph.D. program. In retrospect, Christine related her reaction to the prospect of change. She felt terrified of losing her security and everything tangible she could grasp. If she lost these real things, she'd become an outcast. Her school grant was a secure base. If she left school, she would be penniless.

Christine explained that the experience taught her about her need for security and the "limits of my venturousness." Perhaps this need tempers or compensates her dominant extraverted sensing.

The Telltale Greeting Card

Linda, an ESFP, found her work as a labor relations negotiator exciting and satisfying. She was successful and highly regarded. At one point, she was involved in a particularly demanding and stressful negotiation situation that went on for several months. She was often tired and distracted because of the long hours she had to put in at work. In spite of this, however, she and Don, her boyfriend of several years, decided to go forward with their plans to live together. So they rented a house, moved their belongings in, and set about unpacking and organizing their things.

Linda was unpacking a box of Don's books when a greeting card envelope fell out of a book. She glanced at the return address, noticed that it was from a woman who lived in Don's hometown, which he frequently visits on business, and handed it to him. Don quickly took the card without looking at it and went into the kitchen, saying nothing. Linda recounted her response in this way:

> I was suddenly overwhelmed with anxiety, convinced that Don had been carrying on an affair with someone in his hometown, that our living together was a terrible mistake. I thought about all the times he's been out of town on business, phone calls he made and received when I was at his apartment, things in his past he wouldn't talk about. It all added up. At the same time I was convinced of this, I also knew it was irrational and really didn't add up to anything. But I couldn't stop myself from being flooded with these dark ideas and the frightening conclusion they led to.
>
> I wrestled with this for several hours, gradually becoming calm enough to look rationally at all the consistently loving things in my relationship with Don. I remembered that Don becomes particularly uncommunicative when he's busy with details, and that telling him about the card was merely an unwelcome interruption. My distress went away and I was back to normal.

Looking for Escape Routes

Steve, an ESTP sports journalist, was excited and happy about the impending birth of his and his wife's first child. Although it was the height of football season, he was confident he would be able to get someone to cover for him at a moment's notice should Cindy go into labor earlier than expected. He figured that his uncharacteristic distractibility at work and at home were the result of anticipation and his heavier work load.

Cindy had their baby a week after her official due date. Steve comforted her during her long and difficult labor. Both parents were thrilled with their new baby girl and, though they were quite exhausted, were happy to bring her home. That first night home with her, however, Steve awoke suddenly and was overwhelmed with the thought that a fire might break out in the house. He recalled:

> I was in a panic. I got up and roamed all over the house trying to identify possible escape routes. After satisfying myself that we could escape, I went back to sleep.
> But the next night and every night for a week, the same thing happened. I awoke, roamed the house confirming escape routes, and finally went back to sleep. I knew my concerns were unusual for me, but at the time the chances of a fire, the danger to our baby, and my need to protect her, were all-consuming.

Steve recalls that some time after this episode of terror, he realized that his overly happy-go-lucky demeanor prior to his daughter's birth was perhaps a denial of his anxiety about becoming a father and being responsible for a helpless baby. It occurred to him that this new role in life forced him to explore and become more comfortable with a previously unfamiliar area—a long-term vision of the future.

Return of Equilibrium

Extraverted sensing types report that inferior function episodes occur moderately frequently but are typically quite brief. Perhaps their relative frequency is due to the fact that society's demands for regularity, predictability, and security conflict with the natural predilections of their type. The brevity of the episodes is likely influenced by extraverted sensors' distaste for dwelling on things and their tendency to search for the positive in any situation.

As with other types, the influence of the auxiliary function in the process of reestablishing equilibrium is evident. An ESFP's need to get back in control is quickly aided by the tendency to come up with contingency plans to deal with the anxiety-provoking situation—"if I lose my job, I'll move in with my mother; if she won't have me, I'll get a job as an apartment manager." Just having a plan can be calming, even if she later changes it. Her auxiliary introverted feeling thus focuses on what is important and finds solutions to ground out-of-control negative intuitions.

In the case of the disaffected ESFP minister, needing to get a job to support his family (feeling judgment) encouraged his extrication from the nonfunctional state he was engulfed in. Tertiary thinking was probably also involved—it was logical for him to get a job to help him care for the family he loved. Both kinds of reasoning helped ground him in the real world and reconnect him with his dominant extraverted sensing.

Other extraverted sensing types mention needing others to help them set priorities and provide insight and perspective. One ESTP recognized that he needed others "to understand that I have feelings, too. It helps if they can listen and be less critical and judgmental." Being reassured that dire consequences won't happen can be helpful. One ESFP relies on her sister for reassurance:

> When I can't decide what to do, I let her decide for me. She never judges me, but she's very direct in telling me when something I do is wrong. But she won't dwell on it. She says, "That was stupid. Let's go out to lunch." Pretty soon I put it behind me and am back to my normal, happy self.

Solitary activities such as exercising or gardening can help extraverted sensing types reestablish control over themselves. The solitude allows them to regain confidence in their inner auxiliary thinking or feeling judgment. Security here then permits them to reconnect with their familiar and reliable comfort in the outer world.

As with most experiences of being in the grip of an inferior function, humor does not provide a good way to help extraverted sensing types return to normal. Most report that they lose their sense of humor when in their altered state. However, one ESTP was aware of the somewhat perverse humor she uses to deal with her infrequent depressions. At those times, she reflects on the fact that eventually she will die anyway, so she might as well enjoy life now and not get too upset about things!

Expressions in Midlife

Ideally, midlife is accompanied by a positive and progressive integration of inferior introverted intuition, and along with it tertiary thinking or feeling. For some extraverted sensing types, however, this may not always be the case.

Older ESFPs and ESTPs who instead become stuck in their dominant sensing and auxiliary feeling or thinking often resemble adolescents who have never grown up. They may bore family and friends by retelling tales of their youthful exploits, buy the clothing and pursue the activities associated with much younger people, and in general appear to deny and resist the aging process. A successful ESTP insurance agent often entertained his clients with tales of his youthful exploits as a semiprofessional baseball player. When he reached fifty and continued to wear his baseball cap and carry his "lucky glove" to appointments with customers, he was seen as inappropriately adolescent and an embarrassment to his colleagues in the insurance agency.

Others may find their natural development inhibited by losing their spontaneous relationship to the environment, instead choosing to adhere rigidly to out-dated formulas that once worked but are no longer appropriate. This may have been the response of the ESFP minister who was seen as rigid and restrictive by his parishioners.

The more adaptive route to integration of inferior intuition and tertiary thinking or feeling is aided by extraverted sensing types' increasing attraction to quiet contemplation. Some extraverted sensors may find themselves drawn to literature and television programs involving hypotheses and theories. One 55-year-old ESTP thoroughly enjoyed reading books on chaos theory and astronomy, areas that were of little interest to him in his youth.

Others notice an unfamiliar interest in their own internal mental processes. A 52-year-old ESFP elementary teacher entered individual psychotherapy to explore some of her psychological reactions, which in the past had only mildly puzzled her. She felt a growing need to understand these strange responses in order to feel comfortable with herself now and in the future.

Summary

In the grip of inferior introverted intuition, extraverted sensors experience internal confusion that often results in uncharacteristically strange fantasies. They find meaning and significance in everyday, benign events, and may have insights of cosmic proportions. Auxiliary thinking or feeling often aids their return to equilibrium. ESTPs may analyze an overwhelming situation and use logic to extricate from it, or they may seek the advice of a thinking type as a reality check on the problem. This helps to delimit

TABLE 12   **Major Features of Inferior Introverted Intuition**

Triggers	Forms	New Knowledge
Excessive focus on the future	Internal confusion	Less fear of possibilities
Closing off of options	Inappropriate attribution of meaning	Appreciation of the unknown
Excessive structured activity	Grandiose visions	Access to their own intuition

the disturbing issue and encourages a more balanced view. ESFPs may regain control of a situation when they recognize their own and others' feeling values. Both ESTPs and ESFPs find contingency plans helpful in reestablishing their groundedness in external reality.

As a result of important inferior function experiences, extraverted sensing types become more comfortable with and less fearful of possibilities. This enables them to make difficult decisions in ambiguous situations, accept the reality of the decision, and avoid looking back. They also become more appreciative of the unknown and mysterious, and gain respect for intuitive approaches. Extraverted sensors report seeking out the company of intuitive colleagues and acquaintances and finding new pleasure in these relationships. Table 12 above provides a brief overview of the major features of inferior introverted intuition.

CHAPTER 11

Introverted Intuitive Types
INTJ and INFJ

BASIC TYPE DYNAMICS

Dominant introverted intuition

Auxiliary extraverted thinking or feeling

Tertiary feeling or thinking

Inferior extraverted sensing

Introverted Intuition
Versus Extraverted Sensing

THIS CHAPTER EXAMINES THE way effective introverted intuitives experience their inferior function, and the temporary transformation they make into ineffective, inferior extraverted sensing types when they are "in the grip." The following review of the characteristics of introverted intuition and extraverted sensing will be helpful to our discussion.

Important Features of Dominant Introverted Intuition

Introverted intuitives are the most intellectually independent of the types. They have a theory to explain everything, prefer innovative solutions over established ones, and are adept at seeing situations from an unusual perspective. Their skill at taking a very broad, long-range view of things contributes to their reputation as visionaries. Regardless of whether their auxiliary judging preference is thinking or feeling, their dominant intuition tends to be sharp, quick, and often uncannily correct. It is as if they have antennae out that enable them to detect things long before other people do.

People often count on INTJs and INFJs for insightful analyses and forthright judgments. They are adept at appropriately discounting distracting details and honing in on the essential meaning of complex, confusing situations.

Introverted intuitives report being puzzled by others' perception of them as rigid and intractable. This perception may result from their tendency to express their views directly and forcefully. This is especially true for INTJs. Misinterpretation of their forthright communication style as inflexibility may make others reluctant to present alternatives or argue their own point of view. But, as described in Chapter 3, dominant perceiving types are unlikely to be wedded to their decisions, since they give greater weight to data (perceptions) than to conclusions (judgments). Experience bears this out for the most part. Introverted intuitives readily modify their incorrect conclusions when they receive contradictory new information.

The spiritual, sometimes mystical bent of introverted intuitives has been frequently noted. At the very least, they seem to be aware of subtle cues or nuances long before others notice them. INFJs are especially sensitive to unexpressed anger and conflict, whose presence is usually denied by others. This contributes to the sense of separateness from others that many introverted intuitives report, which may lead them to doubt their own mental stability.

Introverted intuitives, especially INTJs, readily see the big picture in crisis situations and know how to direct others to take the most effective action.

Important Features of Dominant Extraverted Sensing

The qualities associated with extraverted sensing that are relevant to our discussion of its form as an inferior function are an emphasis on:

- External data
- Desire for sensual and aesthetic pleasure
- Delight in the outer world

For a detailed description of dominant extraverted sensing, read the beginning of Chapter 10, "Extraverted Sensing Types: ESTP and ESFP," and the type descriptions for ESTP and ESFP that appear in Appendix A. This will provide you with the background needed to explore the various ways in which inferior extraverted sensing is expressed in INTJs and INFJs.

The Everyday Extraverted Sensing of Introverted Intuitives

The inferior function affects our personalities in several different ways. These include everyday sensitivities, projections, and ways of relaxing, as well as the dramatic manifestations that can be seen when the inferior erupts and a full-blown episode occurs.

Typical Sensitivities and Projections

Introverted intuitives easily gloss over facts and details in their everyday behavior but can be hypersensitive about this. When they become aware that they have made a "sensing" mistake, or an error of fact is pointed out to them, they are likely to become annoyed and defensive. Like their extraverted intuitive counterparts, they may compensate for their uneasiness in this area by becoming expert in some highly specific area. This can sometimes resemble a fetish. An INFJ who had little interest in most aspects of housekeeping knew all the ingredients of different household detergents; an INTJ was pleased with his ability to identify any kind of cloud formation.

In the next chapter, we will discuss how introverted sensing types worry about dire possibilities occurring in the future. In contrast, introverted intuitives focus on relentless realities in the present. There is a readiness to distrust the outer world and to assume that things or people will fail them. An INFJ dreaded an impending vacation trip because she was sure the highway signs would be inadequate or confusing; an INTJ father prepared to teach his daughter long division because he was convinced that her teacher would not instruct her correctly. Another INTJ questioned whether the electrician installing new wiring at his office had used the proper grounding.

To deal with these kinds of concerns, introverted intuitives may acquire detailed knowledge about the issue at hand—carefully studying highway routes, modern arithmetic teaching methods, electrical wiring, and so on.

Discomfort with the environment can also be seen in an overconcern with keeping track of things. One INTJ reported having to check his pocket two or three times to be sure his keys were there. Introverted intuitives try very hard to avoid losing things and experience a disproportionate sense of loss when their efforts fail, frequently accusing others of being responsible for their own carelessness.

Introverted intuitives readily project their own distrust of the environment onto others. They may frequently comment on other people's failure to notice details, or assume that the anxieties they experience when dealing with an unfamiliar environment are characteristic of other people as well. They may therefore be overly cautious in giving people directions and provide too many—often irrelevant—details. One INFJ instructed his 28-year-old son as he was about to head out on a long trip in the car, "And when you smoke, you use the ashtray."

Giving directions to her new house to a friend, an INTJ detailed the following:

> Take Central Avenue to Fifth Street and turn right. Go two blocks to Smith Street and make a left at the next corner, Avenue M. Go three blocks and turn right into Mulberry. That's my street. About half way down the block you'll see a blue house with a two-car garage and a "For Sale" sign on the lawn. Next door to that house is a small cottage with a peaked roof. My house has no address number on it, but it's diagonally across from the blue house....Oh, and did I mention that my house is the only two-story house on the block?

Expressions Through Interests and Hobbies

Relaxing their dominant and auxiliary functions may occur through such sensual pleasures as eating, exercising, and gardening. One INTJ especially enjoys and appreciates sunshine in spring, autumn, and winter. INFJs often mention the pleasant luxury of taking an afternoon nap. Other introverted intuitives describe craving very hot curries, or escaping by becoming totally absorbed in a mystery or adventure novel. "Escape literature" seems to be a particularly effective way for introverted intuitives to suspend their intense inner focus and to vicariously enjoy adventures in the external environment.

An INTJ reports that at times she feels exceptionally relaxed and able to focus totally on observing her environment. Unlike her usual goal-oriented approach, at these times she does not feel she must immediately do something with her observations. Often doing aerobic exercise precedes and stimulates this relaxed state.

Introverted intuitives mention going for walks or drives and noticing interesting details, such as the shapes of houses, the designs on garage doors, the arrangements of trees and flowerbeds in parks. One INFJ described taking walks by himself and noticing how many different shades of green he could identify on a nature trail, or closing his eyes and trying to see how many different sounds he could identify.

Using sensing for relaxation seems to be particularly enjoyable because there is no pressure to achieve any particular goal. "Gardening is an activity I love. I don't worry about performance or doing it perfectly," said an INFJ. "I like pulling weeds, smelling flowers, removing dead flower heads, admiring the colors. All of this nurtures me." Another INFJ enjoys the aesthetic aspects of gardening, the shapes and colors of the flowers, as opposed to the straightness of the planting rows. And an INTJ's hobby is making flower arrangements. She tries to achieve an overall look with the colors of the flowers, rarely wanting to learn their names.

Eruptions of Inferior Extraverted Sensing

When one or more of the preconditions for eruption of the inferior function are present, extraverted sensing appears in its more exaggerated, disruptive form. In addition to the general conditions described in Chapter 4, introverted intuitives are vulnerable to the type-specific factors described below.

Typical Provocations or Triggers

Dealing with details, especially in an unfamiliar environment, can trigger inferior extraverted sensing in introverted intuitives. In fact, introverted intuitives frequently mention that feeling overwhelmed by details often provokes characteristic inferior function reactions. Unexpected events that interrupt planned activities can also unsettle INTJs and INFJs enough to arouse their inferior.

An INFJ reported that she has the following response when she has to deal with unfamiliar details like taxes and finances:

TABLE 13 Dominant Versus Inferior Extraverted Sensing

	Qualities Associated With Extraverted Sensing
As Dominant Function	Focus on external data
	Seeking sensual/aesthetic pleasure
	Delight in the outer world
As Inferior Function	Obsessive focus on external data
	Overindulgence in sensual pleasure
	Adversarial attitude toward the outer world

> I feel like I become instantly stupid. I truly don't seem to be able to take in explanations and process them. I have such anxiety I can't get through it. I feel panicky inside and desperately look for help from someone who can talk to me on my level so that I can slowly begin to understand.

Of the four dominant introverted types, it is introverted intuitives who most frequently mention that "too much extraverting" is a common trigger for inferior function responses. They retreat inside themselves in this state and become intolerant of intrusions by others. They either express irritation at people's questions or do not respond at all to others' attempts to communicate with them.

The Form of the Inferior

As dominant introverted intuition loses its position of primacy, INTJs and INFJs start to lose their characteristic wide-ranging, global perspective. Their field of operation narrows considerably, and their range of acknowledged possibilities becomes limited and idiosyncratic. They may make more factual mistakes and become careless with spelling and grammar. As their hold on their dominant and auxiliary further diminishes, the qualities of inferior extraverted sensing become manifested in obsessive focus on external data, overindulgence in sensual pleasures, and an adversarial attitude toward the outer world. The comparison between dominant and inferior extraverted sensing is shown above in Table 13.

Jung (1976a) incorporates all of these qualities in the following comment about inferior extraverted sensing:

> What the introverted intuitive represses most of all is the sensation of the object, and this colours his whole unconscious. It gives rise to a compensatory extraverted sensation function of an archaic character. The unconscious per-

sonality can best be described as an extraverted sensation type of a rather low and primitive order. Instinctuality and intemperance are the hallmarks of this sensation, combined with an extraordinary dependence on sense-impressions. This compensates the rarefied air of the intuitive's conscious attitude. (p. 402)

Obsessive focus on external data Effective dominant extraverted sensing types are open to the widest variety of information from the environment—the more the better for them. Fully experiencing the outside world is their greatest pleasure. For an introverted intuitive in the grip of inferior extraverted sensing, data from the outside world can seem overwhelming. Facts and details in the world demand the attention of the introverted intuitive in the grip, so he or she obsesses about them. This may be experienced by both INTJs and INFJs as a state of intensity and drivenness. Their attempts to control the details in their environment are often expressed in activities such as feverishly cleaning the house, moving furniture, or organizing records and other materials. They may show an adamant concern about minute details and an unrelenting effort to control everything in their immediate vicinity.

An INFJ described her obsessiveness and withdrawal from her usual interests this way: "I stew about what's going on. I can't sit still and am restless. I am mentally fatigued and find myself compulsively putting things in order and trying to control everything around me."

An INTJ said that when he is in this state, he feels like a top spinning faster and faster. If he is working with tools and getting frustrated and angry, he has learned that it is best for him to stop or he will get hurt or break something.

An INFJ said, "I alphabetize my compact discs; or suddenly it's time to do that thing I thought about doing two months ago. I drop everything and do it; or I fixate on smells and sounds."

"I organize or clean. I feel pressured and can't think clearly," reported another INFJ. "I nitpick about things in the environment. I bombard people verbally and obsess out loud."

An INTJ said, "I start tripping over things and feel out of control in the external world. I feel like I'm under a dark cloud. I get hung up on some false fact and distort it. I get stressed out about time—too many things and not enough time. I attack others with words and then feel guilty."

Often the external data that becomes the object of obsession is something someone said or even failed to say. When the last client of an unusually busy day left without saying her usual, "See you next week," an

INTJ therapist became convinced she had made a mistake during the psychotherapy session. She spent many hours going over and over the content of the session. She felt the only reason the client had not terminated therapy that day was out of politeness, so as not to hurt the therapist's feelings.

A common focus, particularly for INTJ and INFJ women, can be an aspect of their physical appearance. They may become convinced that they have prominent skin blemishes, that others are noticing that they don't dress very well, or that they look fat. In combination with the "overindulgence" manifestation described below, a powerful effect can occur.

Overindulgence in sensual pleasures In effective dominant extraverted sensing types, the enjoyment of sensual pleasures is natural, spontaneous, and quite consistent with their focus on the reality of the immediate environment. In introverted intuitives in the grip of inferior extraverted sensing, this quality takes the form of sensual excess rather than sensual pleasure. Overdoing gratification of the senses is a commonly mentioned behavior for INTJs and INFJs in the grip of their inferior. They may overeat or binge. They see themselves as obsessively doing harm to their bodies. A typical "tactic" is to overindulge compulsively, and immediately after—if not during the episode—berate themselves for their uncontrolled, shallow, destructive behavior.

An INTJ described the experience in this way:

> There is a clear preliminary state where I am totally apart from the real world. I am not even an observer, and I can completely ignore anything real. It's a nice fantasy, that's all—just absorbing. But later I become excessively indulgent, getting totally immersed in physical experiences—eating, exercise, pulp fiction, TV. But I don't enjoy it. It feels like a dangerous roller coaster, but I'm immobilized and can't get off.

An INFJ said: "I have to get away from reality. I do too much of something—one thing. I eat more or stop eating; I shop for useless things."

An INTJ said her pattern is to overeat, feel guilty about it, wake up in the night and feel worse, get too little sleep, causing her to feel more vulnerable, and then eat more. Another INTJ feels bad about her overeating but not guilty: "I hate it when people brag about how much they exercise!" she said.

Adversarial attitude toward the outer world　Effective dominant extra-verted sensing types approach the outer world with eager anticipation of all the wonderful experiences awaiting them. For introverted intuitives in the grip of inferior extraverted sensing, the immediate reality of the outer world spells difficulty and danger. They expect obstacles and problems to plague them as they move through a strange and potentially hostile environment. Anticipating the worst can often elicit anger and blame in introverted intuitives.

The altered state of any inferior function is typically accompanied by a lessening of social controls and therefore more frequent expressions of anger. However, the character of the anger may be different for different types. For introverted intuitives, the "cause" of distress is often one or more "objects" in the environment. The anger directed at either things or people may therefore be more focused, intense, and extreme than with other inferiors. Introverted intuitives may be unable to recognize alternative possibilities so that their perspective becomes extremely narrow. This tunnel vision and externalization of blame can produce ruthless results.

One INTJ said, "I get into verbal raving and am out of control. I regress emotionally and act childish. I feel anxious, exposed, childlike."

An INFJ describes experiencing deep anger: "I am emotionally aroused and am terribly critical of others. I accuse people of never helping me. I become dogmatic and blast people with facts. If no one is around to attack, I write a scathing letter to someone."

An INFJ observed, "I am angry, unreasonable, totally irrational, close-minded, and impatient. I feel vulnerable, and then become angry at others for it. I can't communicate with anyone. I am hard, callous, unfeeling, and I have no energy to be bothered with anyone else."

Grip Experiences

The stories included in this section illustrate one or more forms of inferior extraverted sensing as experienced by introverted intuitives. It is interesting to notice that introverted intuitives, whose dominant focus is typically global, diffuse, and complex, relate their experiences of the inferior in that same style. The two examples that appear in the form of specific "stories" were actually contributed by the spouses of the introverted intuitives involved.

"Help, I Can't Change the Channel!"

Gretchen is an INTJ whose work requires intense, uninterrupted extraversion not only of her auxiliary thinking but also of her dominant intuition and her tertiary feeling. Although she excels at her job and very much enjoys it, it tends to "unbalance" her. When she experiences a lack of sleep and increased stress, her inferior extraverted sensing occurs in the following ways:

> I seem to get stuck on one sensory channel, often a visual one, like watching TV. I watch but am unable to extract any meaning from it, and because it lacks meaning, it is unacceptable to my usual criteria. I think, What kind of person engages in this meaningless pap? I must be careful to keep my worthless behavior from other people because it reveals my lack of competence. If other people knew about it, they would not like me.

> Sometimes I get stuck on something auditory, like listening to one audiotape over and over again. The tapes are often those with a sentimental twist. My judgment then is, Who with any brains would listen to this garbage?

Sometimes Gretchen makes good use of the extraverted sensing that takes over her personality. "Even though I do some task obsessively, I actually accomplish something," she explained. "I'm less upset with myself then, even though I know I haven't made the best use of my time and that my method was inefficient." She may be aware that she is doing something inefficiently or in a harder way than is necessary, but she feels compelled to continue in spite of this: "If my inefficient obsessiveness doesn't accomplish something, I become self-critical and really angry at myself."

Because so much extraverting is a continuing aspect of her work, Gretchen has found some ways to use extraverted sensing in relaxing, nonthreatening ways. She believes her efforts have resulted in a decrease in the intensity and length of her grip experiences.

"The Harder I Work, the More You Criticize Me!"

In Chapter 4 we noted that skill in one's least preferred process did not prevent its eruption as an inferior function. This can be particularly baffling to other people, especially those closest to the person.

Jane, an ENFP, manages her husband's repair business. She takes care of the bookkeeping, makes appointments, and does all the other many tasks associated with running a successful repair shop. She is satisfied with her work and especially enjoys her warm relationships with customers. Her INTJ husband, John, appreciates her skills and the fact that her enjoyment of people relieves him from having to make small talk.

But Jane found one thing about John quite puzzling and difficult to cope with. She described it this way:

> John is a skilled repairman by life circumstances rather than by choice. He is incredibly good at his work. He discovers the source of a repair problem by visualizing it, but he cannot describe what he visualizes. He is also excellent with the meticulous detail his repairs require. He is therefore much sought out by people who have experienced his very exceptional repairs.
>
> The problem is that he is supersensitive about his work. He is touchy, and readily interprets comments as criticism. In short, one cannot talk to him about his work. He says, "The harder I work and the better I do, the more you criticize me." I have to walk on eggshells on the topic of John's work. It's not even okay to compliment him, since he manages to find something negative even in this. He dismisses expressions of appreciation from his clients as insincere politeness.
>
> In most other things, John is objective and good humored. He enjoys politics and philosophy, and his hobby is Civil War history. In these areas he welcomes discussion and is not overly sensitive when people disagree with him or criticize his conclusions.

Jane got a glimmer of understanding when she discovered the form in which inferior extraverted sensing is expressed. She recognized that John spent most of his waking hours using his least preferred extraverted sensing. His innovative use of dominant intuition in detecting repair problems was certainly an asset. However, contrary to what is more common and desirable, his dominant intuition was being used in the service of his inferior sensing, rather than his inferior sensing being used in the service of his dominant introverted intuition.

John consciously uses his least preferred process. He is usually not in the grip when he works; however, his inferior comes out when things are not going well or when he is stressed, fatigued, or otherwise vulnerable. A comparably vulnerable ESFP technician would probably respond to stress in a quite different way.

"Being Autistic or Catatonic Sounds Good to Me!"

Polly, an INFJ, has given a lot of thought to her reactions when she is off center. Like many other introverted intuitives, her description of her reactions is not oriented to specific incidents. Rather, she provides an integrated, global analysis. She related the following:

> If I have too much contact with people in one day, especially if I am doing the kind of reality-based crisis management that used to be a large part of my job, it can be extremely draining for me. I just want to withdraw—being autistic or catatonic sounds good to me at that point! I lose my focus and my energy center when I have to extravert too much, especially around facts and people.

> When I am fully "in the grip," I don't get anything done. I try to obsessively control every detail, I notice everything that is disorganized or needs cleaning in my outer world, and I want to fix it all perfectly and immediately. I eat too much, don't enjoy it, and feel guilty about losing control.

> I feel like nobody helps me; I have to do it all myself and nobody appreciates me. I can't see any possibilities or alternatives around negative facts. I *really* focus on negative facts. I feel immobilized and unproductive, and have trouble concentrating.

> I think this side of me comes out in my dreams in both pleasant and unpleasant ways. My dreams tend to be in color with a lot of emotion, feeling, action, and detail in them. It is almost like all the sensory details I overlook or don't even recognize in my conscious life exist in my unconscious. I have very beautiful and very horrible images in my dreams.

"He's Cheating on His Taxes"

Rudolfo, a 66-year-old INTJ, and his longtime business partner, Clarence, decided to dissolve their partnership, since both wanted to retire. Their lawyer took care of all the details. All that remained was for the ex-partners to reconcile their personal income tax returns for that year to reflect the sale of their co-owned real estate.

Clarence bought a sailboat to fulfill his lifelong dream of sailing around the world. Rudolfo was a bit unnerved without the business that had been the center of his life, but he was hopeful that his mild depression and irritability would diminish as he got used to the unfamiliar free time.

In the early spring, Rudolfo's wife Norma noticed that he was more than usually nervous, withdrawn, and uncommunicative. She tried her best to be supportive and provide him every opportunity to discuss what was bothering him, but he persistently rejected her efforts.

Late one night, Norma awakened to find Rudolfo pacing the living room in great agitation. "I insist that you tell me what's wrong!" she said adamantly. Rudolfo burst out, "I'm convinced that Clarence is cheating on his taxes. This man I've known as honest and forthright all these years turns out to be a crook! I don't understand it and I don't know what to do!"

Rudolfo hung his head in despair. He explained that in looking at his partner's tax return he found that Clarence had written in an incorrect, inflated amount for a real estate-related deduction.

"What did he say when you asked him about it?" asked Norma.

Rudolfo was puzzled by her question. "Of course I can't ask him about it," he said. "First I must be clear in my own mind about reporting it to the authorities so I can tell him what I'm going to do. That is the appropriate and honorable thing to do."

Norma pointed out all the alternative explanations for the income tax reporting—an arithmetic error, some facts of which Rudolfo was unaware, some other honest mistake. She convinced her husband to discuss the matter with Clarence. It turned out that Clarence's accountant had transposed a number, discovered the error, and had just sent Clarence a corrected income tax return.

Rudolfo's several weeks of agitation and obsessive focus on one isolated "fact" and the "inevitable conclusion" that logically resulted from it were no doubt stimulated by his difficulties in adjusting to retirement. He was surprised when alternative explanations were suggested and confessed that they had never entered his mind.

"Let Me Help You Diagnose My Illness"

Angie, an INFJ, who had always been plagued with allergies and frequent infections, became ill one winter with some new symptoms. Numerous specialists and clinicians were unable to diagnose her condition. They agreed that she was ill and growing worse, and many had theories about the possible causes, but what she eventually heard from each one was something along the lines of, "I don't know what's wrong with you. And I don't know what to suggest."

Though often ill and discouraged about her situation, Angie began a systematic study of all of the medical literature relevant to each of her puzzling symptoms, singly and in combination. She pored over volumes in the medical library, sent for all of her own medical records from childhood on, and racked her memory for even remotely relevant past symptoms or events that might have triggered or influenced her current condition. She explained the nature of her search:

> My dining room table was piled high with neatly arranged insurance forms, physician's reports, synopses of medical articles, and a chronological accounting of my medical history—all the facts I could find. Before each appointment with yet another specialist, I summarized the relevant facts and brought them along. But all save a few doctors didn't welcome my help. They seemed overwhelmed with it. Most seemed to believe that because I was so knowledgeable about my condition, I must be a hypochondriac. Of course I was an expert on my symptoms. After three years of seeing doctors who didn't have a clue, I figured they needed all the help I could give them!

Angie's way of coping with her illness by collecting facts was consistent with inferior extraverted sensing as a response to stress. In this case, however, the data she so meticulously collected was an adaptive approach to her situation. But most of her doctors treated her behavior as excessive and pathological. No doubt this judgment was abetted by her single-minded intensity in trying to help her physicians arrive at a diagnosis.

Return of Equilibrium

Introverted intuitives need space and a low-pressure environment to regain dominant intuition and auxiliary thinking or feeling. Like extraverted intuitives, they are not amenable to suggestions and deny the possibility of alternatives. Stuck in some negative, omnipresent "reality," they are unable to process contradictory information. They may respond to those who offer it with anger and rejection, adamantly insisting that no alternatives exist. In fact, INTJs and INFJs agree that the worst thing others can do when they are in this state is to give them advice.

All types engage in self-criticism at some point during or after an episode of the inferior function. However, the focus of that criticism may vary according to type. Introverted intuitives are especially hard on themselves, later viewing their obsessive concerns or angry intensity as signs of unacceptable personal imperfections. One INFJ said that in this state, she needs others to remind her that she is as human as the next person and that she should not be so hard on herself.

A change of scene or activity can help break the negative, obsessive focus. This may entail getting outside, exercising, walking in the woods, or seeing a movie. As with other types, often a good night's sleep helps.

Some examples of methods introverted intuitives use for returning to normal include submerging themselves in peaceful, quiet, natural surroundings, being outdoors and looking at nature, cancelling activities, lightening their schedules, making more spaces for being alone, and taking time out to "recharge" and sort things out.

One INTJ said:

> A Sunday afternoon nap is a wonderful escape. I make an obsessive list of all the things I'm thinking about, do some light reading, or reading I "should" do, and I go right to sleep. If I write in a journal just before I go to sleep, I will often dream and that calms me and helps me find a solution to my troubles. In addition, my cat purring and sleeping next to me is a great way to put life in perspective. I know my equilibrium has returned when I can't find my list of things to do, and I don't care!

INTJs may call upon auxiliary thinking by strategizing to help extricate from obsessiveness. One described forcing himself to get control of at least one situation. This calms him down sufficiently so he can start to regain a broader perspective. Another used her thinking to develop a plan to get something done.

Auxiliary feeling helps INFJs by encouraging acceptance of their less serious side. They can then give in to the urge to cry during "trash" movies. Or they can read bad novels and recognize that doing so is normal and acceptable. Recognizing that others are hurt and distressed by their out-of-character actions often signals that the process of extricating from the inferior is occurring. Both INTJs and INFJs report that they know they are coming out of it when they become bored and frustrated with themselves.

Expressions of understanding, sympathy, and empathy aid the return of equilibrium for some, but not for all introverted intuitives. Gentle humor can be helpful as well. An INFJ said she found it helped to remind herself to be as kind and accepting of herself as she would be of another person in the same situation.

Expressions in Midlife

Ideally, midlife is accompanied by a positive, progressive integration of inferior extraverted sensing, and along with it tertiary thinking or feeling. This unfortunately does not occur for all aging introverted intuitives.

Some introverted intuitives retreat into themselves in midlife. Attention to their inferior sensing and tertiary thinking or feeling may be limited to idiosyncrasies. They may devote a lot of energy to an ill-conceived project and get lost in its details. They then become frustrated and despairing when they find that others are less and less understanding and appreciative of their efforts. This creates a sense of isolation and alienation.

After retirement, an INTJ political scientist devoted all of her time to working out the details of an obscure social interaction theory. Her attempts to publish her work failed. But she became more and more focused on it, until it became her major topic of conversation with family and friends. They began to avoid her or "tune her out." Sensing this, she became bitter and withdrawn.

Other introverted intuitives are more successful in incorporating previously neglected aspects of themselves. They are likely to find new pleasures in the environment and with people. They may take up a new form of exercise, like hiking or fishing, or enjoy a hobby like model building, gardening, or photography. They may also cultivate more moderate and therefore enjoyable ways of gratifying their sensual desires. One INFJ found that she enjoyed watching pro football:

> I am amazed at how physical a sport it is and how crazy the fans get. I don't understand a lot of the rules, but I get a kick out of following the antics and fortunes of my team. When I was a teenager and young adult I hated sports and thought jocks were stupid. In midlife, this is an unexpected source of enjoyment for me.

An INTJ and her ENTJ husband, both in their mid-forties, took ballroom dancing lessons together. Though learning the intricate and detailed dance step sequences was difficult for them, they very much enjoyed getting to the point where a new step became skilled and automatic. Until they got to that point, however, they engaged in heated but enjoyable arguments about who was making the most mistakes.

Summary

In the grip of inferior extraverted sensing, introverted intuitives obsess about details in the outside world, overindulge in sensual pleasures, and externalize blame to outside objects. Their auxiliary thinking or feeling can be the vehicle through which they regain equilibrium. INTJs develop a strategy for analyzing what they are experiencing, achieving distance and objectivity from it, while INFJs examine the important meanings and

TABLE 14   Major Features of Inferior Extraverted Sensing

Triggers	Forms	New Knowledge
Dealing with details	Obsessiveness with external details	Adaptability to outer details
Unexpected events	Sensual overindulgence	Pleasure in temperate sensuality
Excessive extraverting	Adversarial attitude to the world	More realistic goals

feeling connections involved and are therefore able to regain their normal wide-ranging perspective.

As a result of important inferior function experiences, introverted intuitives may better adapt to changing surroundings, incorporate sensual experience into their lives in a satisfying way, and moderate a perhaps overly ambitious, visionary stance into one that is more realistic and possible. Table 14 above summarizes the major features of their inferior extraverted sensing experience.

CHAPTER 12

Introverted Sensing Types
ISTJ and ISFJ

BASIC TYPE DYNAMICS

Dominant introverted sensing

Auxiliary extraverted thinking or feeling

Tertiary feeling or thinking

Inferior extraverted intuition

Introverted Sensing
Versus Extraverted Intuition

THIS CHAPTER EXAMINES THE way effective introverted sensing types experience their inferior function, and the temporary transformation they make into ineffective, inferior extraverted intuitives when they are "in the grip." The following review of the characteristics of introverted sensing and extraverted intuition will be helpful to our discussion.

Important Features of Dominant Introverted Sensing

Introverted sensing types are careful and orderly in their attention to facts and details. They are thorough and conscientious in fulfilling their responsibilities. They may sometimes even do the work of others rather than leave important tasks undone. They are typically seen as well grounded in reality, trustworthy, and dedicated to preserving traditional values and time-honored institutions. With their focus on the reality of the present, they trust the evidence of their senses, and rely on carefully accumulated past and present evidence to support their conclusions and planned courses of action. They achieve great pleasure from perfecting existing techniques with a goal of maximum efficiency and cost effectiveness.

They tend to take a skeptical, critical attitude to information that has not been verified by the senses and are likely to distrust people who are careless about facts, sloppy about details, and favor imagination and novelty over accuracy and solid substantiation. Both ISTJs and ISFJs are uncomfortable moving beyond sense experience until they have thoroughly absorbed and understood it. They want to review and assimilate the facts and events of a movie or book before discussing its meaning with others.

In a crisis that does not constellate their inferior function, introverted sensing types typically appear calm and unruffled, efficient and pragmatic. Others may marvel at their serene demeanor, but the introverted sensors themselves report that they may be feeling quite anxious and distressed and that their visible behavior may not match their inner state.

Important Features of Dominant Extraverted Intuition

The qualities associated with extraverted intuition that are relevant to our discussion of its form as an inferior function are an emphasis on:

- Comfortable inattention to sensing data
- Flexibility and adaptability
- Optimism about future possibilities

For a detailed description of dominant extraverted intuition, read the beginning of Chapter 13, "Extraverted Intuitive Types: ENTP and ENFP," and the type descriptions for ENTP and ENFP that appear in Appendix A. This will provide you with the background needed to explore the various ways in which inferior extraverted intuition is expressed in ISTJs and ISFJs.

The Everyday Extraverted Intuition
of Introverted Sensing Types

The inferior function affects introverted sensing types in several different ways. These include everyday sensitivities, projections, and ways of relaxing, as well as the dramatic manifestations that can be seen when the inferior erupts and a full-blown episode occurs.

Typical Sensitivities and Projections

Inferior extraverted intuition seems to color the everyday personality of introverted sensing types. They see themselves and are seen by others as worriers. They are ready to notice and comment on negative possibilities even in everyday, nonstressful situations. A new plan, a previously unexperienced event—or perhaps anything new—is likely to elicit all the negative possibilities or all the things that might go wrong. Whatever is not grounded in past experience is suspect. The introverted sensor, however, may merely need time to reflect and recognize the connections between anticipated new experiences and the known past. Once that connection is made, the ISTJ or ISFJ can be comfortable pursuing actions that initially may have seemed potentially dangerous.

As parents, introverted sensing types may appear unreasonably overprotective, especially in situations where the child wants to do something new, test his or her independence, or take any degree of risk. The untried and untested may automatically raise the specter of disaster, in spite of the parents' awareness that they may be overreacting to a reasonable request.

A 10-year-old boy asked his ISFJ mother if he could spend the night at his friend's house. "Where will you sleep?" his mother asked. "He has double-decker bunk beds," the child replied. "You can't go, then. You'll convince him to let you sleep on the top—you're not used to sleeping on the top. You'll fall off and break your leg. No!"

Although this is often the initial parental response to minor risktaking, children of introverted sensing parents report that when their parents received additional factual information and reassurance about precautions, they would amend their original decisions.

In projecting their inferior onto others, the introverted sensing type may engage in self-pity, blaming the outer environment and other people for whatever difficulties they are experiencing. This is in marked contrast to their typical willingness to accept responsibility and solve problems calmly and methodically. Their uneasiness with the unknown may also be reflected in suspiciousness about others' motives and fears that the environment will somehow betray them. They may thus see extraverted intuitives' natural comfort with the outer world as foolish risktaking, judging ENTPs and ENFPs to be irresponsible, immature show-offs.

Expressions Through Interests and Hobbies

Poetry, music, and art may be one way for introverted sensors to engage their "other side." Their choice of artists and styles within the arts may tend toward the expressive and dramatic, and they often prefer romantic musicians and artists. The favorite opera of one rather austere and conventional ISTJ is "La Boheme."

Some introverted sensors are attracted to astrology and the more occult spiritual movements. The evidence presented for such systems often involves detailed eyewitness testimony collected over long time periods. Perhaps this sensing method lends the data legitimacy, thus providing a comfortable, acceptable way to develop familiarity with the vagaries of intuition. In some introverted sensors, the interest in such areas can become excessive and obsessive, and could be an attempt to control unruly, disorganized, and frightening eruptions of intuition. However, as long as it does not take too much energy away from the person's dominant introverted sensing, even such interest may prove adaptive.

Introverted sensing types may enjoy relaxing their use of sensing by reading fantasy fiction, watching science fiction movies, or entertaining themselves with idle speculation and daydreams.

Eruptions of Inferior Extraverted Intuition

When one or more of the preconditions for eruption of the inferior function are present, extraverted intuition appears in its more exaggerated, disruptive form. Not only can the general conditions described in Chapter 4 stimulate an inferior function episode, but some type-specific factors may also serve as triggers.

Typical Provocations or Triggers

Things likely to push the inferior "button" of introverted sensing types can be described as issues of reality. Dealing with people whose approach denies facts and actualities (often identified as extraverted intuitives) serves as a trigger for eruptions of harsh, negative, extreme reactions to whatever is being proposed. With the usual preconditions in operation, even slight deviations from present reality or minor suggestions for future change will provoke introverted sensors to intractable anger and stubborn immovability.

One ISFJ said, "If I'm watching the devastating effects of an ongoing crisis and someone says to me, 'Don't worry, everything is going to be fine,' I come unglued. I steamroll over the person and mow them down!"

An ISTJ reported that her usual calm demeanor is replaced by cold fury and biting sarcasm when someone tries to convince her that the evidence of her senses is wrong: "I'm seeing and smelling the ash from this guy's cigar and smelling the smoke on his breath and he's telling me he doesn't smoke cigars!"

The prospect of unknown, previously unexperienced activities and situations is a common trigger for introverted sensing types. The anxiety associated with the unfamiliar and unimaginable future acts directly on their most unconscious arena. Careful contingency plans and attention to details normally tempers such an unconscious reaction. But when the new possibility comes up suddenly, an inferior function response is likely.

"Overdoing" their own type may also provoke the response in introverted sensors. When this takes the form of doing other people's assigned duties, working long and hard, and being unappreciated or taken for granted, the stage is set for an extreme, spontaneous eruption of inferior extraverted intuition. "I get to feeling used and abused," said an ISFJ. "Then I explode and say awful things that I'm embarrassed about later."

The Form of the Inferior

Introverted sensing types' characteristic task orientation and calm attention to responsibilities begin to disappear as command over dominant introverted sensing is lost. As their hold on their dominant and auxiliary further diminishes, the qualities of inferior extraverted intuition become

TABLE 15   Dominant Versus Inferior Extraverted Intuition

	Qualities Associated With Extraverted Intuition
As Dominant Function	Comfortable inattention to sense data Flexibility, adaptability, risktaking Optimism about future possibilities
As Inferior Function	Loss of control over facts and details Impulsiveness Catastrophizing

manifested in a loss of control over facts and details, impulsiveness, and catastrophizing. The comparison between dominant and inferior extraverted intuition is shown above in Table 15.

The following statement by Jung (1976a) addresses the first and last of these manifestations:

> Whereas true extraverted intuition is possessed of singular resourcefulness, a "good nose" for objectively real possibilities, this archaisized intuition has an amazing flair for all the ambiguous, shadowy, sordid, dangerous possibilities lurking in the background. (p. 398)

Loss of control over facts and details   Effective dominant extraverted intuitives are comfortable glossing over facts and details as they focus on the complexities of an engaging new idea. Their strength lies in emphasizing generalities; the particulars can be dealt with later. In the grip of inferior extraverted intuition, however, the introverted sensing type's relationship to details becomes problematic. As they begin to lose trust in dominant sensing and auxiliary thinking or feeling, introverted sensors have difficulty attending to relevant factual information and arriving at rational conclusions.

On the last afternoon of a difficult training session, an ISTJ imagined that a small-group exercise in which trainees practiced their presentation skills was preparation for each class member to give a presentation to the entire class. He became anxious and agitated as the time to return to the workshop room approached. He later admitted that he did not feel adequately prepared to present the material publicly and feared he would be humiliated. What he failed to recognize was the fact that no such activity was listed on the schedule (sensing data) and that with only 60 minutes left to the workshop, 35 people could not possibly make presentations (thinking judgment). His general anxiety and fatigue at the end of a stressful day contributed to his abandonment of his sensing and thinking.

Impulsiveness Flexibility and adaptability are assets to effective dominant extraverted intuitives. These qualities permit them to manage the multiple activities and interests characteristic of their operating style. As expressions of inferior extraverted intuition, however, these same qualities take on an aspect of thoughtlessness and impulsiveness, not unlike the qualities introverted sensors project onto dominant extraverted intuitives. When they experience a gradual slide into their inferior, introverted sensing types may become uncharacteristically spontaneous, sometimes to the point of later judging themselves to have been irresponsible and reckless.

One ISFJ reported giving in to the urge to leave work in the middle of the day and go to the movies. An ISTJ made a spur-of-the-moment decision to buy a new computer without thoroughly researching the options ahead of time. He returned it later, assessing the purchase as rash and foolish.

Increasing lack of focus, confusion, anxiety, and even panic may be experienced by introverted sensing types, even though their outer demeanor remains calm and seemingly unperturbed. Their uncharacteristic spontaneity, however, may come out in snappishness and terse, hurtful comments to others, or in out-of-character behavior. After being divorced by his wife of twenty years, an ISTJ dated forty different women in six months. It was as if his inexperienced intuition went haywire, and his tertiary feeling judgment was unequal to the task of deciding among the overwhelming relationship possibilities available.

Catastrophizing Whereas effective dominant extraverted intuitives thrive on the exciting possibilities the future will bring, when in the grip of inferior extraverted intuition, introverted sensing types anticipate the future with fear and trembling. As the descent into the grip proceeds, they become ever more negative, unwilling to tolerate the unfamiliar, and more wildly imaginative about disastrous outcomes. One ISFJ described this as "awfulizing." In its full-blown state, inferior extraverted intuition anticipates all the catastrophes that might happen in an unsafe, threatening world and focuses on dire possibilities in the future (Remember that the other introverted perceiving type, the introverted intuitive, focuses on negative realities in the present.) Introverted sensors imagine that anything not previously experienced—any unfamiliar place, any new activity—will provoke horrifying consequences. In the full grip of the inferior, even familiar, previously safe areas may be reassessed as fraught with danger. This level of catastrophizing is the hallmark of inferior extraverted intuition.

An ISFJ school choir director is usually in a good mood when she awakens—except when a choir performance is scheduled for that day. On such occasions, she experiences a general feeling of dread and impending disaster, even though there is no specific content associated with her forebodings.

After having knee surgery, which resulted in a good deal of pain and immobility, an ISTJ was convinced that he would never feel any better: "I couldn't stop expressing my pessimism and was a real pain to one and all. Before that I'd always been a pretty optimistic person."

An increase in fatigue and stress often lowers the introverted sensing type's tolerance and patience when faced with others' inattention to or denial of important facts and details. A full-blown exhibition of negative possibilities is likely to ensue.

One ISFJ said, "I am given to very sarcastic humor, slashing and unpredictable explosions of cold, hard statements about here-and-now reality. I get stubborn and let loose a negative barrage covering all the bad consequences of what is being proposed."

When her work situation becomes particularly stressful, another ISFJ's recurrent fear is that her most recent promotion will be rescinded, or that she will receive a letter from her college informing her that her degree had been granted by mistake, and they are going to have to take it back.

One evening in May, an ISTJ returned home tired after a long day of hiking in the mountains. He was distressed to discover that his garage door would not open. He immediately imagined all the effects of this—he would have trouble getting to work on time, he wouldn't be able to go on vacation in the summer, and he certainly could not make it to his niece's wedding in August!

Introverted sensors report having strange or paranoid thoughts when they are in this state, feeling overwhelmed and irritable, and imagining that a current stressful situation will go on forever, as will their inability to handle both the stress and the situation. However, they may also come up with off-the-wall, unrealistic positive possibilities when faced with unfamiliar situations. They then must deal with the extreme disappointment that results when the unrealistic positive events don't happen. For example, an ISTJ was quite attracted to a young woman he talked to briefly at a party one evening. He planned to get her phone number from his friend so he could ask her out. He imagined where they would go, what they would talk about, and how pleasant their date would be. On calling his friend, therefore, he was upset to learn that the young woman was engaged to be married and had left town that morning to return home to plan her wedding.

Grip Experiences

The stories included in this section illustrate one or more forms of inferior extraverted intuition as experienced by ISTJs or ISFJs. Although the last example demonstrates evidence of all three forms of the inferior, most of the introverted sensing experiences reported are relatively brief and to the point, often focusing on only one aspect of the inferior. This is consistent with the pragmatic, singular focus of introverted sensors.

Loving Concern or Secret Wish?

Warren, an ISTJ, reported that once he became worried because his wife was unexplainably late returning home from a shopping trip. He imagined that she had been involved in a fatal accident, and fantasized in great detail her funeral, his raising their children by himself, and so on. Losing all contact with his usual reasonable thought process, he then experienced tremendous guilt, concluding that his quickness to fantasize his wife's demise meant that he harbored a secret wish that she would die.

On other occasions, he would imagine that she had been kidnapped or that she really wanted a divorce and was at that very moment consulting a divorce lawyer.

Warren reported that when he "came back to his senses" and reflected on the situations that led up to his catastrophic fantasies, they were typically in the context of decreased time spent at home and overinvolvement in work activities. The bout with his inferior stimulated a renewed appreciation of his wife and the importance of their relationship, and reminded him to broaden his perspective on life in general.

Both inferior intuition and tertiary feeling came out in Warren's experience. His anxieties involved the loss of an important relationship, consideration of feeling values that he might be unaware of, and guilt about his imagined negative motives. His reevaluation of his life's priorities regarding work and family also revolved around broadening his perspective and appreciating relationships.

From Anxiety to Indignation

In a similar scenario, Deborah, an ISTJ, recalled an incident that occurred early in her marriage as she was waiting for her husband to pick her up from work:

> It was pouring rain and I was standing at a transfer point of a bus stop. Even though I was under an awning, I was getting really wet. He was late. At first I worried that he had gotten into an accident. But that soon switched to anger at my own plight. As I told him later—"I buried you; then I dug you up and divorced you!"

The Worry Wart

An ISTJ army chaplain in his early sixties recognized the influence of his inferior function in the following facts about himself:

- He has always been interested in apocalyptic literature.
- He and others believe he is overconcerned about his retirement options.
- An important prayer in his personal devotions is, "Lord remind me, 'Don't worry about the future.' "
- He recalls that his mother's earliest admonition to him was, "Quit being a worry wart!"

Explained the chaplain: "I felt quite liberated by discovering that this familiar but distressing part of me is natural and adaptive. It hasn't stopped my habitual worrying, but I'm relieved to know that my reactions make sense and are predictable, normal parts of my personality."

Is a Better Job Worth It?

A career counselor had a young ISFJ client who was contemplating a career change. The career that most interested him, however, might have involved moving to another state. There were few external impediments to such a move, since he was unmarried and had no romantic involvements. However, he expressed great concern that if he got married before he changed his work, then changed careers, and then met a more compatible woman in his new work and living environment, his happy home would be broken up and he would have to get a divorce! The counselor's attempts to point out the unreality of his concerns were ignored.

In a somewhat similar scenario, an ISTJ man was moving to a new city because he had received a coveted work promotion. He became increasingly anxious, imagining all kinds of terrible things that would happen: His car would break down on the freeway and no one would stop to help him; he would get mugged on the street; no one would ever talk to him; or he would become ill and die in his lonely apartment.

ESFP's New Experience or ISFJ's Worst Nightmare?

Annette, an ISFJ, and Dan, an ESFP, were having a drink before dinner in one of those revolving cocktail lounges at the very top of a twenty-story hotel in Texas. The clear glass walls on all sides of the lounge gave customers a full view of the city. It was an early August evening. As they talked, the skies darkened, heavy clouds appeared, and the wind started blowing very hard.

Dan, leaning against the glass outer wall, said, "Hey, this is great. I can feel the glass vibrating from the wind!"

"Let's go inside the main part of the restaurant," said Annette.

"Why would you want to do that? We won't have the beautiful view," said Dan.

"I want to move away from all this glass and go into the central part where the restaurant is," insisted Annette.

Dan was puzzled. "But I don't understand why?" he asked.

"Because it's August—we're in Texas, the wind is blowing hard, those clouds look ominous, and it's tornado season!" she declared vehemently.

Replied Dan, "But if there's a tornado, this is a wonderful place to watch it from!"

"Let's Be Realistic!"

Steve, an ISFJ, was managing director of a major division in a large international company. During a routine audit it was discovered that his assistant, a trusted employee of fifteen years' tenure, had been systematically embezzling funds for five years. This was devastating to everyone in the company, especially Steve, who felt the credibility of his department had been dealt a mortal blow. He held himself responsible for not seeing his assistant's criminal behavior.

As the police handcuffed the embezzler and hauled him off to jail, John, an ENFJ company vice president said to Steve, "This really isn't a bad situation, Steve. Look at everything we've learned from this and how much better we'll be for the experience."

Replied Steve heatedly, "Let's be realistic, John. We're not having a developmental opportunity here. We're having a crisis!"

Stop! Don't Think About Anything!

Alice, an ISTJ, was having her dream house built. After a two-month delay, the house was close to completion. Alice was looking forward to moving out of her temporary housing and into her long-awaited dream house. When asked to provide an example of her reactions when her inferior extraverted intuition was in operation, she was at a loss until the following sequence of events occurred:

> The stress of building the house was ongoing. The delay made the closing date uncertain, and I was working within a contract deadline. There was high stress at work as well: My department was being downsized and I would have to lay people off; I was behind in reviewing proposals; and I was put in charge of a new program that I disapproved of, but would have to implement anyway.
>
> I was concerned because there were still construction tasks to be done. I had fleeting thoughts that Curtis, my contractor, was purposely slowing down work on the house, but I couldn't imagine why. Early that evening, Dick, a friend who was in the construction business and knew Curtis, told me he had heard that Curtis was delaying completing my house until after the contract had expired so he could

charge me more money. He told me Curtis had failed to meet three previous promised completion dates on other houses.

I knew in an instant that this must be true. I recalled that Curtis was known for taking his time on finishing touches. He would play on my desperation to leave my temporary housing, and I would give in and agree to a higher price, which I couldn't afford. I would lose the house. After waiting all this time and designing just what I wanted, someone else was going to live in my house. I would have to find another, inadequate house. And then interest rates would rise and I could never afford to live in a house I really wanted. Besides, I would have to sue Curtis to get back the money I had already paid other contractors to do the landscaping and fireplace, so I would have much less money available to invest in a house I wanted.

Throughout the evening I tried desperately to fight off my anxiety by focusing on other tasks, but those thoughts kept creeping back in and I would find myself on the verge of tears. I calmed myself down enough to get to sleep, but woke up at 2:30 A.M. and couldn't go back to sleep. I spent the night tossing and turning as I thought about how I would be moving out of my temporary housing, but wouldn't have a house to move into. Plus my furniture was going to be delivered on Tuesday, but they would have to leave it on the side of the road because the house wouldn't be mine. But then there was always the possibility that the moving company had lost my furniture and wouldn't be able to deliver it anyway. And then I'd be too upset to implement the new program and we wouldn't get it done by the deadline, so my boss would get in trouble, and then I'd get in trouble, too.

I was finally able to calm myself down enough to get some rest, though not sleep. To do that, I had to think through contingency plans (auxiliary thinking) for how I would handle various scenarios should they occur, just to convince myself that I wasn't totally at the mercy of others' whims. I also convinced myself that I had to be willing to walk away from the contract in order to maintain any bargaining power in the situation—and to withhold some of the contract cost in escrow until all items were finished to my satisfaction.

On the other side of this grip experience, I think of these contingency plans as appropriate and necessary, though I feel a little silly about my anxiety attack. I must say it helped to talk to two people in the construction business today who were able to confirm that my negative fantasy about Curtis' deviousness was just that—a negative fantasy. But this morning as I prepared to sign the contract with my landscaper, I had to consciously fight off the inclination to cancel the appointment, though I knew this would further impede closing on the house.

This was an awful experience. I rarely have a sense of panic like that, and it seemed that any direction I turned to counter my negativity, there were more frightening fantasies lurking to increase my panic. I was in a negative spiral and it was moving faster and faster. At one point I remember telling myself, "Stop! Don't think about anything!" It wasn't 'till this morning that I realized I had been in the grip.

Return of Equilibrium

Although many introverted sensing types report that they need to play out their worries to completion internally, the natural pathway out of the inferior function seems to be through their auxiliary extraverted thinking or feeling. This may take the general form of engaging in physical activity with others or perhaps changing their environment. ISTJs report using their thinking to remind them of what is real—that they can take control and that things always work out. ISFJs find it helpful when they (with great difficulty) talk to someone and reveal their irrational fears, and then receive quiet reassurance.

As with other types, ISTJs and ISFJs report needing to "hit bottom" before they can extricate comfortably from the experience. One ISFJ used the metaphor of being sucked into a whirlpool. "The worst thing to do is to fight it," he said. "That will guarantee you'll drown. Instead, you have to let yourself be drawn into it and pulled all the way down to the bottom. Then you will emerge alive."

Both types report that they need others to take them seriously, not to patronize or judge them as irrational. Being allowed to vent with an active listener who resists offering solutions is useful. Unobtrusive help with some of the overwhelming details contributing to the introverted sensor's fatigue and stress is also welcome.

Expressions in Midlife

During the first half of life, many introverted sensors come across as workaholics, demonstrating their devotion to family by providing financial security, and setting and meeting realistic goals. In their relationships with their children, they may emphasize duty, accountability, and rules as the best ways to fulfill their parental responsibility to raise independent, successful future members of society. Because of this, they may be seen as disinterested and distant in the case of ISTJs; or as demanding, overprotective, and guilt-inducing in the case of ISFJs. Others can experience both introverted sensing types as controlling and rigid.

Ideally, midlife is accompanied by a positive and progressive integration of inferior extraverted intuition, along with tertiary thinking or feeling. However, this ideal may not always occur.

Some introverted sensors become more exaggerated versions of them-selves in their older years. There may be a sharpening of the otherwise natural qualities of introverted sensing, causing the individuals to appear as a caricature of their type. They may develop rigid rules and unvarying routines, insisting that everyone else conform to their way of doing things. This can prove quite painful for family members and others, often leading relatives and friends to avoid dealing with an aging introverted sensing person. The older introverted sensor may experience this avoidance as confirmatory of his or her real or imagined failures in the first half of life, furthering a sense of despair and isolation.

Introverted sensors who are able to add intuition to their resources seem to "mellow" in the second half of life. They appear more flexible and open to new experiences, more accepting of alternative viewpoints and lifestyles, and more interested in exploring previously rejected or ignored aspects of themselves and the world in general. Things that they were likely to ignore in their earlier years may now intrigue them.

One ISTJ reported that in her early efforts at cooking she followed recipes exactly. In her mid-thirties she began deviating from written instructions in minor ways and doing some mild experimenting. Now in her forties, she makes up her own recipes, using published ones only to give her ideas. When guests rave about her creations, she feels especially pleased and affirmed.

An ISFJ recalled that in his younger years he gave little thought to what he now recognizes were eruptions of his inferior function. They were too disruptive and unlike him to be explainable. However, in middle age he became curious about these episodes and gave them a good deal of thought. Even before becoming aware of the concept of the inferior function, he learned to predict when episodes would occur and what triggered them:

> I had a really terrible fall season last year. And then for several days in a row I woke up and told my wife I'd better not go to work because I would lose control. I felt like a coffee pot that percolates and then boils over all of a sudden.

Older introverted sensing types also seem more tolerant of others' "fail-ings." The daughter of one 78-year-old ISTJ noted that her mother had become quite relaxed and philosophical about people not coming to her house on time and promises not being kept—events that would have greatly annoyed her years earlier. This same ISTJ recalled her own mother

TABLE 16   **Major Features of Inferior Extraverted Intuition**

Triggers	Forms	New Knowledge
Denial of reality	Loss of control over facts and details	Broadened perspective
Anything unknown	Impulsiveness	Clarified values
Overdoing their own type	Catastrophizing	Flexibility in relationships

(probably also an ISTJ or an ESTJ) criticizing her own grandmother (another likely STJ) for moderating her views and loosening her standards as she aged!

Many "mellowing" introverted sensors devote more attention to personal interactions with family members and friends, become more flexible and accepting of lifestyle and value differences, and often form the kind of close, warm relationships with their grandchildren that their own children would have welcomed.

Summary

In the grip of inferior extraverted intuition, introverted sensing types lose control over facts and details, become impulsive, and catastrophize about the unknown, especially the future. Auxiliary thinking or feeling aids their return to equilibrium. ISTJs use objective analysis to begin to control their anxious imaginings, while ISFJs solicit the reassurance of trusted companions and friends to modify their perceptions.

As a result of important bouts with inferior extraverted intuition, introverted sensors recognize and incorporate a broader, flexible perspective into their lives. They are better able to stand back from the absorbing tasks and responsibilities of daily living and reconsider what is most important to them. Often the awareness involves a renewed appreciation of family and other close relationships. Table 16 above highlights the main features of the inferior function experience of introverted sensing types.

CHAPTER 13

Extraverted Intuitive Types
ENTP and ENFP

BASIC TYPE DYNAMICS

Dominant extraverted intuition

Auxiliary introverted thinking or feeling

Tertiary feeling or thinking

Inferior introverted sensing

Extraverted Intuition
Versus Introverted Sensing

THIS CHAPTER EXAMINES THE way effective extraverted intuitives experience their inferior function, and the temporary transformation they make into ineffective, inferior introverted sensing types when they are "in the grip." The following review of the characteristics of extraverted intuition and introverted sensing will be helpful to our discussion.

Important Features of Dominant Extraverted Intuition

ENTPs and ENFPs have a passion for new ideas and especially enjoy the pursuit of possibilities in the world. They prefer what might be over what is, approach the outer world with trust and optimism, and see the environment as welcoming, safe, and exhilarating. They are bored by facts, details, and repetitive activities, especially those irrelevant to their current interests. However, an incoming fact may stimulate their intuition and lead to new theories or models.

They seem to have a natural trust in the environment as supportive of all things possible. They may therefore ignore sensory data that might portend danger or take risks that others might avoid. As a rule, new challenges are more appealing to them than what is known and verified. They have an uncanny instinct for trends and future developments, often before others are even mildly aware of them. Some may, in fact, predict future programs or outcomes and be told they are really "out in left field." Months, sometimes years later, they may see those ideas come into their own.

Their enthusiasm for a current project can be so compelling that they may be oblivious to time and energy limitations, often ignoring their own and others' needs to take breaks from the activity for food and rest. At an extreme, they may become so physically run down that they are forced to stop their work or risk serious illness.

Extraverted intuitives tend to enjoy the company of like-minded intuitives, and may be somewhat disdainful of their opposite types, finding them drab, predictable, and conventional. They may see introverted sensing types as overconcerned with health, safety, and comfort.

Their noninferior mode of responding to mild or moderate crises can verge on the dramatic, sometimes accompanied by a wealth of either affect or critical intensity that may seem excessive to others.

Important Features of Dominant Introverted Sensing

The qualities associated with introverted sensing that are relevant to our discussion of its form as an inferior function are an emphasis on:

- Solitude and reflection
- Attention to facts and details
- An awareness of internal experience

For an understanding of introverted sensing in its dominant, well-differentiated form, read the beginning of Chapter 12, "Introverted Sensing Types: ISTJ and ISFJ," and the type descriptions for ISTJ and ISFJ that appear in Appendix A. This will provide you with the background needed to explore the various ways in which inferior introverted sensing is expressed in ENTPs and ENFPs.

The Everyday Introverted Sensing of Extraverted Intuitives

The inferior function affects extraverted intuitives in a variety of ways—from everyday sensitivities, projections, and ways of relaxing, to the dramatic manifestations that can be seen when the inferior errupts and a full-blown episode occurs.

Typical Sensitivities and Projections

Extraverted intuitives report varying degrees of concern about whether others see them as having substance, stability, and depth. Because they are sensitive to indications that people may not be taking them seriously, they tend to be somewhat defensive about glossing over details and dismissing facts.

One ENFP becomes so deeply involved in the details of a new project that she obsesses about it, searching out supporting evidence in the form of ever more facts, which often turn out irrelevant to the goals of the project.

An ENTP lawyer acknowledged that she often feels unprepared with data to support her legal arguments, so she makes sure she has at least a few facts she can bring forth at appropriate moments to convince others of her thoroughness. An ENFP teacher says she always overprepares for lectures, bringing enough material for twice the amount of time she actually has to present.

When a strongly held value is involved, extraverted intuitives willingly attend to important facts and details. Those who disagree with their viewpoints, however, may accuse them of overvaluing relevant facts. They may therefore begin to doubt their own perceptions and judgments and seek confirmation from others. For example, an ENFP whose company was planning a major move became increasingly concerned because critical financial facts were being ignored by management. When her expressed concerns were discounted, she began to doubt her perceptions, even though a few of her colleagues shared them. Only after the move actually resulted in a financial crisis did she (and others) accept the validity of her fact-based perceptions.

Less mature extraverted intuitives may sometimes present themselves as "experts" about some factual area, eager to educate others about it. This can prove embarrassing for all if they try to impress a true authority in a particular field. An ENTP at a basic training session for volunteer firefighters complained that the level of information being presented was "too elementary for someone of my level of knowledge and experience. After all," he explained, "I've already witnessed a forest fire and helped put out a couple of brush fires!"

Sensitivity can also emerge in a focus on one or two specific areas that involve facts or sensory data. One ENFP was characteristically picky about making selections from a restaurant menu. He invariably requested some alteration in the standard fare, adding or deleting a vegetable, grilling rather than broiling, and so on. His companions at these events would be subjected to a lengthy explanation of his finely discriminating gourmet tastes.

In mildly stressful or fatiguing situations, an uneasiness about facts comes out in projected form by a pickiness and obsessiveness about what would otherwise be judged by the extraverted intuitive as irrelevant detail. Often there are irritated complaints about others' failure to attend to "important" details like typos, misplaced footnotes, motel beds that are too soft or too hard, or fussiness about food. One ENTP was surprised to learn from his wife that every time they discussed household finances, he would ask the same questions about their insurance policies—using exactly the same tone of voice.

Expressions Through Interests and Hobbies

For many extraverted intuitives, the least preferred function may be expressed through the development of expertise in one or two specific areas that require the use of sensing. One ENFP who doesn't care much for cooking is known for her superb pie crusts; another takes great pride and pleasure in doing all her own business accounting; and one ENTP's passion is for meticulous gardening and landscaping.

Another ENTP described his lifelong hobby of model railroading:

> It connects me to facts and reality. I literally create a world in a very direct way, and I run that world. I operate it and manipulate it. It is also pure relaxation of my usual intense cognitive activity. When I stop working on my railroad, I can't remember a single thought, only what I actually did.

Another appeal of his hobby is its connection to his grandfather, who was an acclaimed master woodcarver. The hobby thus provides a strong sense of connection to his past.

Eruptions of Inferior Introverted Sensing

When one or more of the preconditions for eruption of the inferior function are present, introverted sensing emerges in its more exaggerated, disruptive form. In addition to the general conditions described in Chapter 4, extraverted intuitives are vulnerable to the type-specific factors described below.

Typical Provocations or Triggers

Fatigue and pressure from overcommitment often trigger an inferior function reaction in extraverted intuitives. Not surprisingly, given the typical expressions of their type, they mention physical exhaustion as an inferior function trigger more frequently than other types. Often the enthusiasm of extraverted intuitives encourages them to overextend themselves and neglect their physical needs for food and rest. The result may be a physical illness that forces them to stop overdoing things, and also may serve as a trigger for an inferior function experience.

Other frequent triggers are having to do a lot of detail work or attending to practical matters for long periods. This is an especially effective provocation if the extraverted intuitive's efforts meet with failure. Dealing with bureaucratic red tape can be especially noxious for extraverted intuitives who are likely to dig in their heels and refuse to capitulate to "ridiculous rules."

For some extraverted intuitives, violation of important values can constellate a reaction. Explained one ENFP, "It happens when I feel the pain of others who are the victims of someone's extreme aggressiveness." An ENTP economist's severe inferior function reaction was triggered by working on a theoretical model that had negative social implications.

TABLE 17   Dominant Versus Inferior Introverted Sensing

	Qualities Associated With Introverted Sensing
As Dominant Function	Solitude and reflection
	Attention to facts and details
	Awareness of internal experience
As Inferior Function	Withdrawal and depression
	Obsessiveness
	A focus on the body

The Form of the Inferior

As the connection with dominant intuition diminishes, so does the extraverted intuitive's characteristic enthusiasm, optimism, and energetic approach to life. When their hold on their dominant and auxiliary continues to taper off, the qualities of inferior introverted sensing become manifested in withdrawal and depression, obsessiveness, and a focus on the body. The comparison between dominant and inferior introverted sensing is shown above in Table 17. In the following statement, Jung (1976a) describes the appearance of obsessiveness and a focus on the body:

> They take the form of intense projections which are...chiefly concerned with quasi-realities, such as sexual suspicions, financial hazards, forebodings of illness, etc....
> [The extraverted intuitive may] fall victim to neurotic compulsions in the form of oversubtle ratiocinations, hair-splitting dialectics, and a compulsive tie to the sensation aroused by the object....But sooner or later the object takes revenge in the form of compulsive hypochondriacal ideas, phobias, and every imaginable kind of absurd bodily sensation. (p. 370)

Withdrawal and depression   Effective dominant introverted sensing types are in their element when they spend time alone in reflection. Processing their stored information is familiar and pleasurable, and they are energized by their introverted sensing activities. For extraverted intuitives in the grip of inferior introverted sensing, the inward focus of energy is unfamiliar and disturbing. The diminution of extraverted energy results in feelings of sadness and despair. Tertiary thinking or feeling may emerge as well. For ENTPs this comes out in a conviction that no one understands them or cares about them; they may become emotional and vulnerable in this state. ENFPs may demonstrate perverse logic and accuse others of not being rational, insisting that logic is the only acceptable criterion for making a decision.

In this condition, one ENTP describes feeling isolated, convinced that no one loves her or ever has. Another reports feeling hollow, turned off, "fixated on a narrow linear trap." Another ENTP is plagued by an uncharacteristic emotionalism. "When things don't go well, I resort to emotion to get my point across," he explained.

"There is a sense of feeling numb and frozen with no way out," said an ENFP. "I have tunnel vision and lose my sense of time." Another noted that when under too much pressure, verbal skills deteriorate until "eventually, I become almost mute."

Many ENFPs describe turning inward, eventually becoming grumpy, depressed, and putting people off. Their feeling side seems to disappear. One ENFP said, "I realized I had become numb and frozen inside—there was no light, no energy—just a wasteland of a landscape, and I was plodding through it."

Both ENTPs and ENFPs report a loss of enthusiasm and motivation, accompanied by low energy. They are prone to an uncharacteristic, uncomfortable pensiveness and are unable to find pleasure in the things they normally enjoy. This may lead to self-neglect and, ultimately, illness. This kind of approach to life is particularly alien to them, for they are usually enthusiastic, fun-loving, and full of energy.

One ENFP noted that twice a year, in winter and summer, she regularly experiences ten days to three weeks where she retreats into herself and broods. Others describe periods of becoming withdrawn, critical, un-friendly, and cold. Isolation can exacerbate this reaction. An ENFP who was forced to spend a lot of time alone while recuperating from a badly broken leg was put on antidepressants after a month of increasingly lengthy periods of sobbing and despair.

Obsessiveness   Effective dominant introverted sensing types are adept at dealing with many facts and details and in putting their knowledge to practical use. In the psyche of extraverted intuitives in the grip of inferior introverted sensing, this appears as obsessiveness, characterized by tunnel vision. Although some variation of tunnel vision is associated with all of the inferior functions, it is especially notable here because extraverted intuitives are typically oriented to the broadest of perspectives. But having perspec-tive requires the kind of energy that is absent when people are in the grip of their inferior. All sense of possibilities is eliminated. An ENTP said that sometimes the details involved in a major project deadline overwhelm her so much that she feels herself slipping into an obsessive focus on how much time is left to work on the project: "I get it down to minutes and keep repeating the time frame over and over."

When their intuition is not working, sensory data become the all-encompassing objects of perception for extraverted intuitives. But their lack of expertise in this area usually leads to an inappropriate selection of sensory data. And because "the future is now" in a very distorted way, they take the data at hand and project it into a vague, oppressive future. They may focus on a thought such as, I'm alone now and will always be alone, rather than the dominant intuitive's more typical response of, I'm alone now. I wonder what interesting things I can find to do, and what exciting people I'll find in the world.

It seems that when their inferior sensing focuses on a single fact, dormant extraverted intuition intrudes and generalizes it. Because the extraverted intuitive is disadvantaged by low energy, he or she cannot recognize the fact in question as one possibility among many. No perspective exists to the person beyond the one fact. Extraverted intuitives in this state report being unable to respond to alternatives presented to them by others. The present fact is projected into forever—be it pain, depression, or whatever occupies the central focus at that moment.

Extraverted intuitives report one or more of the following ways of obsessing: being overly picky, getting upset about little things, becoming irritable and cranky, escalating small irritations into major issues, getting finicky over unimportant things, getting nervous and jumpy with people, and becoming fussy, crabby, short-tempered, and rigid. "I am usually a very happy and relaxed person," said one ENFP. "But people tell me that when I'm in my negative mode I become terse and clipped in my interactions with others. I give orders and delegate in a very autocratic manner." An ENTP described becoming outraged by minor errors, irritated by detail, intolerant of interruptions and people—"the very things I usually welcome." Another told of feeling overwhelmed and out of control, being unable to sort out priorities, and thus becoming inflexible.

An ENFP described becoming curt with people, insensitive, literal, logical, and critical, especially becoming insensitive and pedantic about language and vocabulary. Other ENFPs report doing obsessive recordkeeping, organizing data from their checkbooks, making endless lists of things to do, and putting minute details in order.

Many ENFPs report fanatically cleaning house and being unable to stop themselves, even though they typically view this activity as relatively unimportant and avoid it. Others devote the same kind of passion to mowing the lawn.

An ENFP described the following reaction as very distressing:

> I cannot respond to another's conversation. I pace, the traffic is loud, the clock is loud, sounds I never noticed before are deafening and very slow. It's almost as though time is standing still. My usual self is calm, patient, and friendly. I would classify not responding to the conversation of another as exceedingly rude behavior. And I'm generally oblivious to noise.

Another ENFP becomes picky and critical of himself and others. Usually, he sees the bigger picture, is flexible, and allows others to be who they are without trying to control or change their behavior.

On the day before the final examination in a workshop, when anxieties typically run high, a minor typesetting error was discovered in a table of data in the test manual. The instructor commented that there were two or three other errors in the text that would be corrected in the next edition. One ENFP heatedly stated that he wanted the publisher to prepare a document listing all the typos in the text and to send it to him so he wouldn't have to buy a new text when the errors were corrected.

A focus on the body   When effective dominant introverted sensing types describe the nuances of their internal sensory experiences, one can marvel at the exquisite, evocative images that emerge. When an extraverted intuitive in the grip of inferior introverted sensing focuses on inner sensations and internal experiences, it often translates into exaggerated concern about physical "symptoms" whose diagnostic meaning is always dire and extreme. Extraverted intuitives frequently overinterpret real or imagined bodily sensations as indicative of illness. When they are in full command of their dominant and auxiliary functions, extraverted intuitives easily ignore or minimize messages from their bodies. So when they do focus on the body, it is done to the exclusion of everything else. A particular symptom can have only one cause, which must be life threatening or incurable: A pulled muscle is taken as a sign of heart disease; indigestion signifies an impending heart attack; and a headache is believed to be a brain tumor. It seems that when their intuition isn't working, messages from their bodies are reacted to rigidly and absolutely.

An ENTP had been in a rare bad mood for several days but was unable to identify any cause. One morning while shaving, he noticed that when he turned his eyes to the left, the white in his right eye crinkled. He had never noticed that before and was terrified that something terrible was wrong with his eyes. Before making an appointment with an eye doctor, however, he decided to observe other people's eyes to determine just how bad his were. To his relief, but chagrin, he found that everyone's eyes moved the same way his did. He had merely never bothered to look at eyes—his own or other people's—that closely before.

An ENFP fell and injured a small bone in her back, which she could feel as a bump. She asked a friend, who was a nurse, what it could be, and was told that it was probably a cyst. She quickly translated the cyst into cancer and imagined herself on Medicaid dying alone in a squalid hospital ward. In fact, all that was necessary was a visit to a chiropractor to have the bone put back in place.

During a particularly stressful time, another ENFP insisted that her husband have an otherwise innocent-appearing wart removed because she feared it was malignant. Another ENFP reported that in times of great stress he becomes obsessed with illness. Once, when he had a routine liver function test, he became convinced he was dying of liver cancer before the test was even performed. Yet another ENFP told of owning a blood pressure cuff he rarely uses—except when he becomes very stressed, at which times he takes his blood pressure three times a day.

One ENTP described taking any fact and blowing it out of proportion, such as imagining an illness in his child as a fatal disease. Others report having a low pain threshold, fearing the dentist, and reacting to stress with a number of somatic symptoms. In fact, though physical symptoms as an expression of stress are common across types, it may be possible that "somaticizing" is more prevalent among extraverted intuitives. One ENTP had digestive problems for fifteen years. During a period of extreme stress, he developed a life-threatening bleeding ulcer. An ENFP and an ENTP discovered in a discussion that they both have medical conditions that force them to attend to their bodies—something they did not do prior to having the conditions. As a result, they more readily attend to their other physical needs as well.

Grip Experiences

The stories included in this section illustrate one or more forms of inferior introverted sensing as experienced by ENTPs or ENFPs. Notice how these grip experiences often include dominant extraverted intuition in an excessive, inappropriate degree. The wild but detailed imagination of these extraverted intuitives adds to the believability of their experience. There is also a characteristic drama revealed in relating the experiences.

"All Those Doctors Are Wrong!"

Theresa, an ENTP opera singer who had temporarily retired from singing to raise her children, was told by a physician that the kind of persistent ear problem she reported to him occasionally indicated a possible brain tumor. Though she was soon given a clean bill of health, she continued to obsess about her ear, interpreting every twinge and momentary dizziness as signaling that the physician was wrong and she indeed was going to die of a tumor. She consulted other physicians, who found nothing seriously wrong, but who suggested that in light of her continuing concerns, she consult a psychologist.

"In talking about my life situation," she explained, "I realized just how extremely different it was compared to the time before I had children. I was doing practically nothing to satisfy my artistic needs, except sometimes singing songs for my daughter's preschool class."

She was forced to realize that, although she very much enjoyed being with her children, she was perhaps overdoing her devotion to them to the exclusion of her own needs. In order to change her one-sided approach, Theresa arranged for more childcare, rented a small studio, and started giving singing lessons two mornings a week. Gradually, her obsession with her ear symptoms diminished and she felt more relaxed, less pressured, and generally more satisfied with her daily life.

"If I Ever Tell You I'm in Love Again...."

Harold, a 50-year-old ENFP, was recovering from his fourth divorce, and as had happened before, was depressed about his failure to succeed at yet another marriage. His negative self-image generalized to all aspects of his life—his work, his relationships with friends and relatives, and his prospects for the future.

"I feel like I'm in a dark hole and there's no light for miles around," he tearfully said to a long-time friend. "I feel humiliated and unworthy, unable to control anything in my life. I never have, and I never will."

Harold's pattern when he was single and living alone was to seriously overextend himself at work and in community activities. He avoided personal relationships, especially with women. Ultimately, his fatigued, stressed state would leave him feeling vulnerable and he would find himself attracted to some woman whom he saw as perfect for him—often generalizing her appropriateness from some minor quality like her hair color. What he sought was a soul mate, a perfect union. "I'm hopelessly in love with the most wonderful woman," he would tell his friends. During this "in love" period, he would ignore old friends and long-term relationships, alienating people who cared about him. He also became cavalier about his work, careless about time, schedules, commitments, and other "details." As a result, he put his career in jeopardy.

Showering them with gifts, poems, attention, and promises of his undying devotion forever, Harold scared off many women. Those who responded positively to his excesses (the ones he married) tended to be quite different from his distorted image of them, and had unrealistic perceptions of Harold as well. Not surprisingly, the marriages failed, often because of some trivial disagreement, such as where to go on a vacation.

Harold was determined to get to the root of his obsessive attachments to inappropriate women. He resolved to resist his usual pattern of frenetic overwork with inevitable poor perception and judgment. "Please," he begged his best friend. "If I ever tell you I'm in love again—shoot me!"

"Will I Have to Take Antidepressants for the Rest of My Life?"

Diane, a young mother of three children, had been seeing a psychotherapist for several months in order to deal with her reactions to her recent difficult divorce. She found herself questioning her competence as a wife and mother, and felt rather shaky and inadequate in making decisions for herself and her children. She took the MBTI personality inventory early in therapy and verified ENFP as her type. She was gradually regaining her positive sense of herself, and both she and her therapist were quite satisfied with her progress.

One evening, she called her therapist in tears, and related the following story:

> I was visiting with a friend this afternoon. We shared some wine, talked about our mutual friends, our children, and so on. I felt really calm and relaxed. As I was getting ready to leave, my friend said, "You know, Diane, you seem really depressed"!
>
> I didn't feel depressed, and I was unaware I was acting depressed. Do you think I'll have to take an antidepressant for the rest of my life?
>
> No, I'm quite confident an antidepressant is not necessary," her therapist replied. "You haven't needed one before and don't need one now. But tell me something about your friend."
>
> "Well," said Diane, "she's about my age and has two children and she's recently divorced."
>
> "Oh?" said the therapist. "Tell me, how is she doing with the divorce?"
>
> "Well, to tell you the truth," said Diane, "I think she's depressed."

In reviewing and discussing this incident, Diane recognized that her friend was projecting her own depression onto Diane. Diane was vulnerable to accepting her friend's judgment because she herself was distrustful of her own inner feeling judgment. Her distrust was a consequence of her tendency to extravert her feeling judgment rather than introvert it, as would be desirable for effective type development. Extraverts who extravert both of their preferred functions are often ready hosts for others' projections.[9] So she "tunneled in" on her friend's statement, accepted it as true, and extended it over her entire future life span.

The experience was valuable for Diane because it made her aware of her readiness to fall into the grip of inferior sensing. When in that state, she was quite prone to accepting others' projections. She gradually became more trusting of her own inner judgment and less gullible about others' assessments of her.

"And I'll Have to Put the Animals to Sleep!"

Sarah, a divorced ENFP mother, had been working very hard, was under a lot of stress, and had just caught a cold. On coming home one evening she found a letter from the Internal Revenue Service informing her that her income tax return would be audited. She described her response in the following way:

I could feel myself physically sinking. Absorbed in this feeling, it suddenly became clear to me that I would have to sell my house in order to pay the additional taxes that would result from the audit. I then imagined the one room apartment I would have to rent. Of course, the children would have to live with their dad, since I wouldn't have room for them.

I kept feeling physically really awful. I thought about all the boxes I would have to collect to make the move to the apartment and imagined going from store to store to collect them; then I realized my corner cupboard, which I loved, would not fit in an apartment, and I would have to sell it. I planned the garage sale where I would have to sell all my extra things that wouldn't fit in the apartment.

As dusk approached and the outside world became somewhat dark and gloomy, I felt overwhelmed with all the details I would have to attend to. It was then that I realized that I would have to have our two dogs and three cats put to sleep. That felt really awful. I got to thinking about whether it would be less painful to take them to the vet one at a time or whether I should take them all at the same time.

About that time a friend, Elise, also an ENFP, dropped in on Sarah. Immediately noting Sarah's blank expression, she asked what was wrong. Sarah handed her the letter from the I.R.S. and said dejectedly, "I'm going to have to sell the house."

To her credit, Elise did not laugh. She instinctively knew that Sarah could not recognize her premature conclusion and the absurdity of her reasoning. In the grip of the inferior function, there is no such thing as a sense of humor.

Instead, Elise said, "Oh, that must feel really bad."

"Yes," said Sarah, bursting into tears, "and I'm going to have to put the animals to sleep!"

Again, using good instincts, Elise did not argue with Sarah's remark, but invited her to go for a walk. As they walked, Sarah felt things loosening up, and felt better by the time they returned home. Her friend left, promising to return the next day to help Sarah decide how to handle her audit.

In reflecting on the meaning and impact of this experience, Sarah acknowledged her chronic uneasiness about her recordkeeping and attention to the everyday details of living.

"I realized that perhaps I had been overdoing my laid-back approach to things and that maybe my quick descent into a negative state meant that my approach was too extreme," reasoned Sarah.

She resolved to improve her recordkeeping, and grew to feel more comfortable about this aspect of her life.

Return of Equilibrium

Extraverted intuitives seem to need time to reflect, fully experience themselves, and even "wallow" in their inferior state. Meditating, which can be a useful way for all extraverted types to attend to their introverted functions, is particularly appealing to extraverted intuitives in the grip of their inferior.

As is the case for most types, extraverted intuitives need others to back off and avoid patronizing them. It can be helpful if some of the burden of overwhelming details are attended to, but attempts to assist by taking over and "solving the problem" for them are not appreciated. Talking to trusted friends helps, as long as the friends don't offer advice (or if they do offer it, not expect the advice to be taken), make judgments, or try to talk them out of their negative state.

Movement out of the inferior often is aided by a positive engagement of the sensing function, especially in situations where a neglect of behavior associated with sensing has provoked an inferior function experience. Physical exercise, such as jogging, engaging in some quiet sensing, or visualizing a place of peace and silence, can be helpful. Attending to physical needs, such as sleeping a lot, eating good food, and getting massages, also accompany the gradual diminishing effects of the inferior.

The role of the auxiliary may be underscored for ENTPs who find it helpful to try to analyze what is happening, either alone or with a close friend who is able to accept the ENTP's emotion and help the person to sort out priorities. One ENTP suggested that others "talk to me *as I am,* combining the normal me and the anxious me." For ENFPs who may be communicating uncharacteristic coldness and indifference, what is needed from others is warmth, kindness, and approval.

Extraverted intuitives often respond to an inferior episode by resolving to pay more attention to details, especially the kind involved in their recent negative experience. They may also gain a new respect for their bodies and their physical limitations. They report being better able (at least for a while) to maintain a more balanced perspective regarding their often overly ambitious expectations of themselves. They may create a plan to attend to their bodies with things such as an exercise regimen, and to develop their inner judgment, with such things as formal meditation or regular quiet time. They may also resolve to notice and deal more quickly with the overload that can signal an impending inferior function episode.

Expressions in Midlife

Ideally, midife is accompanied by a positive, progressive integration of inferior introverted sensing, and along with it tertiary feeling or thinking. This ideal, however, may not occur for all extraverted intuitives.

When they have not satisfactorily accomplished their adult goals, extraverted intuitives' demeanor and behavior may appear increasingly inappropriate. They may be seen as immature, "flaky," and irresponsible. Their way of dressing and choice of activities often overemphasize the youthfulness they no longer possess. They are not seen by others as aging gracefully.

Even if their personality is seemingly the same as it has always been, they may be rigid and inflexible in their insistence on an extraverted intuitive approach. A 50-year-old ENFP wore her teenaged daughter's clothing, moved from one dissatisfying career to another, and avidly pursued each new intellectual fad that came along. A 55-year-old ENTP had married and divorced three women in ten years, with each wife being younger than her predecessor.

Extraverted intuitives who are more ready to integrate inferior sensing and tertiary feeling or thinking may find themselves struggling with the internal pull to develop their introversion. They are so much a part of the external world and have found so much stimulation and enjoyment in it that there is almost a sense of loss as they find themselves paying more attention to internal things. One ENFP said:

> I realized that I was having internal conversations much more often than I did when I was younger. I didn't really *want* to—I like talking to other people—but after a while it felt less like I was cutting myself off from an external experience and more like there was some real energy in my internal dialogue.

Extraverted intuitives can find surprising pleasure in accomplishments related to their tertiary and inferior functions. ENTPs may gain great pleasure from the warmth, closeness, and satisfying harmony they find in relationships; ENFPs may pride themselves on newly developed organizational skills and be especially pleased when others comment on their successful use of logical analysis in solving problems.

Movement from the tertiary to the inferior may appear in the form of an increasing desire and pleasure in being alone and quiet. There is greater

TABLE 18 Major Features of Inferior Introverted Sensing

Triggers	Forms	New Knowledge
Violation of values and principles	Withdrawal and depression	Acceptance of physical limitations
A focus on facts	Obsessiveness	Value of facts and details
Physical exhaustion	A focus on the body	Increased structure and planfulness

enjoyment of solitary activities that require an appreciation of one or more of the five senses. One ENFP in her fifties was vacationing on an island on the East Coast. Each day while walking on the beach, she noticed a rock bed exposed by the outgoing tide. Each day she felt compelled to explore the bed. Finally, one day she sat down and found herself picking up and holding individual rocks—noting their texture, subtle colors, the feel of them in her hands. "It was a very sensual experience," she later recalled. "It had great meaning internally and was deeply satisfying."

Summary

In the grip of inferior introverted sensing, extraverted intuitives withdraw and become depressed, obsess about details, and become focused on their bodies. When obsessing about one or two inner facts, their dominant extraverted intuition may intrude in the form of a theory projecting the few facts into the distant future. Auxiliary thinking or feeling accompanies their return to equilibrium. ENTPs use logical analysis to do so, and ENFPs reconnect with their inner value structure and its relationship to their dominant intuition.

As a result of important inferior function experiences, extraverted intuitives acknowledge the limitations of their physical and mental energies, resolve to take better care of themselves, and integrate a greater appreciation for details, facts, structure, and careful planning. Table 18 above summarizes the major features of the inferior function experience of extraverted intuitive types.

CHAPTER 14
When Hidden Personalities Meet

THERE ARE MANY EXAMPLES of the puzzling and often distressing situations that can arise when a person is gripped by his or her inferior function. Not the least of these relate to their effects on other people and the way others respond to the person who is "in the grip" of his or her inferior.

One can respond to someone else's expression of the inferior in a variety of ways, including judging them incompetent, unreliable, eccentric, unpredictable, crazy, and the like. But a common reaction to someone else's inferior is to fall into the grip of one's own! Even when this does not occur, however, dealing with others "in the grip" can be quite difficult, be they spouses, parents, children, bosses, colleagues, or friends.

This chapter provides examples of interactions between two activated inferiors in couples, parents and children, and people in work settings. It demonstrates how one person's inferior can stimulate another person's inferior and identifies some of the beneficial effects of knowing about the characteristics of the inferior function when interacting with other people.

Many of the incidents and characterizations described here are composites of situations and people. Some were dealt with in the context of psychotherapy, and, as a result, represent only a brief and simplified description of an often complex relationship. Other examples were contributed by the people who experienced them or by people who observed others who appeared to be "in the grip." In all cases, the stories may be taken as illustrative of the ways people interact when they are in the grip of their inferior functions. The descriptions do not describe or explain everything that was relevant for the situation or the people described. Bear in mind that, enlightening though it can be, the inferior function doesn't explain everything.

Couples

In Chapter 9, we saw an interaction between the inferior functions of Luis, an INTP (inferior extraverted feeling), and Judy, an ENFJ (inferior introverted thinking). For this couple, each partner's dominant function is the other's inferior. When both are tired, stressed, or otherwise vulnerable to their unconscious, they readily project or directly express their least developed, unreliable side. In such a scenario, nothing can be resolved. Two "partial personalities" do the acting and projecting, leaving their more balanced selves confused, drained, and ineffectual.

Here are some other examples of what happens to couples when one or both partners is in the grip of their inferior function. To help you follow the "action" of the stories, each interaction begins with a listing of the key features of the inferior functions of both people involved in the interaction. Note that all three features of each person's inferior are not necessarily revealed in any one incident described.

"If You Love Me, You Won't Pick on Me!"

Edna, INFJ
Inferior Extraverted Sensing

KEY FEATURES OF INFERIOR FUNCTION

- Obsessive focus on external data
- Overindulgence in sensual pleasures
- Adversarial attitude toward the outer world

Clark, INTP
Inferior Extraverted Feeling

KEY FEATURES OF INFERIOR FUNCTION

- Logic emphasized to an extreme
- Hypersensitivity to relationships
- Emotionalism

Edna and Clark are the parents of four young children. They are devoted to their children, their professional lives, and several time-consuming civic and recreational activities. Stress and fatigue are familiar companions in their lives.

In the grip of inferior extraverted sensing, Edna accuses Clark of not helping her around the house or with their children. As she continues to obsess about his lack of participation, she becomes convinced that he cares more for his work than he does for his family. She notices she is being short-tempered and impatient with their children. She feels overburdened and guilty in her conviction that she is alone as their parent. Her anger toward Clark mounts, and she becomes silent and withholding when she is not being actively critical of him.

Clark's inferior extraverted feeling interprets Edna's criticism and withholding as a lack of appreciation and rejection of him as a husband and father. He says that being loved and appreciated by Edna is more important to him than anything else.

In discussing this repetitive cycle, both acknowledged feeling inadequate and guilty about how they perform as spouses and parents. They therefore readily project doubts about themselves onto each other as faults and inadequacies. Both served as willing hosts for their mutual projections.

Over an extended time period, they aired their innermost doubts and fears, which helped defuse their anger and resentment and remind them of their underlying positive feelings for each other. They agreed to try to stay more aware of their tendencies to resent each other, yet knowing their history, they accepted the likelihood that it would happen again, even though they might be able to detect early warning signs more readily.

The "Downside" of Compatibility

When both partners in an intimate relationship share the same dominant function, they also share the same inferior function. Therefore, when fatigue and stress levels are great, two similar immature personalities are likely to emerge and interact.

Annette, ISTP
Inferior Extraverted Feeling

Beth, INTP
Inferior Extraverted Feeling

KEY FEATURES OF INFERIOR FUNCTION
- Logic emphasized to an extreme
- Hypersensitivity to relationships
- Emotionalism

Annette and Beth had lived together for ten years and shared a close, satisfying relationship. They each worked very hard at their demanding careers and were frequently at their worst when they arrived home on workdays. Inadvertently, one or both would say the wrong thing, so that the others' feelings would get hurt. Their vulnerable condition frequently brought on tearful recriminations, the dredging up of a complete past history of insults and hurtful comments, and the like.

Though they very much liked being similar types, awareness of their shared vulnerabilities brought a mixed reaction. They were distressed to find they were experts at hurting each other! In time, however, they were able to bypass the more minor insensitivities and wounds. Talking through major bouts with their inferior functions after an episode occurred was helpful for each individually as well as for their relationship as a couple.

Letty and Rob at Their Worst

Letty, ESFJ
Inferior Introverted Thinking

KEY FEATURES OF INFERIOR FUNCTION

- Excessive criticism
- Convoluted logic
- Compulsive search for the truth

Rob, ISFJ
Inferior Extraverted Intuition

KEY FEATURES OF INFERIOR FUNCTION

- Loss of control over facts and details
- Impulsiveness
- Catastrophizing

Letty and Rob were planning to get married. They were devoted to each other and very much in love. But because both were divorced and each had two nearly grown children, there were several complicated personal and business matters that needed to be settled, especially in Rob's case.

As Christmas approached, Letty noticed that Rob was procrastinating about taking care of some legal matters. She did not say anything about this for several weeks. Then one evening when Rob called her to say that he wouldn't be coming over for the third night in a row because he was "too tired and stressed out," Letty lost control. She unleashed a barrage of angry recriminations, accusing Rob of being weak, ineffectual, and moody.

"You never keep your promises," she fumed. "If you're so wishy-washy about taking care of business matters, you must be just as ambivalent about our relationship! Maybe we should call the whole thing off!"

Rob was crushed by Letty's outburst. He later explained that he was indeed feeling rather down because Christmas always brought forth both happy and sad memories of life with his ex-wife and their children. He became focused on the thought that since his first marriage had failed, perhaps the new one would, too. He imagined all the things that could go wrong in his relationship with Letty: The children would resent their stepparents, his business might fail and they wouldn't have enough money to do enjoyable things together, they would grow to hate each other, and so on.

As his obsession with a negative future intensified, he was overwhelmed by the conviction that he would be unable to love Letty in the way she deserved. Perhaps the most sensible thing to do was to release her from her agreement to marry him so that she could be free to find a more worthy life partner.

In despair, he talked to Letty about his fears. At first she was shocked at his irrational response, but she later remembered that in other very stressful times Rob had overreacted and arrived at unwarranted conclusions. And when it was pointed out to her, she recognized her own hypercritical outburst as her usual reaction to feeling shut out of an important relationship. The couple was eventually better able to deal with the realities of their situation in a more rational and effective way.

"I Know How to Get There!"

Aaron, ENFP
Inferior Introverted Sensing

KEY FEATURES OF INFERIOR FUNCTION

- Withdrawal and depression
- Obsessiveness
- A focus on the body

Marlene, ISTJ
Inferior Extraverted Intuition

KEY FEATURES OF INFERIOR FUNCTION

- Loss of control over facts and details
- Impulsiveness
- Catastrophizing

Aaron and his wife Marlene were preparing for a special evening to celebrate Aaron's long-awaited promotion. Aaron's boss had invited them to dinner at a new and reputedly excellent restaurant on the outskirts of the city.

"Do you know how to get to the restaurant?" asked Marlene. "You know you always have trouble following directions."

"Yes, yes," replied Aaron. "I looked on the map. It's quite simple."

"I'll bet it is," muttered Marlene under her breath.

"What's that?" asked Aaron. "I said I'll get dressed," she answered.

They were planning to meet his boss and her husband at the restaurant at 7 o'clock. "A half hour will be more than enough time to get there," said Aaron.

"Maybe," replied Marlene. "But you'd better leave another half hour for getting lost!"

Aaron sighed. He was quite used to Marlene's jibes about his sense of direction, his underestimation of time, and his generally easygoing style. He was usually good-humored when she teased him in this way. Both of them were able to joke about their different ways of doing things. But tonight he was happy and excited and did not want anything negative to spoil his good humor.

"I know how to get there!" he said rather irritably. "Just lay off me, will you?"

"Touchy, aren't we," Marlene teased.

Sure enough, Aaron ended up in an unknown area and had to confess that they were lost. "Oh, let me see the map!" snapped Marlene.

"I didn't bring it," said Aaron. "It was a very straightforward route. I know I figured it out right. The map must have been wrong. Or maybe it was an old map and the highway department changed the road signs. It's not my fault!"

Marlene was furious: "We have ten minutes to get there and we don't know where we are. Your boss will think we are totally incompetent and irresponsible. She'll take away your promotion. Or she'll blame me for it and think I'm the stereotype of an empty-headed, slow wife. The whole thing is a disaster! Just drive till we find a gas station and we'll ask for directions."

For his part, Aaron unleashed a detailed accounting of every mistake Marlene had made in the last five years, from bouncing a check several years ago to parking the car where a pick-up truck scraped the side of it. "And I don't need to ask directions. I know how to get there!" he snapped.

After driving around aimlessly for a few minutes, Aaron came upon a familiar-sounding road. It led them directly to the restaurant. They arrived at 7:15. His boss and her husband arrived at 7:20.

"Sorry to keep you waiting," said Aaron's boss. "We got lost trying to find this place."

The evening went well after that. Aaron and Marlene were able to laugh at themselves and their familiar reactions to each other's habits. They resolved to do it better next time, knowing that the right circumstances would once again provoke a recurrence of their "car syndrome."

Using Knowledge of the Inferior in Couple Relationships

Knowing which "buttons to push" often means knowing what to say or do to provoke an inferior function response in our loved ones. When people are familiar with the form of their own and each other's inferiors, they can use this knowledge either negatively or positively. Awareness of another person's vulnerabilities can give one power over that person, and awareness of our own vulnerabilities can tempt us to use them to excuse some of our own unpleasant behavior.

But the potential for enhancing the intimacy of a relationship far outweighs the negative possibilities that can accompany a knowledge of the inferior function. When only one partner is "in the grip," the other may be able to respond in a helpful way, thus encouraging the other person to benefit from the experience. When both partners are "beside themselves," as in the above examples, the opportunity for new understanding comes only *after* both have emerged from their inferior state. It is then that discussion, review, and a new level of intimacy is likely to occur.

Knowing how the other person's inferior is expressed can provide one with a helpful perspective. It can prevent the recipient of exaggerated, unfounded, hurtful statements from taking them as literal and enduring. We can stand back from the situation and observe it somewhat objectively and dispassionately. We can recognize the partial personality we are faced with as only somewhat representative of the person we usually experience. In the best of circumstances, this can help us to avoid falling into our own inferior in response to our partner's.

Parents and Children

Parents and children can also provoke each others' grip response throughout childhood, adolescence, and far into their adult years. People who know each other very well instinctively know what "buttons" will catapult the other person into an inferior function response or some other equally unconscious personal complex.

"It's Not My Opinion, It's a Fact!"

Sam, ENFJ
Inferior Introverted Thinking

KEY FEATURES OF INFERIOR FUNCTION

- Excessive criticism
- Convoluted logic
- Compulsive search for the truth

Anita, INTJ
Inferior Extraverted Sensing

KEY FEATURES OF INFERIOR FUNCTION

- Obsessive focus on external data
- Overindulgence in sensual pleasures
- Adversarial attitude toward the outer world

At the age of 28, Sam was struggling with career decisions. His mother, Anita, had been divorced for many years from Sam's father. She had raised Sam virtually by herself. Anita and Sam lived in different states. Sam was in the process of exploring career options and had applied for a range of different positions.

On the day his mother was to arrive for a weekend visit, Sam heard that he would not be hired for a coveted job as a science administrator. His alternative was to accept a position working with adolescents in a mental hospital, another good job, but one less compelling to him. He also had the option of turning down the mental health job and awaiting funding for another science job. But if he chose this option, the wait could be as long as six months.

Anita was becoming increasingly concerned about her only son's lack of career direction. Her goal was to support and encourage him in his struggle, and Sam trusted his mother's good intentions. But their highly vulnerable states held the potential for disaster.

As soon as she arrived, Sam filled his mother in on his recent career developments. Her immediate response was, "You don't understand about mental hospitals. Let me explain it to you. That's a terrible place to work. People will take advantage of you. You'll hate it. I know because I worked in one 20 years ago. They are all the same! What you ought to do is become a teacher, like me. You know you'd be very good at it."

Sam replied heatedly, "That was your experience and your opinion. I'll make my own decision. What was right for you is not necessarily right for me. I've told you over and over that I have no interest in being a teacher and why. You know from your own experience that it's a dead-end job. I expect you to have some respect for my judgment. You're treating me like a child and an idiot!"

Anita said, "It's not my opinion. I'm giving you facts. I'm just trying to support you by telling you the facts. You just don't understand about mental hospitals. And I know you better than you know yourself, so I know you're capable of making the right decision."

Anita gave Sam more and more "facts." Sam grew increasingly resentful of her overbearing, deprecatory manner. Sam went to the library and brought back books and articles about mental hospitals. Anita refused to look at them. Their weekend together was spent in repetitions of the same accusations and attacks on both sides, relieved by occasional neutral moments. The tension did not end until Anita's departure.

In retrospect, both were able to see that Anita's anxiety and concern for her son came out in her adhering to a few questionable "facts" from her own experience and using them to try to talk her son out of what she saw as a poor career choice. Sam was already ambivalent about taking the job, but his ambivalence took second place to his perception of his mother's criticism of him. His response was to provide her with the "real truth" in published form. But since what was factual or true was not the issue, neither tactic resolved anything.

Though neither knew about the inferior function at the time this incident occurred, hearing it interpreted in this way lessened their lingering hurt and anger. They hoped that knowledge of their own and each other's typical out-of-character responses would help them resolve future conflicts more productively.

"The First Time You Wear It the Whole Thing Will Fall Apart"

Camille, ENFP
Inferior Introverted Sensing

KEY FEATURES OF INFERIOR FUNCTION
- Withdrawal and depression
- Obsessiveness
- A focus on the body

Her Mother, ISTJ
Inferior Extraverted Intuition

KEY FEATURES OF INFERIOR FUNCTION
- Loss of control over facts and details
- Impulsiveness
- Catastrophizing

Camille contributed the following:

"In thinking about my type and my mother's type, I believe that much of our interaction time during my teenage years was spent in our inferior functions. The pattern looked like this.

"I would be caught up in my extraverted intuition—this party or dance would be so wonderful! All my fantasies of popularity and social acceptance would come true, I would be beautiful and charming, people would compete for my attention. Then I would ask my mother if I could go to the event. She would immediately begin presenting all her negative fantasies—only riffraff would be there, no one from my crowd would go, I would use poor judgment and get into trouble, terrible things would happen.

"I would then give her detail after detail, 'Jane is going, Judy's mother said..., Susan gets to go, I wouldn't do this and that,' etc. Finally, I would explode and go to my room to brood, recounting to myself every detail of my life, every word my mother and I had said, every instance of my mistreatment.

"Here is a typical encounter: When I was 14, I had a vision of a skirt that would change my life—a pink, very full, gauzy skirt. I could see myself looking very romantic—perhaps worn with an off-the-shoulder peasant blouse. My mother, an accomplished seamstress, had done her best to teach me to sew. But I had to sew *her* kind of clothes, tailored, subtle plaids or checks, and always practical clothing—and in her way, step-by-step, with careful attention to detail.

"Using babysitting money, I went shopping, got the pattern for the skirt and yards of exactly the right gauzy pink material. I went home to begin my creation. But as I began laying out the material, pinning pattern pieces, getting ready to cut, I became possessed with the need to do it right. I pinned and repinned and repinned. My mother had never been as picky as I was being. Watching me, my mother began to pace, and was soon saying, 'The material will soon be worn out and unusable,' 'the first time you wear it the whole thing will fall apart,' 'the seams will pucker and you will never be able to....' She painted at least twenty different negative fantasies for me, as grim lipped, I perspired and pinned."

Camille said that this was just one of many similar mother-daughter encounters, which she and her mellowing ISTJ mother can now laugh about.

"You Should Know Me Better than That!"

Mary, ISFJ
Inferior Extraverted Intuition

KEY FEATURES OF INFERIOR FUNCTION
- Loss of control over facts and details
- Impulsiveness
- Catastrophizing

Sean, INTP
Inferior Extraverted Feeling

KEY FEATURES OF INFERIOR FUNCTION
- Logic emphasized to an extreme
- Hypersensitivity to relationships
- Emotionalism

At 77, Mary was growing increasingly concerned about her health. She was nearly blind and suffered from arthritis and numerous other health problems. As a result, it was difficult for her to take care of her own affairs. She was advised to give power of attorney to her 50-year-old son, Sean. In discussing this with him, she commented that perhaps her lawyer should be a cosigner to the power of attorney. "That way you won't be able to take advantage of me," she told Sean.

Sean was silently furious at his mother's remark. Later, in talking to his wife about it, he said, "I felt annihilated by her comment. How could she even think like that for a minute. I don't have many intimate relationships, but I invest myself fully in the ones I do have. My mother and I have had a close relationship for 50 years. She should know me better than that!"

Sean continued to be distressed and despairing about his mother's comment for several days, but he gradually recognized that his mother was doing her typical "worst case analysis" in response to her increasing anxiety about her failing health. He was able to regain his equilibrium and forgive his mother without having to confront her and create more of a problem than the situation warranted.

It was easy to interpret Mary's hurtful remark as her inferior extraverted intuition taking over her perception. When she expressed her least developed side to Sean, she in turn triggered his inferior extraverted feeling response. He felt hurt, demeaned, misunderstood, and unappreciated.

"He Doesn't Seem to Have Any Goals at All"

Paul, ENTJ
Inferior Introverted Feeling

KEY FEATURES OF INFERIOR FUNCTION
- Hypersensitivity to inner states
- Outbursts of emotion
- Fear of feeling

Tom, ESFP
Inferior Introverted Intuition

KEY FEATURES OF INFERIOR FUNCTION
- Internal confusion
- Inappropriate attribution of meaning
- Grandiose visions

Paul was concerned about his 17-year-old son, Tom, who was entering his senior year in high school. He confessed that their relationship had been difficult from the beginning, with Tom seeming to purposely defy every value and principle important to Paul. Nevertheless, Paul admired his son's popularity with his peers and his ease in social relationships.

He was somewhat more uneasy about Tom's ready pursuit of pleasure and rather frenetic level of physical activity. In early elementary school, Tom had been diagnosed as hyperactive and had been put on medication. The diagnosis was later found to be in error.

Paul was also irritated by Tom's lackadaisical approach to school assignments, especially since his tested IQ was in the superior range. "I'm really worried about my son's lack of motivation and direction. He doesn't seem to have any goals at all!" Paul said.

Tom was quite clear about his preferences, which were nearly opposite those of his father. He acknowledged that the two of them rarely saw eye to eye: "He get's really uptight and upset about unimportant things, yells at me and accuses me of not appreciating what I've got and everything he does for me. If I leave a smudge on my car when I polish it, he gets mad and tells me that if I'm this sloppy with my car, how could I ever succeed in life. It's really stupid!"

When particularly tired, Tom is unable to put his father's criticisms in perspective. He becomes overwhelmed with fears about his future and wonders if his father's view of him is true. "It's true I don't plan ahead much," admitted Tom. "Maybe there really is something missing in my character, like Dad seems to think." Tom would then imagine all sorts of unpleasant, unavoidable failures that would occur if he continued on in his own way. But if he tried to emulate his very responsible and serious father, he envisioned a joyless, oppressive life. Either way, he felt doomed.

Paul's experience of his own inferior extraverted sensing prevented him from appreciating all but the surface competencies of his son's type. His fears about his son's competence were far out of proportion, as was his conclusion that his son was not equipped for successful adulthood. He had a hard time envisioning and respecting Tom's talents and values.

Tom despaired of receiving his father's approval, but his rejection and derision of his father's concerns were more than a youthful desire for independence: The two approached life from very different perspectives. Paul readily descended into a raging, despairing state of inferior introverted feeling as he watched Tom's easygoing dominant extraverted sensing lifestyle. In his vulnerable position of inexperienced youth and with his basic respect for his father, Tom was vulnerable to his father's exaggerated emotional judgments, which emanated from his inferior introverted feeling.

"Promise Me You'll Tell Me if I Get to Be Like Him!"

Anna, ISTJ
Inferior Extraverted Intuition

Otis, ISTJ
Inferior Extraverted Intuition

KEY FEATURES OF INFERIOR FUNCTION
- Loss of control over facts and details
- Impulsiveness
- Catastrophizing

Anna called her elderly father Otis to invite him for dinner at a local restaurant.

"I guess I'll come," he said. "But we'll have to go early so I don't get caught in traffic. And you know that place won't take reservations, and I don't want to sit around waiting all night. You don't know if they've changed the menu again, do you? Last time they didn't have my dessert, and I'd just as soon stay home if I can't get what I want when I go out. Money doesn't grow on trees, you know."

Anna groaned internally. "I'm paying for dinner, Dad. I was there a few night's ago and the menu is the same, so you can order your usual. I'll pick you up so you don't have to deal with traffic."

"No, no. Don't bother. It's too far out of your way and you'll waste gas. You've got to watch the pennies."

Anna was a highly paid engineer with a very secure future. "No, I don't have to watch my pennies, Dad. Why can't you just relax and have a good time? You always see the bad side of things."

"Well, you know Anna, you should never take anything for granted," he advised. "You might have an okay job now, but what if the economy gets worse and they lay you off? By the way, do you have any savings? You know I only have my social security, so you won't be able to count on me to help you out."

"Dad, stop it!" shouted Anna into the phone. "You're always putting me down. Everyone else respects my work, but you think I'm going to be fired at any moment. You don't care anything about me. Nothing I do makes you happy. You're the most pessimistic, negative, irritating old man who ever lived, and I don't want to have dinner with you tonight or any night!"

Anna slammed down the phone and then called her best friend Sally and related the latest encounter with her father. "He just gets worse and worse.

Soon we won't be able to talk to each other at all. And I think his memory is going. What if he gets to where he can't take care of himself and I have to take him in? I couldn't stand it. And what if he's right and I do lose my job? He'd really crow about that and say, 'Told you so, told you so,' like he always does when something bad happens."

Sally knew what to do in this situation, which came up regularly for Anna. She listened sympathetically, agreeing that Otis was being his usual crotchety self and recognizing how difficult it must be for Anna to deal with him.

"How about my joining you and your dad at the restaurant tonight? You know he's usually more sociable when I'm around."

"But I called it off," said Anna.

"Call it back on, then. You know he really loves to eat out, and he's probably sorry he upset you. He always is."

The three had a pleasant dinner together with little incident. Anna later observed to Sally that her father's negativity nearly always caused her to imagine the same kinds of unpleasant possibilities he came up with. She shuddered to think that she might get stuck like her father seemed to be, and made Sally promise to tell her immediately if she thought she was becoming like him.

Using Knowledge of the Inferior
With Parents and Children

Anything that promotes understanding between parents and children of any age has to be an asset. Parents who understand psychological type have an objective way of accepting and appreciating differences between themselves and their children. Adolescent and adult children who understand typology have a valuable way of differentiating between parent-child issues and what may be "pseudo issues" attributable to type differences.

An understanding of the habitual out-of-character reactions of parents and children adds greatly to the value of psychological type knowledge. Family life can be stressful for many people, but it can also represent the comfort and security of ultimate acceptance. It is thus a safe place for people to be at their worst. Family members tend to be adept at identifying and handling each other's idiosyncrasies, but they often lack an accurate understanding and comfortable acceptance of their own and each other's foibles. Recognizing the influence of the inferior function can objectify such aberrations and enable family members to view extreme behavior within the context of normal personality.

At Work

It should come as no surprise that the workplace frequently bears witness to incidents where people's inferior functions emerge and interact. This can be more devastating than in the case of intimate relationships. In intimate relationships, one can usually trust that love and the strength of the bond will mitigate any negative effects of the episode.

There are several examples of work-stimulated grip experiences in the preceding eight chapters. There was Eleanor, the INTP CPA, and Jenny, the ESTJ manager. Eleanor did not know much about typology when her grip experience occurred. When she discovered that it could be well explained as an inferior function episode, she was relieved. At the time of Jenny's experience, she was knowledgeable about all aspects of typology. Nevertheless, she was vulnerable to the stress that pushed her into her inferior function.

In some circumstances, however, knowing the form of one's own and one's co-workers' inferior functions can minimize their effects and even prevent unpleasant and unproductive confrontations from occurring at work. The following example illustrates this point.

Frank and Zeke

Frank, ENFP
Inferior Introverted Sensing

KEY FEATURES OF INFERIOR FUNCTION
- Withdrawal and depression
- Obsessiveness
- A focus on the body

Zeke, ESTP
Inferior Introverted Intuition

KEY FEATURES OF INFERIOR FUNCTION
- Internal confusion
- Inappropriate attribution of meaning
- Grandiose visions

Frank, a police sergeant in the criminal division, was having difficulty in his relationship with Zeke, a legal adviser he worked with. Zeke persistently questioned and criticized Frank's communication style and competence in a demeaning, combative manner. Frank was in great distress during an eight-month period that Zeke verbally attacked him on a daily basis.

As a result, Frank's generally positive self-image of competence and ability to communicate effectively changed to extreme self-doubt. He felt especially distrusting of his intuition, which had always been his most reliable guide in his work. He found himself obsessing about every memo he wrote, questioning his interrogation methods, and making minute revisions of his case reports.

It was in this context that an important but difficult and complicated case came up that required Frank and Zeke to work closely together. As the case dragged on, Frank observed Zeke coming up with all kinds of doomsday predictions about the case, based on improbable, inappropriate theories. Zeke imagined bizarre legal and medical ramifications, despite the fact that these matters were far outside his area of expertise.

Frank, who knew about the manifestations of the inferior function, guessed that the stress of the case might well account for Zeke's aberrant behavior. He was concerned, however, that if Zeke continued talking in this strange manner, the case might be jeopardized. He therefore made every effort to appease Zeke and prevent him from bringing even worse repercussions into the situation.

Frank also realized that sooner or later, he and Zeke would have to confront each other and that, with his negative experiences with Zeke and his ongoing diminished self-confidence, he could easily slip into the grip of his own inferior function. He knew what would happen to him if he did: He would become upset, argumentative, hostile, and confrontational. He would lash out at everyone around him, make off-the-wall accusations, and obsess about his own and everyone else's inattention to facts. Frank knew that "losing it" would not serve him or his department well.

Being aware and prepared for this probability circumvented a likely inferior function episode for Frank. By anticipating things, he was able to distance himself and deal with the situation in a quiet, objective, and reasonable manner.

Knowing When to Stop

Patsy, ENFP
Inferior Introverted Sensing

KEY FEATURES OF INFERIOR FUNCTION

- Withdrawal and depression
- Obsessiveness
- A focus on the body

Ginny, INTP
Inferior Extraverted Feeling

KEY FEATURES OF INFERIOR FUNCTION

- Logic emphasized to an extreme
- Hypersensitivity to relationships
- Emotionalism

Patsy and Ginny are business partners. By mutual agreement, Ginny takes care of all the finances of the business—making deposits to the right accounts, balancing the accounts, paying the bills on time, figuring the taxes, filling out forms, and so on. Though the business is doing very well, the cash flow is uneven, and staying current on all bills requires some real maneuvering at times.

Ginny has learned that it works best if she just takes care of all this without discussing it with Patsy. For Patsy, there is no good time for financial discussions. Talking about it first thing in the morning "spoils what was going to be a nice day." Talking about it last thing in the day means "I'll be awake all night." It doesn't seem to matter if it's positive information or negative information that's at issue—just talking about money is painful for her. And specifics seem to be taken out of context. A statement by Ginny that, "We're a little overextended right now, so let's be careful just to purchase things we really need," may lead to phone calls from Patsy saying, "I'm at the office supply and I just bought a box of paper clips for $1.99, but now I'm feeling guilty. I think we have a bunch of papers in our files with clips on them that we could take off and reuse. Should I return this box?"

Patsy prefers not to know very much about the finances of their business. She says, "Just tell me, do we have money?" The desired answer is yes or no, with no other information. Most of the time, Patsy and Ginny deal with the financial issues pretty well, but there is one pattern they have noticed that gets both of them dangerously close to being beside themselves. Here is how it typically goes.

Patsy wants to go on a trip or buy something, and Ginny has to tell her to hold back because their finances are tight.

Ginny: "We've only got $1,000 in the bank, and we can't expect to receive the check from X for another couple of weeks, and the American Express bill that's due next week is for $950."

Patsy: "Why is that bill so high; we didn't charge anything, did we?"

Ginny: "It's for your plane tickets for those two business talks you did out of town last month."

Patsy: "But we were reimbursed for those last month. Where are the reimbursement checks? Why don't we save the reimbursement checks to pay the bills when they come due?"

Ginny: "It would be nice if we could put all the reimbursement checks into a savings account and draw the money out when we get the bills. Unfortunately, we needed those checks to pay the rent on the first of the month because we hadn't gotten the check from the state government. It wouldn't make sense to be late on the rent, get a penalty, and damage our credit rating, while we're holding onto $800 in checks. The money comes in and then goes out. That's the logic of it."

After many repetitions of this scenario, Patsy and Ginny have learned to end their conversations when they get to this point. In the past, however, as these discussions went on, Patsy would become more and more insistent that the crux of the problem was Ginny's mishandling of reimbursement checks. Ginny would eventually become hurt and tearful and accuse Patsy of not appreciating how hard she worked to keep their finances in order. And the cycle would go on and on. Their understanding of their own and each other's response to the stress associated with finances has enabled them to inhibit their inferior functions before they get past the point of no return.

The INFP Psychotherapy Supervisor

Work settings tend to be pretty stressful places, regardless of the nature of the work being performed or the competence and devotion of the people involved. It is not unusual, therefore, for people to deal on a daily basis with a supervisor who is chronically operating out of his or her inferior function, as the next example illustrates.

Carol, ESFJ
Inferior Introverted Thinking

KEY FEATURES OF INFERIOR FUNCTION

- Excessive criticism
- Convoluted logic
- Compulsive search for the truth

Andrew, INFP
Inferior Extraverted Thinking

KEY FEATURES OF INFERIOR FUNCTION

- Judgments of incompetence
- Aggressive criticism
- Precipitous action

Carol, a family therapist in a mental health center, was pleased to discover that her unit's new supervisor, Andrew, was an INFP. Carol values her friendships with INFPs and is particularly appreciative of the therapeutic insights of her INFP colleagues. She therefore became increasingly puzzled and distressed when early encounters with Andrew became frequently destructive and hostile.

In performing his job as supervisor, Andrew appears obsessively concerned with recordkeeping and client confidentiality, and is meticulous about following established cautionary procedures. His primary focus is on the prevention of possible lawsuits against the mental health facility. Consequently, when suicide, homicide, or any other severe acting-out behavior is even slightly hinted at for a client, Andrew insists on pages of documentation on all interactions, treatment plans, and so on.

When Carol approaches Andrew for therapeutic advice, Andrew invariably inquires only about the accuracy of the records and whether Carol had said or done anything "dangerous." This response from Andrew makes Carol doubt her own value as a therapist and question what Andrew expects of her. When Carol is not overwhelmed by her concerns about her therapeutic skills, she feels frustrated, angry, and shortchanged by Andrew. Any attempt on Carol's part to establish harmony, seek out Andrew's knowledge as a therapist, or provide some common sense evaluation of a situation is met by increased criticism and negativity from Andrew.

Andrew seems to be chronically in the grip of inferior extraverted thinking. His self-doubt about his competence to do his job and the pressure of being responsible for a number of therapists and many clients are apparently overwhelming for him. His response overemphasizes minute details that might "trip him up" and inevitably lead to the discovery of his incompetence and a dreaded lawsuit for failure to treat some client appropriately.

Carol's feelings about this continuing situation vary from sympathy for Andrew's obvious unhappiness to irritation and resentment about Andrew's failure to give his best to his staff members. The continuing situation is distressing for everyone involved.

"Are These People Really Adults?"

Felice, ISFP
Inferior Extraverted Thinking

KEY FEATURES OF INFERIOR FUNCTION
- Judgments of incompetence
- Aggressiveness
- Precipitous action

Glen, INTJ
Inferior Extraverted Sensing

KEY FEATURES OF INFERIOR FUNCTION
- Obsessive focus on external data
- Overindulgence in sensual pleasures
- Adversarial attitude toward the outer world

Felice has been the administrator of a large church for more than fifteen years. She is good at her job, which is broad and complex. She manages church membership, religious school operations, space rentals for weddings and other events, and volunteers. In short, she stays on top of everything. Her accounting methods are not terribly systematic, but after twenty years, she knows everything so well that even with unorthodox recordkeeping, church finances are always in order and the church is consistently solvent.

Felice is directly responsible to the church's minister, Glen. Glen is thankful that Felice takes care of all the financial data and handles the day-to-day affairs of the church in a manner that pleases the congregation and frees him from having to get involved in areas he doesn't enjoy.

Felice and Glen get along fine most of the time. But Felice confessed to her son that sometimes Glen is completely unreasonable, usually when he has to present church affairs at a finance meeting of church officers. The day before such meetings, he gets into a frenzy and demands detailed, specific financial information about every aspect of the church's activities.

"Just get it off the computer!" he demands. "That's what you have it for!" Glen does not know how to operate a computer, but he has great respect for its capabilities. Felice has never been able to convince him that a person can't simply get something out of a computer that hasn't been put in. He believes all you need to do is push some button and whatever you need will magically appear.

Felice believes that to be an effective administrator, she must accommodate Glen's wishes. But she cannot do this because what he wants often cannot be produced. She has never confronted him about this, for, in her mind, it would not be proper.

Glen heaps more and more verbal abuse on Felice as she fails to provide the desired financial figures. So, in her distress, frustration, and resentment, she turns into a tyrant, taking it out on everyone in the church—employees, volunteers, parishioners, delivery people, and so on. She becomes rigid, dictatorial, and withholding.

One spring, the church school had requested and approved a sum for a summer picnic for seventy-five children. Two days before the picnic, the teacher came to Felice to get the check. Little did the teacher know that the day before, Glen had (erroneously) decided the church was in debt and told Felice there was no money for anything.

Felice angrily told the teacher that there was no money at all and she would have to cancel the picnic. There was nothing anyone could do about it and if she had any complaints, she should go to the minister. The angry teacher then berated the minister, who got angry at Felice, who in turn took it out on her staff, who became puzzled, hurt, and demoralized.

"Everyone is at their worst," said a long-time church volunteer. "Especially Glen and Felice. It's as if they both turn into eight year olds, and immature ones at that!"

Using Knowledge of the Inferior in the Workplace

The workplace is an arena where people demonstrate their best and worst selves. We show our competence in areas where we are skilled and experienced and where we are appreciated by co-workers and rewarded by employers for competent work performance. But the stress that is chronic in most work situations can thwart our best efforts and elicit our own and others' least effective sides. Understanding the forms of different inferior functions can provide the potential for understanding, predicting, and explaining out-of-character behavior at work.

Power relationships in the workplace add a particularly potent, often destructive dimension to expressions of the inferior function. An employee who is beside himself may be fired for being unreliable; a co-worker may be judged as impossible to work with at times and therefore be avoided even when at her best; and a supervisor's out-of-character behavior may just be "something you have to watch out for and fear."

Characterizing people and judging them on the basis of their most aberrant behavior is wasteful and often unwarranted. It is here that knowledge of the inferior function can prove particularly beneficial. Extreme out-of-character reactions to the stresses of the workplace can be viewed in the context of the *consistency* of personality rather than its unpredictability. This can provide the rationality necessary to distinguish between true unreliability, poor performance, and faulty leadership and intermittent episodes of the inferior function.

People who recognize their own and others' inferiors at work report that they are better able to keep things in perspective for themselves and others. This can have a positive effect on productivity and employee satisfaction, which in turn may reduce some of the stresses of the workplace.

Conclusion

The "gripping" experiences described in this chapter are but a few of the many ways that personal and professional interactions can trigger an inferior function. Remember, however, that even though activation of the inferior may contribute to an exaggerated reaction on someone's part, the content involved should not be ignored. Important truths often emerge when a usually reticent person relinquishes social inhibitions, or when a normally cheerful and confident individual reveals his or her innermost doubts and fears.

CHAPTER 15

In and Out of the Grip

THIS CHAPTER INCLUDES DISCUSSIONS of some remaining issues related to the inferior function experience, some intriguing areas for further exploration, and some recommendations for applying the inferior function concept in everyday life. The following areas will be discussed:

- Living life in your inferior function
- The role of the inferior in job burnout
- Questions about the role of the auxiliary
- Maturity and the grip
- Trivializing the inferior
- Overusing the concept of the inferior
- The value of opposites

Living Life in Your Inferior Function

Life circumstances sometimes require a person to operate in his or her inferior function for extended periods. Some develop excellent skills in their fourth function and also put their dominant function to innovative use. However, when in a vulnerable state, they can easily slip into a full-blown inferior function experience.

When people chronically work out of their inferior function, we might expect to see exaggerated, perhaps inappropriate, demonstrations of the function involved. Sometimes a person who seems to be a caricature of his or her type, whose type qualities are extreme, is really the opposite or near opposite type—perhaps trying too hard to do it well.

This was the case for Joe, the director of training in a large corporation. His reputation in the company was as a hard-nosed, rigid, often punitive person who insisted that rules be followed meticulously. He was particularly callous when personal problems arose for employees, such as marital difficulties or sick children. He insisted that as adults, people must learn to separate their work lives from their personal lives.

Several people familiar with type were convinced that Joe was an ESTJ with a marked inability to use his tertiary intuition and inferior feeling functions in any adaptive way. When a consultant administered the MBTI personality inventory to senior members of the firm, they were amazed to discover that Joe had verified his reported type as INFP. Later discussions with Joe revealed that his role model was his very effective predecessor, Bill. Bill was a mature ESTJ.

It is not uncommon for the demands of a career to force development and frequent use of our least preferred processes. If the demands are not excessive, this is not necessarily problematic. Whether serious problems develop depends on a variety of factors, such as satisfying avocations, good income, family life, and friends. Limited opportunity to fully develop or satisfy one's personality preferences is but one of the disappointments people are likely to experience during their lives. Sad as this may be, though, it is heartening to see the innovative ways in which some people manage to exercise and validate their own type.

There are also some general societal pressures that encourage people to live out of their inferior functions. For example, men with a preference for feeling may get a message that their style is unacceptable because it is not "masculine," and may therefore develop an exaggeratedly critical thinking approach, coming across as excessively "macho," or even crass and abusive toward women.

Men with a preference for thinking who are in "feeling" professions may show a seemingly artificial overconcern for people. An ENTJ minister recalled that during his six months in a pastoral counseling training program, he focused on his and his client's emotions, even though he felt uncomfortable, condescending, and phony about doing so. He saw himself as emotionally and intellectually incompetent in comparison to other ministers, who appeared comfortable in their roles as counselors.

Women in our society must also deal with the pressures of cultural expectations. Women who prefer thinking may be seen by others and see themselves as lacking in those feminine qualities that society considers essential to being an acceptable woman. In response, they may over-compensate with an exaggerated focus on fulfilling family expectations, helping others, and demonstrating "feminine" interests. This may be especially true for women with a thinking preference who include the traditional roles of wife and mother in their lives. Their style of dress may tend toward lace and pastel colors, and they may feign ineptitude about such traditionally "masculine" things as mechanical devices and finances.

Women with a feeling preference who choose traditionally male-dominated careers may also find themselves operating out of their inferiors, for a thinking approach is often touted as the path to success in such cases. Like male feeling types, they may develop exaggerated thinking character-istics—an abrasive, critical manner, very tailored clothing, and a harsh approach to expressions of emotion and feeling concerns. An INFP senior lawyer was viewed by new associates as unrelenting in her criticism of their work, and lacking any softness or social graces.

Additional examples of some of the above situations can be found in N. L. Quenk (1989) and A. T. Quenk and N. L. Quenk (1982).

The Role of the Inferior in Job Burnout

I noted in Chapter 14 that the preconditions for the inferior function experience are often present in the workplace and can force people to spend an extended period of time in the grip of their inferior function. But the influence of the inferior may also be evident when people work out of their preferred functions in their jobs. In fact, job burnout symptoms can be interpreted to be the result of (or at least to be influenced by) *overuse* or one-sided use of one's personality type. The characteristics of job burnout in different types reveal a predictable pattern consistent with inferior function attributes.

The definitive work in this area was done by Anna-Maria Garden (1985, 1988). Garden's initial research questioned the generalizability of research conclusions about burnout because the subject samples used in such research were drawn primarily from the human services professions—groups generally overrepresented with feeling types. Garden noted that a major reported effect of job burnout is negative, hostile, and "depersonalized" reactions to people—responses quite opposite to those that are typical of people-oriented feeling types.

Garden's research (1988) explored the relationship between personality type preferences (specifically the functions S, N, T, F) and the ways people experienced and expressed job burnout. She found a similar reversion or reversal for each of the four functions—that is, there was a "loss of the attributes typically expected of that type." She identified the "type" of burnout for each of the four preferences she examined as follows:

- For feeling types, a loss in (or lower level of) the inclination to care for others

- For thinking types, a loss in achievement orientation or ambitiousness

- For sensing types, a loss in groundedness

- For intuitive types, a loss of enthusiasm and originality (p. 13)

Further, Garden (1988) found that "in some instances, an increase in the characteristics associated with one's opposite was apparent. Thinking types, for example, showed higher levels of concern for others and sensing types showed an increase in the level of boredom" (p. 14).

The qualities of burnout identified by Garden's innovative and careful research show at least some of the major characteristics described in this book. Perhaps a consideration of such burnout evidence, in conjunction with knowledge of the inferior function of each type, can lead to increased understanding of the burnout phenomenon and more effective approaches to intervention.

Questions About the Role of the Auxiliary

Does a well-developed auxiliary "protect" a person from readily falling into the grip or speed the return of equilibrium once a person is in the grip? If the inferior function sometimes occurs simply as a response to an extreme state, and not for some self-regulating purpose, are "less developed" people more vulnerable than people who are "well developed"? For example, are ENFPs who extravert their auxiliary feeling as well as their dominant intuition more vulnerable to their inferior than other ENFPs who more adaptively introvert their auxiliary feeling? There is some anecdotal evidence to suggest this (N. L. Quenk, 1985b).

Can one actively try to engage the auxiliary as a way to end the experience and thus shorten it—or once constellated, does the inferior have to play out fully and completely before it dissipates naturally?

Some people report an interesting effect if their business or life partner's dominant function is the same as their own auxiliary function. In this circumstance, one partner is likely to say or do "the right thing" to help the other when he or she is in the grip. Thus, an ESTJ (dominant extraverted thinking, auxiliary introverted sensing) might mention the logical consequences of the fact an INTJ (dominant introverted intuition, auxiliary extraverted thinking) is stuck on, or an ISFP (dominant introverted feeling, auxiliary extraverted sensing) might offer quiet reassurance and emotional support to his ESFP (dominant extraverted sensing, auxiliary introverted feeling) partner. If this is generally true, it provides further evidence for the role of the auxiliary in the restoration of psychological balance.

Maturity and the Grip

People of all types report that the frequency and intensity of their grip experiences tend to decrease with age, notwithstanding the often startling episodes characteristic of our middle years. Even without specific knowledge of psychological type theory or the adaptive nature of inferior function experiences, people tend to become familiar with and often benefit from these experiences.

Sometimes "familiarity breeds contempt," however, and a mature person learns to ignore and reject these kinds of experiences. If this becomes habitual, they may miss out on important developmental information. For others, repetition of the form of the inferior can encourage development of a repertoire of helpful responses. These may include stopping what they are doing, taking time to attend to neglected sides of themselves, and reflecting on some aspect of their lives. When this occurs, the psyche may receive the stimulation necessary to permit the person to proceed in his or her personal growth and development.

Trivializing the Inferior

Often when we name an experience, we run the risk of minimizing and trivializing it. Then when we experience it we say, "Ah, yes. I know what this is. It's nothing but my midlife crisis—or my grief process, or my empty nest syndrome, or my inferior function." We may then disregard the experience and miss out on an important opportunity to develop our awareness of ourselves and our lives.

If Jung is correct about the role of the inferior in the self-regulation of the psyche, then it would be an error to treat it in a dismissive, trivial manner. We might rather approach encounters with our least developed side with the utmost respect, neither avoiding it nor attempting to forcibly overcome it.

Overusing the Concept of the Inferior

Have you ever had the experience of learning a new word and then seeing and hearing it everywhere? Once our awareness is heightened, we begin to notice words or other things we didn't see before. Often when we learn a new concept we try to apply it everywhere and feel compelled to try to explain everything with it. Done judiciously, this is a good way to become familiar with a new idea as well as recognize its limitations. People who have been newly introduced to typology often stretch the limits of the theory by insisting that virtually everything is related to one's type.

It's well to remember, therefore, that typology, including the inferior function, is only one, albeit very rich and intriguing, way of understanding individual differences. There are many other useful explanatory systems. It is probably a testimony to the incredible complexity of human beings that no one personality theory proves entirely adequate to the task of explaining us.

It has been wisely said that, "If the only tool you have is a hammer, you'll treat everything as if it were a nail." Avoiding that pitfall will encourage our best use of Jung's personality theory and his concept of the inferior function.

The Value of Opposites

An opposite by definition requires opposition. Thus, the inferior and dominant functions need each other and are reflections of each other. When we consider those things we despise, we can assume that their opposites are what we very much value; by considering what we value, we implicitly identify the things we despise. Awareness of both sides is equally important.

For those of us who characteristically emphasize the positive, recognizing the negative side of things can be distressing, but it can also stimulate valuable insights into ourselves and others. Those who most naturally focus on the negative and objectionable things around them can find in this perspective a way to appreciate the positive and satisfying counterparts that can moderate this limited view.

At the end of Chapter 1, I indicated what you could expect from this book—its nonpathological approach and its focus on the valuable limitations of consciousness. I hope that you have come away with a richer awareness of those unconscious, inferior parts of ourselves that embody our own wisdom.

Acknowledgments

PEOPLE OF ALL SIXTEEN types have contributed to this book by sharing their own experiences or by reviewing the chapter about their own type. I am most grateful to them for confirming and enhancing my understanding of the eight inferior functions. Among them are Scott Anchors, MaryAnn Andrews, Sally Carr, Lelys Ceballos, Gene Dickman, John DiTiberio, Karen Dorris, Carolyn Earnest, Catherine Fitzgerald, Diane Ganze, Sandra Hirsh, Ruth Johnson, Barbara Johnston, Betsy Kendall, Jean Kummerow, Kay Kummerow, Pam Lorenz, Jan Mitchell, Jim Newman, Connie Otis, Gerald Otis, Kaleb Quenk, Karin Quenk, Roberta Rice, Betsy Schmidt-Nowara, Audrey Schuurmann, Julie Sparks, Kim Spencer, Jeanne Street, SueLynn, Eric Rounds, Derek Updegraff, and Sondra Van Sant.

Nancy Barger, Sue Clancy, Linda Kirby, Wayne Mitchell, and Alex Quenk read a series of drafts of the manuscript. Their excellent suggestions greatly enhanced the final product.

Rachel Quenk edited the manuscript before it was submitted to the publisher. Her excellent editorial and content suggestions greatly improved the manuscript, as well as my subsequent writing style. Karin Quenk contributed original artwork.

Finally, I am indebted to the many unnamed people—colleagues, clients, workshop participants, and friends—who over the years have freely shared their knowledge of themselves. I hope my many composite stories of their experience have done them justice.

Descriptions of the Sixteen Personality Types

ESTJ
Extraverted Thinking With Sensing

ESTJ PEOPLE USE THEIR thinking to run as much of the world as may be theirs to run. They like to organize projects and then act to get things done. Reliance on thinking makes them logical, analytical, objectively critical, and not likely to be convinced by anything but reasoning. They tend to focus on the job, not the people behind the job.

They like to organize facts, situations, and operations related to a project, and make a systematic effort to reach their objectives on schedule. They have little patience with confusion or inefficiency, and can be tough when the situation calls for toughness.

They think conduct should be ruled by logic, and govern their own behavior accordingly. They live by a definite set of rules that embody their basic judgments about the world. Any change in their ways requires a deliberate change in their rules.

They are more interested in seeing present realities than future possibilities. This makes them matter-of-fact, practical, realistic, and concerned with the here-and-now. They use past experience to help them solve problems and want to be sure that ideas, plans, and decisions are based on solid fact.

They like jobs where the results of their work are immediate, visible, and tangible. They have a natural bent for business, industry, production, and construction. They enjoy administration, where they can set goals, make decisions, and give the necessary orders. Getting things done is their strong suit.

Like the other decisive types, ESTJs run the risk of deciding too quickly before they have fully examined the situation. They need to stop and listen to the other person's viewpoint, especially with people who are not in a position to talk back. This is seldom easy for them, but *if* they do not take time to understand, they may judge too quickly, without enough facts or enough regard for what other people think or feel.

ESTJs *may* need to work at taking feeling values into account. They may rely so much on their logical approach that they overlook feeling values—what they care about and what other people care about. If feeling values are ignored too much, they may build up pressure and find expression in inappropriate ways. Although ESTJs are naturally good at seeing what is illogical and inconsistent, they may need to develop the art of appreciation. One positive way to exercise their feeling is to appreciate other people's merits and ideas. ESTJs who make it a rule to mention what they like, not merely what needs correcting, find the results worthwhile both in their work and in their private lives.

ENTJ
Extraverted Thinking With Intuition

ENTJ people use their thinking to run as much of the world as may be theirs to run. They enjoy executive action and long-range planning. Reliance on thinking makes them logical, analytical, objectively critical, and not likely to be convinced by anything but reasoning. They tend to focus on the ideas, not the person behind the ideas.

They like to think ahead, organize plans, situations, and operations related to a project, and make a systematic effort to reach their objectives on schedule. They have little patience with confusion or inefficiency, and can be tough when the situation calls for toughness.

They think conduct should be ruled by logic, and govern their own behavior accordingly. They live by a definite set of rules that embody their basic judgments about the world. Any change in their ways requires a deliberate change in their rules.

They are mainly interested in seeing the possibilities beyond what is present, obvious, or known. Intuition heightens their intellectual interest, curiosity for new ideas, tolerance for theory, and taste for complex problems.

ENTJs are seldom content in jobs that make no demand upon their intuition. They are stimulated by problems and are often found in executive jobs where they can find and implement new solutions. Because their interest is in the big picture, they may overlook the importance of certain details. Since ENTJs tend to team up with like-minded intuitives who may also underestimate the realities of a situation, they usually need a person around with good common sense to bring up overlooked facts and take care of important details.

Like the other decisive types, ENTJs run the risk of deciding too quickly before they have fully examined the situation. They need to stop and listen to the other person's viewpoint, especially with people who are not in a position to talk back. This is seldom easy for them, but *if* they do not take time to understand, they may judge too quickly, without enough facts or enough regard for what other people think or feel.

ENTJs *may* need to work at taking feeling values into account. Relying so much on their logical approach, they may overlook feeling values—what they care about and what other people care about. If feeling values are ignored too much, they may build up pressure and find expression in inappropriate ways. Although ENTJs are naturally good at seeing what is illogical and inconsistent, they may need to develop the art of appreciation. One positive way to exercise their feeling is through appreciation of other people's merits and ideas. ENTJs who learn to make it a rule to mention what they like, not merely what needs correcting, find the results worthwhile both in their work and in their private lives.

ISTP
Introverted Thinking With Sensing

People with ISTP preferences use their thinking to look for the principles underlying the sensory information that comes into awareness. As a result, they are logical, analytical, and objectively critical. They are not likely to be convinced by anything but reasoning based on solid facts.

While they like to organize facts and data, they prefer not to organize situations or people unless they must for the sake of their work. They can be intensely but quietly curious. Socially they may be rather shy except with their best friends. They sometimes become so absorbed with one of their interests that they can ignore or lose track of external circumstances.

ISTPs are somewhat quiet and reserved, although they can be quite talkative on a subject where they can apply their great storehouse of information. In everyday activities they are adaptable, except when one of their ruling principles is violated, at which point they stop adapting. They are good with their hands, and like sports and the outdoors, or anything that provides a wealth of information for their senses.

If ISTPs have developed their powers of observing the world around them, they will have a firm grasp on the realities of any situation, and show a great capacity for the important and unique facts of a situation. They are interested in how and why things work and are likely to be good at applied science, mechanics, or engineering. ISTPs who do not have technical or mechanical interests often use their talents to bring order out of unorganized facts. This ability can find expression in law, economics, marketing, sales, securities, or statistics.

ISTPs *may* rely so much on the logical approach of thinking that they overlook what other people care about and what they themselves care about. They may decide that something is not important, just because it isn't logical to care about it. If ISTPs always let their thinking suppress their feeling values, their feeling may build up pressure and find expression in inappropriate ways. Although good at analyzing what is wrong, ISTPs sometimes find it hard to express appreciation. But if they try, they will find it helpful on the job as well as in personal relationships.

ISTP people are in some danger of putting off decisions or of failing to follow through. One of their outstanding traits is economy of effort. This trait is an asset if they judge accurately how much effort is needed; then they do what the situation requires without fuss or lost motion. *If* they cannot judge accurately, or if they just don't bother, then nothing of importance gets done.

INTP
Introverted Thinking With Intuition

People with INTP preferences use their thinking to find the principles underlying whatever ideas come into their awareness. They rely on thinking to develop these principles and to anticipate consequences. As a result, they are logical, analytical, and objectively critical. They are likely to focus more on the ideas than the person behind the ideas.

They organize ideas and knowledge rather than situations or people, unless they must for the sake of their work. In the field of ideas they are intensely curious. Socially, they tend to have a small circle of close friends, and like being with others who enjoy discussing ideas. They can become so absorbed with an idea that they can ignore or lose track of external circumstances.

INTPs are somewhat quiet and reserved, although they can be quite talkative on a subject to which they have given a lot of thought. They are quite adaptable so long as their ruling principles are not violated, at which point they stop adapting. Their main interest lies in seeing possibilities beyond what is present, obvious, or known. They are quick to understand and their intuition heightens their insight, ingenuity, and intellectual curiosity.

Depending on their interests, INTPs are good at pure science, research, mathematics, or engineering; they may become scholars, teachers, or abstract thinkers in fields such as economics, philosophy, or psychology. They are more interested in the challenge of reaching solutions to problems than of seeing the solutions put to practical use.

Unless INTPs develop their perception, they are in danger of gaining too little knowledge and experience of the world. Then their thinking is done in a vacuum and nothing will come of their ideas. Lack of contact with the external world may also lead to problems in making themselves understood. They want to state the exact truth, but often make it so complicated that not everyone can follow them. If they can learn to simplify their arguments, their ideas will be more widely understood and accepted.

INTPs *may* rely so much on logical thinking that they overlook what other people care about and what they themselves care about. They may decide that something is not important, just because it isn't logical to care about it. *If* INTPs always let their logic suppress their feeling values, their feeling may build up pressure until it is expressed in inappropriate ways.

Although they excel at analyzing what is wrong with an idea, it is harder for INTPs to express appreciation. But if they try, they will find it helpful on the job as well as in personal relationships.

ESFJ
Extraverted Feeling With Sensing

People with ESFJ preferences radiate sympathy and fellowship. They concern themselves chiefly with the people around them and place a high value on harmonious human contacts. They are friendly, tactful, and sympathetic. They are persevering, conscientious, orderly even in small matters, and inclined to expect others to be the same. They are particularly warmed by approval and sensitive to indifference. Much of their pleasure and satisfaction comes from the warmth of feeling of people around them. ESFJs tend to concentrate on the admirable qualities of other people and are loyal to respected persons, institutions, or causes, sometimes to the point of idealizing whatever they admire.

They have the gift of finding value in other people's opinions. Even when these opinions are in conflict, they have faith that harmony can somehow be achieved and they often manage to bring it about. To achieve harmony, they are ready to agree with other's opinions within reasonable limits. They need to be careful, however, that they don't concentrate so much on the viewpoints of others that they lose sight of their own.

They are mainly interested in the realities perceived by their five senses, so they become practical, realistic, and down-to-earth. They take great interest in the unique differences in each experience. ESFJs appreciate and enjoy their possessions. They enjoy variety but can adapt well to routine.

ESFJs are at their best in jobs that deal with people and in situations where cooperation can be brought about through good will. They are found in jobs such as teaching, preaching, and selling. Their compassion and awareness of physical conditions often attracts them to health professions, where they can provide warmth, comfort, and patient caring. They are less likely to be happy in work demanding mastery of abstract ideas or impersonal analysis. They think best when talking with people, and enjoy communicating. They have to make a special effort to be brief and businesslike and not let sociability slow them down on the job.

They like to base their plans and decisions upon known facts and on their personal values. While liking to have matters decided or settled, they do not necessarily want to make all the decisions themselves. They run some risk of jumping to conclusions before they understand a situation. *If* they have not taken time to gain first-hand knowledge about a person or situation, their actions may not have the helpful results they intended. For example, ESFJs beginning a new project or job may do things they assume should be done, instead of taking the time to find out what is really wanted or needed. They have many definite "shoulds" and "should nots," and may express these freely.

ESFJs find it especially hard to admit the truth about problems with people or things they care about. *If* they fail to face disagreeable facts, or refuse to look at criticism that hurts, they will try to ignore their problems instead of searching for solutions.

ENFJ
Extraverted Feeling With Intuition

People with ENFJ preferences radiate sympathy and fellowship. They concern themselves chiefly with the people around them and place a high value on harmonious human contacts. They are friendly, tactful, and sympathetic. They are persevering, conscientious, and orderly even in small matters, and inclined to expect others to be the same. ENFJs are particularly warmed by approval and are sensitive to indifference. Much of their pleasure and satisfaction comes from the warmth of feeling of people around them. ENFJs tend to concentrate on the admirable qualities of other people and are loyal to respected persons, institutions, or causes, sometimes to the point of idealizing whatever they admire.

They have the gift of being able to see value in other people's opinions. Even when opinions are in conflict, they have faith that harmony can somehow be achieved, and they often manage to bring it about. To bring harmony, they are ready to agree with other's opinions within reasonable limits. They need to be careful, however, not to concentrate so much on the viewpoints of others that they lose sight of their own.

They are mainly interested in seeing the possibilities beyond what is present, obvious, or known. Intuition heightens their insight, vision, and curiosity for new ideas. They tend to be interested in books and moderately tolerant of theory. They are likely to have a gift of expression, but may use it in speaking to audiences rather than in writing. They think best when talking with people.

They are at their best in jobs that deal with people, and in situations that require building cooperation. ENFJs are found in jobs such as teaching, preaching, counseling, and selling. They may be less happy in work demanding factual accuracy, such as accounting, unless they can find a personal meaning in their work. They have to make a special effort to be brief and businesslike and not let sociability slow them down on the job.

They base their decisions on their personal values. While they like to have matters decided or settled, they do not necessarily want to make all the decisions themselves. ENFJs run some risk of jumping to conclusions before they understand a situation. *If* they have not taken time to gain first-hand knowledge about a person or situation, their actions may not have the helpful results they intended. For example, ENFJs beginning a new project or job may do things they assume should be done, instead of taking the time to find out what is really wanted or needed. They have many definite "shoulds" and "should nots," and may express these freely.

ENFJs find it especially hard to admit the truth about problems with people or things they care about. *If* they fail to face disagreeable facts, or refuse to look at criticism that hurts, they will ignore their problems instead of searching for solutions.

ISFP
Introverted Feeling With Sensing

People with ISFP preferences have a great deal of warmth, but may not show it until they know a person well. They keep their warm side inside, like a fur-lined coat. When they care, they care deeply, but are more likely to show their feeling by deeds rather than words. They are very faithful to duties and obligations related to things or people they care about.

They take a very personal approach to life, judging everything by their inner ideals and personal values. They stick to their values with passionate conviction, but can be influenced by someone they care deeply about. Although their inner loyalties and ideals govern their lives, ISFPs find these hard to talk about. Their deepest feelings are seldom expressed; their inner tenderness is masked by a quiet reserve.

In everyday activities they are tolerant, open-minded, flexible, and adaptable. If one of their inner loyalties is threatened, though, they will not give an inch. They usually enjoy the present moment, and do not like to spoil it by rushing to get things done. They have little wish to impress or dominate. The people they prize the most are those who take the time to understand their values and the goals they are working toward.

They are interested mainly in the realities brought to them by their senses, both inner and outer. They are apt to enjoy fields where taste, discrimination, and a sense of beauty and proportion are important. Many ISFPs have a special love of nature and a sympathy with animals. They often excel in craftsmanship, and the work of their hands is usually more eloquent than their words.

They are twice as good when working at a job they believe in, since their feeling adds energy to their efforts. They see the needs of the moment and try to meet them. They want their work to contribute to something that matters to them—human understanding, happiness, or health. They want to have a purpose beyond their paycheck, no matter how big the check. They are perfectionists whenever they deeply care about something, and are particularly suited for work that requires both devotion and a large measure of adaptability.

The problem for *some* ISFPs is that they may feel such a contrast between their inner ideals and their actual accomplishments that they may burden themselves with a sense of inadequacy. This can be true even when they are being as effective as others. They take for granted anything they do well and are the most modest of all the types, tending to underrate and understate themselves.

It is important for them to find practical ways to express their ideals; otherwise they will keep dreaming of the impossible and accomplish very little. *If* they find no actions to express their ideals, they can become too sensitive and vulnerable, with dwindling confidence in life and in themselves. Actually, they have much to give and need only to find the spot where they are needed.

INFP
Introverted Feeling With Intuition

People with INFP preferences have a great deal of warmth, but may not show it until they know a person well. They keep their warm side inside, like a fur-lined coat. They are very faithful to duties and obligations related to ideas or people they care about. They take a very personal approach to life, judging everything by their inner ideals and personal values.

They stick to their ideals with passionate conviction. Although their inner loyalties and ideals govern their lives, they find these hard to talk about. Their deepest feelings are seldom expressed; their inner tenderness is masked by a quiet reserve.

In everyday matters they are tolerant, open-minded, understanding, flexible, and adaptable. But if their inner loyalties are threatened, they will not give an inch. Except for their work's sake, INFPs have little wish to impress or dominate. The people they prize the most are those who take the time to understand their values and the goals they are working toward.

Their main interest lies in seeing the possibilities beyond what is present, obvious, or known. They are twice as good when working at a job they believe in, since their feeling puts added energy behind their efforts. They want their work to contribute to something that matters to them—human understanding, happiness, or health. They want to have a purpose beyond their paycheck, no matter how big the check. They are perfectionists whenever they care deeply about something.

INFPs are curious about new ideas and tend to have insight and long-range vision. Many are interested in books and language and are likely to have a gift of expression; with talent they may be excellent writers. They can be ingenious and persuasive on the subject of their enthusiasms, which are quiet but deep-rooted. They are often attracted to counseling, teaching, literature, art, science, or psychology.

The problem for *some* INFPs is that they may feel such a contrast between their ideals and their actual accomplishments that they burden themselves with a sense of inadequacy. This can happen even when, objectively, they are being as effective as others. It is important for them to use their intuition to find ways to express their ideals; otherwise they will keep dreaming of the impossible and accomplish very little. If they find no channel for expressing their ideals, INFPs may become overly sensitive and vulnerable, with dwindling confidence in life and in themselves.

ESTP
Extraverted Sensing With Thinking

People with ESTP preferences are friendly, adaptable realists. They rely on what they see, hear, and know first-hand. They good-naturedly accept and use the facts around them. They look for a satisfying solution instead of trying to impose any "should" or "must" of their own. They are sure a satisfying solution will turn up once they have grasped all the facts.

They solve problems by being adaptable, and often can get others to adapt, too. People generally like them well enough to consider any compromise they suggest. They are unprejudiced, open-minded, and tolerant of most everyone—including themselves. They take things as they are and thus may be very good at easing a tense situation and pulling conflicting factions together.

They are actively curious about objects, scenery, activities, food, people, or anything new presented to their senses. Their expert abilities in using their senses may show in: (a) a continuous ability to see the need of the moment and turn easily to meet it, (b) the ability to absorb, apply and remember great numbers of facts, (c) an artistic taste and judgment, or (d) the handling of tools and materials.

With their focus on the current situation and realistic acceptance of what exists, they can be gifted problem solvers. Because they are not necessarily bound by a need to follow standard procedures or preferred methods, they are often able to see ways of achieving a goal by "using" the existing rules, systems, or circumstances in new ways, rather than allowing them to be roadblocks.

They make their decisions by using the logical analysis of thinking rather than the more personal values of feeling. Their thinking enables them to crack down when the situation calls for toughness, and also helps them grasp underlying principles. They learn more from first-hand experience than from study or reading, and are more effective in actual situations than on written tests. Abstract ideas and theories are not likely to be trusted by ESTPs until they have been tested in experience. They may have to work harder than other types to achieve in school, but can do so when they see the relevance.

ESTPs do best in careers needing realism, action, and adaptability. Examples are engineering, police work, credit investigation, marketing, health technologies, construction, production, recreation, food services, and many kinds of troubleshooting.

ESTPs are strong in the art of living. They get a lot of fun out of life, which makes them good company. They enjoy their material possessions and take the time to acquire them. They find much enjoyment in good food, clothes, music, and art. They enjoy physical exercise and sports, and usually are good at these.

How effective they are depends on how much judgment they acquire. They may need to develop their feeling so that they can use their values to provide standards for their behavior, and direction and purpose in their lives. If their judgment is not developed enough to give them any character or stick-to-it-iveness, they are in danger of adapting mainly to their own love of a good time.

ESFP
Extraverted Sensing With Feeling

ESFP people are friendly, adaptable realists. They rely on what they can see, hear, and know first-hand. They good-naturedly accept and use the facts around them, whatever these are. They look for a satisfying solution instead of trying to impose any "should" or "must" of their own. They are sure that a solution will turn up once they have grasped all of the facts.

They solve problems by being adaptable, and often can get others to adapt, too. People generally like them well enough to consider any compromise they suggest. They are unprejudiced, open-minded, and tolerant of most everyone—including themselves. They take things as they are and thus may be very good at easing a tense situation and pulling conflicting factions together.

With their focus on the current situation and realistic acceptance of what exists, they can be gifted problem solvers. Because they are not necessarily bound by a need to follow standard procedures or preferred methods, they are often able to see ways of achieving a goal by "using" the existing rules, systems, or circumstances in new ways, rather than allowing them to be roadblocks.

They are actively curious about people, activities, food, objects, scenery, or anything new presented to their senses. Their expert abilities in using their senses may show in: (a) a continuous ability to see the need of the moment and turn easily to meet it, (b) the skillful handling of people and conflicts, (c) the ability to absorb, apply, and remember great numbers of facts, or (d) an artistic taste and judgment.

They make their decisions by using the personal values of feeling rather than the logical analysis of thinking. Their feeling makes them tactful, sympathetic, interested in people, and especially good at handling human contacts. They may be too easy in matters of discipline. They learn far more from first-hand experience than from books, and do better in actual situations than on written tests. Abstract ideas and theories are not likely to be trusted by ESFPs until they have been tested in experience. They may have to work harder than other types to achieve in school, but can do so when they see the relevance.

ESFPs do best in careers needing realism, action, and adaptability. Examples are health services, sales, design, transportation, entertainment, secretarial or office work, food services, supervising work groups, machine operation, and many kinds of troubleshooting.

ESFPs are strong in the art of living. They get a lot of fun out of life, which makes them good company. They enjoy their material possessions and take the time to acquire and care for them. They find much enjoyment in good food, clothes, music, and art. They enjoy physical exercise and sports and usually are good at these.

How effective they are depends on how much judgment they acquire. They may need to develop their feeling so that they can use their values to provide standards for their behavior, and direction and purpose in their lives. *If* their judgment is not developed enough to give them any character or stick-to-it-iveness, they are in danger of adapting mainly to their own love of a good time.

ISTJ
Introverted Sensing With Thinking

People with ISTJ preferences are extremely dependable and have a complete, realistic, and practical respect for the facts. They absorb, remember, and use any number of facts and are careful about their accuracy. When they see that something needs to be done, they accept the responsibility, often beyond the call of duty. They like everything clearly stated.

Their private reactions, which seldom show in their faces, are often vivid and intense. Even when dealing with a crisis they look calm and composed. Not until you know them very well do you discover that behind their outer calm they are viewing the situation from an intensely individual angle. When ISTJs are "on duty" and dealing with the world, however, their behavior is sound and sensible.

ISTJs are thorough, painstaking, systematic, hard-working, and careful with particulars and procedures. Their perseverance tends to stabilize everything with which they are connected. They do not enter into things impulsively, but once committed, they are very hard to distract or discourage.

ISTJs often choose careers where their talents for organization and accuracy are rewarded. Examples are accounting, civil engineering, law, production, construction, health careers, and office work. They often move into supervisory and management roles.

If they are in charge of something, their practical judgment and valuing of procedure makes them consistent and conservative, assembling the necessary facts to support their evaluations and decisions. They look for solutions to present problems in the successes of the past. With time they become masters of even the smallest elements of their work, but don't give themselves any special credit for this knowledge.

They *may* encounter problems if they expect everyone to be as logical and analytical as they are. They then run the danger of inappropriately passing judgment on others or overriding less forceful people. A useful rule is to use their thinking to make decisions about inanimate objects or their own behavior, and to use their perception to understand others. If they use their senses to see what really matters to others, so that it becomes a fact to be respected, they may go to generous lengths to help.

Another problem may arise *if* the ISTJ's thinking remains undeveloped. They may retreat, becoming absorbed with their inner reactions to sense-impressions, with nothing of value being produced. They may also tend to be somewhat suspicious of imagination and intuition, and not take it seriously enough.

ISFJ
Introverted Sensing With Feeling

People with ISFJ preferences are extremely dependable and devotedly accept responsibilities beyond the call of duty. They have a complete, realistic, and practical respect for the facts. When they see from the facts that something needs to be done, they pause to think about it. If they decide that action will be helpful, they accept the responsibility. They can remember and use any number of facts, but want them all accurate. They like everything clearly stated.

Their private reactions are often vivid and intense, and sometimes quite unpredictable to others. These private reactions seldom show in their faces, and even when dealing with a crisis, they can look calm and composed. Not until you know them very well do you discover that behind their outer calm they are looking at things from an intensely individual angle, often a delightfully humorous one. When ISFJs are "on duty" and dealing with the world, however, their behavior is sound and sensible.

ISFJs are thorough, painstaking, hard-working, and patient with particulars and procedures. They can and will do the "little" things that need to be done to carry a project to completion. Their perseverance tends to stabilize everything with which they are connected. They do not enter into things impulsively, but once in, they are very hard to distract or discourage. They do not quit unless experience convinces them they are wrong.

ISFJs often choose careers where they can combine their careful observation and their caring for people, as in the health professions. Other fields attractive to ISFJs are teaching, office work, and occupations that provide services or personal care. ISFJs show their feeling preference in their contacts with the world. They are kind, sympathetic, tactful, and genuinely concerned; traits that make them very supportive to persons in need.

Because of their concern for accuracy and organization, ISTJs often move into supervisory roles. If they are in charge of something, their practical judgment and appreciation of what works make them conservative and consistent. They take care to collect the facts necessary to support their evaluations and decisions. As they gain experience, they compare the present problem to past situations.

For an ISFJ, problems may arise if their judgment is not developed. *If* their feeling preference remains undeveloped, they will not be effective in dealing with the world. They may instead retreat, becoming silently absorbed in their inner reactions to sense-impressions. Then nothing of value is likely to come out. Another potential problem is that they tend to be somewhat suspicious of imagination and intuition and not take it seriously enough.

ENTP
Extraverted Intuition With Thinking

People with ENTP preferences are ingenious innovators who always see new possibilities and new ways of doing things. They have a lot of imagination and initiative for starting projects and a lot of impulsive energy for carrying them out. They are sure of the worth of their inspirations and tireless with the problems involved. They are stimulated by difficulties and most ingenious in solving them. They enjoy feeling competent in a variety of areas and value this in others as well.

They are extremely perceptive about the attitudes of other people, and can use this knowledge to win support for their projects. They aim to understand rather than to judge people.

Their energy comes from a succession of new interests and their world is full of possible projects. They may be interested in so many different things that they have difficulty focusing. Their thinking can then help them select projects by supplying some analysis and constructive criticism of their inspirations, and thus add depth to the insights supplied by their intuition. Their use of thinking also makes ENTPs rather objective in their approach to their current project and to the people in their lives.

ENTPs are not likely to stay in any occupation that does not provide many new challenges. With talent, they can be inventors, scientists, journalists, troubleshooters, marketers, promoters, computer analysts, or almost anything that it interests them to be.

A difficulty for people with ENTP preferences is that they hate uninspired routine and find it remarkably hard to apply themselves to sometimes necessary detail unconnected with any major interest. Worse yet, they may get bored with their own projects as soon as the major problems have been solved or the initial challenge has been met. They need to learn to follow through, but are happiest and most effective in jobs that permit one project after another, with somebody else taking over as soon as the situation is well in hand.

Because ENTPs are always being drawn to the exciting challenges of new possibilities, it is essential that they develop their judgment. *If* their judgment is undeveloped, they may commit themselves to ill-chosen projects, fail to finish anything, and squander their inspirations on incompleted tasks.

ENFP
Extraverted Intuition With Feeling

People with ENFP preferences are enthusiastic innovators, always seeing new possibilities and new ways of doing things. They have a lot of imagination and initiative for starting projects, and a lot of impulsive energy for carrying them out. They are stimulated by difficulties and are most ingenious in solving them. ENFPs can get so interested in their newest project that they have time for little else. Their energy comes from a succession of new enthusiasms and their world is full of possible projects. Their enthusiasm gets other people interested too.

They see so many possible projects that they sometimes have difficulty picking those with the greatest potential. Their feeling can be useful at this point to help select projects by weighing the values of each. Their feeling judgment can also add depth to the insights supplied by their intuition.

The ENFP's feeling preference shows in a concern for people. They are skillful in handling people and often have remarkable insight into the possibilities and development of others. They are extremely perceptive about the attitudes of others, aiming to understand rather than judge people. They are much drawn to counseling, and can be inspired and inspiring teachers, particularly where they have freedom to innovate. With talent, they can succeed in almost any field that captures their interest— art, journalism, science, advertising, sales, the ministry, or writing, for example.

A difficulty for ENFPs is that they hate uninspired routine and find it remarkably hard to apply themselves to the sometimes necessary detail unconnected with any major interest. Worse yet, they may get bored with their own projects as soon as the main problems have been solved or the initial challenge has been met. They may need to learn to follow through and finish what they have begun, but are happiest and most effective in jobs that permit one project after another, with somebody else taking over as soon as the situation is well in hand.

Because ENFPs are always being drawn to the exciting challenges of new possibilities, it is essential that they develop their feeling judgment. *If* their judgment is undeveloped, they may commit themselves to ill-chosen projects, fail to finish anything, and squander their inspirations by not completing their tasks.

INTJ
Introverted Intuition With Thinking

People with INTJ preferences are relentless innovators in thought as well as action. They trust their intuitive insights into the true relationships and meanings of things, regardless of established authority or popularly accepted beliefs. Their faith in their inner vision can move mountains. Problems only stimulate them—the impossible takes a little longer, but not much. They are the most independent of all the types, sometimes to the point of being stubborn. They place a high value on competence—their own and others'.

Being sure of the worth of their inspirations, INTJs want to see them worked out in practice, applied and accepted by the rest of the world; they are willing to spend any time and effort to that end. They have determination, perseverance, and will drive others almost as hard as they drive themselves. Although their preference is for intuition, they can, when necessary, focus on the details of a project to realize their vision.

INTJs often value and use confidently their intuitive insights in fields such as science, engineering, invention, politics, or philosophy. The boldness of their intuition may be of immense value in any field, and should not be smothered in a routine job.

Some problems *may* arise from the INTJ's single-minded concentration on goals. They may see the end so clearly that they fail to look for other things which might conflict with the goal. Therefore they need to actively seek the viewpoints of others.

INTJs may neglect their feeling to the point of ignoring other people's values and feelings. If they do, they may be surprised by the bitterness of their opposition. An INTJ's own feeling has to be reckoned with also, for if too much suppressed, it may build up pressure and find expression in inappropriate ways. Their feeling needs to be used constructively, such as through appreciation of other people. Given their talent for analysis, appreciation may be hard for them, but they will find it helpful on the job as well as in personal relationships.

To be effective, INTJs must develop their thinking to supply needed judgment. *If* their judgment is undeveloped, they will be unable to criticize their own inner vision, and will not listen to the opinions of others. They will therefore be unable to shape their inspirations into effective action.

INFJ
Introverted Intuition With Feeling

People with INFJ preferences are great innovators in the field of ideas. They trust their intuitive insights into the true relationships and meanings of things, regardless of established authority or popularly accepted beliefs. Problems only stimulate them—the impossible takes a little longer, but not much.

They are independent and individualistic, being governed by inspirations that come through intuition. These inspirations seem so valid and important that they sometimes have trouble understanding why everyone does not accept them. Their inner independence is often not conspicuous because INFJs value harmony and fellowship; they work to persuade others to approve of and cooperate with their purposes. They can be great leaders when they devote themselves to carrying out a sound inspiration, attracting followers by their enthusiasm and faith. They lead by winning (rather than demanding) acceptance of their ideas.

They are most content in work that satisfies both their intuition and their feeling. The possibilities that interest them most concern people. Teaching particularly appeals to them, whether in higher education, or through the arts or ministry. Their intuition provides insight into the deeper meanings of the subject and they take great satisfaction in aiding the development of individual students.

When their interests lie in technical fields, INFJs may be outstanding in science, or research and development. Intuition suggests new approaches to problems and feeling generates enthusiasm that sparks their energies. Intuition powered by feeling may be of immense value in any field if not smothered in a routine job.

Some problems *may* result from the INFJ's single-minded devotion to inspirations. They may see the goal so clearly that they fail to look for other things that might conflict with the goal. It is also important that their feeling is developed, since this will supply necessary judgment. *If* their judgment is undeveloped, they will be unable to evaluate their own inner vision and will not listen to feedback from others. Instead of shaping their inspirations into effective action, they may merely try to regulate everything (small matters as well as great ones) according to their own ideas, so that little is accomplished.

Selected Quotations From Jung on His Typology

Differentiation of Functions

WHATEVER WE PERSISTENTLY EXCLUDE from conscious training and adaptation necessarily remains in an untrained, undeveloped, infantile, or archaic condition, ranging from partial to complete unconsciousness. Hence, besides the motives of consciousness and reason, unconscious influences of a primitive character are always normally present in ample measure and disturb the intentions of consciousness. For it is by no means to be assumed that all those forms of activity latent in the psyche, which are suppressed or neglected by the individual, are thereby robbed of their specific energy. For instance, if a man relied wholly on the data of vision, this would not mean that he would cease to hear. (1960, p. 124)

So long as a function is still so fused with one or more of the other functions—thinking with feeling, feeling with sensation, etc.—that it is unable to operate on its own, it is...not differentiated, not separated from the whole as a special part and existing by itself. Undifferentiated thinking is incapable of thinking apart from other functions; it is continually mixed up with sensations and fantasies....To the extent that a function is largely or wholly unconscious, it is also undifferentiated; it is not only fused together in its parts but also merged with the functions....Without differentiation direction is impossible, since the direction of a function towards a goal depends on the elimination of anything irrelevant. Fusion with the irrelevant precludes direction; only a differentiated function is *capable* of being directed. (1976a, pp. 424, 425)

Now experience shows that there is only *one* consciously directed function of adaptation. If, for example, I have a thinking orientation I cannot at the same time orient myself by feeling, because thinking and feeling are two quite different functions. In fact, I must carefully exclude feeling if I am to satisfy the logical laws of thinking....I withdraw as much libido as possible from the feeling process, with the result that this function becomes relatively unconscious. Experience shows again, that the orientation is largely habitual; accordingly the other unsuitable functions, so far as they are incompatible with the prevailing attitude, are relatively unconscious, and hence, unused, untrained and undifferentiated. (1960, p. 35)

I do not believe it is humanly possible to differentiate all four functions alike, otherwise we would be perfect like God, and that surely will not happen. There will always be a flaw in the crystal. We can never reach perfection. Moreover, if we could differentiate the four functions equally we should only make them into consciously disposable functions. Then we would lose the most precious connection with the unconscious through the inferior function, which is invariably the weakest; only through our feebleness and incapacity are we linked up with the unconscious, with the lower world of the instincts and with our fellow beings. Our virtues only enable us to be independent. There we do not need anybody, there we are kings; but in our inferiority we are linked up with mankind as well as with the world of our instincts. It would not even be an advantage to have all the functions perfect, because such a condition would amount to complete aloofness. I have no perfection craze. My principle is: for heaven's sake do not be perfect, but by all means try to be complete—whatever that means. (1976b, p. 97)

Experience has shown that it is practically impossible, owing to adverse circumstances in general, for anyone to develop all his psychological functions simultaneously....As a consequence of this one-sided development, one or more functions are necessarily retarded. These functions may properly be called inferior in a psychological but not pathological sense, since they are in no way morbid but merely backward as compared with the favoured function. (1976a, p. 450)

We know that three of the four functions of consciousness can become differentiated, i.e., conscious, while the other remains connected with the matrix, the unconscious, and is known as the "inferior" function. It is the Achilles' heel of even the most heroic consciousness....(1959, p. 237)

It is an empirical fact that only *one* function becomes more or less successfully differentiated, which on that account is known as the superior or main function, and together with extraversion or introversion constitutes the type of conscious attitude. This function has associated with it one or two partially differentiated auxiliary functions which hardly ever attain the same degree of differentiation as the main function, that is, the same degree of applicability by the will. Accordingly they possess a higher degree of spontaneity than the main function, which displays a large measure of reliability and is amenable to our intentions. (1959, p. 238)

Just as adaptation to the environment may fail because of the one-sidedness of the adapted function, so adaptation to the inner world may fail because of the one-sidedness of the function in question. (1960, p. 36)

Primitive Consciousness

You know all our *raisonnement* is done in a way by the primitive but only in his unconscious, because his functions are not yet developed out of his unconscious, so it manifests, of course, in the form of a revelation. It is as if a voice told them in the night what should be done. (1976c, p. 26)

There are individuals whose thinking and feeling are on the same level, both being of equal motive power for consciousness. But in these cases there is also no question of a differentiated type, but merely of relatively undeveloped thinking and feeling. The uniformly conscious or uniformly unconscious state of the functions is, therefore, the mark of a primitive mentality. (1976a, p. 406)

Characteristics of the Inferior

The inferior function is practically identical with the dark side of human personality. The darkness which clings to every personality is the door into the unconscious and the gateway to dreams, from which those two twilight figures, the shadow and the anima, step into our nightly visions or, remaining invisible, take possession of our ego-consciousness. A man who is possessed by his own shadow is always standing in his own light and falling into his own traps. (1959, p. 123)

The fourth function is contaminated by the unconscious and, on being made conscious, drags the whole of the unconscious with it. We must then come to terms with the unconscious and try to bring about a synthesis of opposites. (1953, p. 146)

[The inferior function] may be either unconscious or conscious, but in both cases it is autonomous and obsessive and not influenceable by the will. It has all the "all-or-none" character of an instinct. Although emancipation from the instinct brings a differentiation and enhancement of consciousness, it can only come about at the expense of the unconscious function, so that the conscious orientation lacks that element which the inferior function could have supplied. Thus it often happens that people who have an amazing range of consciousness know less about themselves than the veriest infant, and all because the fourth would not come—it remained down below or up above in the unconscious realm. (1969, p. 166)

[The inferior function] is also found in psychology as the opposition between the functions of consciousness, three of which are fairly differentiated, while the fourth, undifferentiated, "inferior" function is undomesticated, unadapted, uncontrolled, and primitive. Because of its contamination with the collective unconscious, it possesses archaic and mystical qualities, and is the complete opposite of the most differentiated function....(1969, p. 121)

As a rule, the inferior function does not possess the qualities of a conscious differentiated function. The conscious differentiated function can as a rule be handled by intention and by the will. If you are a real thinker, you can direct your thinking by your will, you can control your thoughts....But the feeling type can never do that because he cannot get rid of his thought. The thought possesses him, or rather he is possessed by his thought. Thought has a fascination for him, therefore he is afraid of it. The intellectual type is afraid of being caught by feeling because his feeling has an archaic quality, and there he is like an archaic man—he is the helpless victim of his emotions. (1976b, p. 19, 20)

Positive as well as negative occurrences can constellate the inferior counter-function. When this happens, sensitiveness appears. Sensitiveness is a sure sign of the presence of inferiority. This provides the psychological basis for discord and misunderstanding, not only as between two people, but also in ourselves. The essence of the inferior function is autonomy: it is independent, it attacks, it fascinates and so spins us about that we are no longer masters of ourselves and can no longer rightly distinguish between ourselves and others. (1966, p. 58)

Value of the Inferior

And it is a fact that it has the strongest tendency to be infantile, banal, primitive, and archaic. Anybody who has a high opinion of himself will do well to guard against letting it make a fool of him. On the other hand, deeper insight will show that the primitive and archaic qualities of the inferior function conceal all sorts of significant relationships and symbolical meanings....(1969, p. 165)

The "other" in us always seems alien and unacceptable; but if we let ourselves be aggrieved the feeling sinks in, and we are the richer for this little bit of self-knowledge. (1970a, p. 486)

And yet it is necessary for the development of character that we should allow the other side, the inferior function, to find expression. We cannot in the long run allow one part of our personality to be cared for symbioti-cally by another; for the moment when we might have need of the other function may come at any time and find us unprepared....And the conse-quences may be bad: the extravert loses his indispensable relation to the object, and the introvert loses his to the subject. Conversely, it is equally indispensable for the introvert to arrive at some form of action not con-stantly bedevilled by doubts and hesitations, and for the extravert to reflect upon himself, yet without endangering his relationships. (1966, p. 58)

We know from experience that the inferior function always compensates, complements, and balances the "superior" function....The inferior func-tion is the one of which least conscious use is made. This is the reason for its undifferentiated quality, but also for its freshness and vitality. It is not at the disposal of the conscious mind, and even after long use it never loses its autonomy and spontaneity, or only to a very limited degree. Its role is therefore mostly that of a *deus ex machina*. It depends not on the ego but on the self. Hence it hits consciousness unexpectedly, like lightening, and occasionally with devastating consequences. It thrusts the ego aside and makes room for a supraordinate factor, the totality of a person, which consists of conscious and unconscious and consequently extends far beyond the ego. (1959, p. 303)

The "inferior" function, however, just because of its unconsciousness, has the great advantage of being contaminated with the collective unconscious and can thus restore the vital connection with the latter. (1959, p. 332)

Extraversion and Introversion

Strictly speaking, there are no introverts and extraverts pure and simple, but only introverted and extraverted function-types, such as thinking types, sensation types, etc. There are thus at least eight clearly distinguishable types. (1976a, p. 523)

When we come to analyze the personality, we find that the extravert makes a niche for himself in the world of relationships at the cost of unconsciousness (of himself as subject); while the introvert, in realizing his personality, commits the grossest mistakes in the social sphere and blunders about in the most absurd way. These two very typical attitudes are enough to show—quite apart from the types of physiological temperament described by Kretschmer—how little one can fit human beings and their neuroses into the strait jacket of a single theory. (1954, p. 118)

We can therefore formulate the occurrence as follows: in the introvert the influence of the object produces an inferior extraversion, while in the extravert an inferior introversion takes the place of his social attitude. And we come back to the proposition from which we started: "The value of the one is the negation of value for the other." (1966, p. 58)

Sensation (Sensing)

But the sensation type remains with things. He remains in a given reality. To him a thing is true when it is real. Consider what it means to an intuitive when something is real. It is just the wrong thing; it should not be, something else should be. But when a sensation type does not have a given reality—four walls in which to be—he is sick. (1976b, p. 19)

The specifically compulsive character of the neurotic symptoms is the unconscious counterpart of the easy-going character of the pure sensation type, who, from the standpoint of rational judgment, accepts indiscriminately everything that happens....This coercion overtakes the sensation type from the unconscious, in the form of compulsion....If he should become neurotic, it is much harder to treat him by rational means because the functions which the analyst must turn to are in a relatively undifferentiated state. (1976a, p. 365)

Intuition

The intuitive is always bothered by the reality of things; he fails from the standpoint of realities; he is always out for the possibilities of life. He is the man who plants a field and before the crop is ripe is off again to a new field....Give the intuitive four walls in which to be, and the only thing is how to get out of it, because to him a given situation is a prison which must be undone in the shortest time so that he can be off to new possibilities. (1976b, p. 19)

Thinking

If you know that *thinking* is highly differentiated, then feeling is undifferentiated. What does that mean? Does it mean these people have no feelings? No, on the contrary. They say, "I have very strong feelings. I am full of emotion and temperament." These people are under the sway of their emotions, they are caught by their emotions, they are overcome by their emotions at times. If, for instance, you study the private lives of professors it is a very interesting study. If you want to be fully informed as to how the intellectual behaves at home, ask his wife and she will be able to tell you a story! (1976b, p. 18)

In the pursuit of his ideas [the introverted thinker] is generally stubborn, headstrong and quite unamenable to influence. His suggestibility to personal influences is in strange contrast to this. He has only to be convinced of a person's seeming innocuousness to lay himself open to the most undesirable elements....His style is cluttered with all sorts of adjuncts, accessories, qualifications, retractions, saving clauses, doubts, etc., which all come from his scrupulosity. (1976a, p. 385)

The feeling of the introverted thinking type is extraverted. He has the same kind of strong, loyal and warm feeling described as typical for the extraverted thinking type, but with the difference that the feeling of the introverted thinking type flows toward definite objects. (1976b, pp. 18, 19)

The more the feelings are repressed, the more deleterious is their secret influence on thinking that is otherwise beyond reproach....The self asser-tion of the personality is transferred to the formula. Truth is no longer allowed to speak for itself; it is identified with the subject and treated like a sensitive darling whom an evil-minded critic has wronged. (1976a, p. 350)

Because of the highly impersonal character of the conscious attitude, the unconscious feelings [of the introverted thinker] are extremely personal and oversensitive, giving rise to secret prejudices—a readiness, for instance, to misconstrue any opposition to his formula as personal ill-will, or a constant tendency to make negative assumptions about other people in order to invalidate their arguments in advance—in defense, naturally, of his own touchiness. His unconscious sensitivity makes him sharp in tone, acrimonious, aggressive. Insinuations multiply. His feelings have a sultry and resentful character—always a mark of the inferior function. (1976a, p. 350)

I have frequently observed how an analyst, confronted with a terrific thinking type, for instance, will do his utmost to develop the feeling function directly out of the unconscious. Such an attempt is foredoomed to failure, because it involves too great a violation of the conscious standpoint. Should the violation nevertheless be successful, a really com-pulsive dependence of the patient on the analyst ensues, a transference that can only be brutally terminated, because, having been left without a standpoint, the patient has made the standpoint the analyst....In order to cushion the impact of the unconscious, an irrational type needs a stronger development of the rational auxiliary function present in consciousness (and vice versa). (1976a, p. 407)

Feeling

Disappointment [is] the strongest incentive to differentiation of feeling...[it] can supply the impulse either for a more or less brutal outburst of affect or for a modification and adjustment of feeling, and hence for its higher development. This culminates in wisdom if feeling is supplemented by reflection and rational insight. Wisdom is never violent: where wisdom reigns there is no conflict between thinking and feeling. (1970b, p. 334)

It is true that feelings, if they have an emotional character, are accompanied by physiological effects; but there are definitely feelings which do not change the physiological condition. These feelings are very mental, they are not of an emotional nature. That is the distinction I make. Inasmuch as feeling is a function of values, you will readily understand that this is not a physiological condition. It can be something as abstract as abstract thinking. You would not expect abstract thinking to be a physiological condition. Abstract thinking is what the term denotes. Differentiated thinking is rational; and so feeling can be rational in spite of the fact that many people mix up the terminology. (1976b, p. 30)

If you have a value which is overwhelmingly strong for you it will become an emotion at a certain point, namely, when it reaches such an intensity as to cause a physiological enervation. (1976b, p. 26)

The reverse is true of the feeling type. The feeling type, if he is natural, never allows himself to be disturbed by thinking; but when he gets sophisticated and somewhat neurotic he is disturbed by thoughts. Then thinking appears in a compulsory way, he cannot get away from certain thoughts. He is a very nice chap, but he has extraordinary convictions and ideas, and his thinking is of the inferior kind. He is caught by this thinking, entangled in certain thoughts....On the other hand, an intellectual, when caught by his feelings, says, "I feel just like that," and there is no argument against it. Only when he is thoroughly boiled in his emotion will he come out of it. He cannot be reasoned out of his feeling, and he would be a very incomplete man if he could. (1976b, p. 18, 19)

She begins consciously to feel "what other people think." Naturally, other people are thinking all sorts of mean things, scheming evil, contriving plots....(1976a, p. 391)

The Shadow

The individuation process is invariably started off by the patient's becoming conscious of the shadow, a personality component usually with a negative sign. This "inferior" personality is made up of everything that will not fit in with, and adapt to, the laws and regulations of conscious life. It is compounded of "disobedience" and is therefore rejected not on moral grounds only, but also for reasons of expediency. Closer investigation shows that there is at least one function in it which ought to collaborate in orienting consciousness. Or rather, this function does collaborate, not for the benefit of conscious, purposive intentions, but in the interests of unconscious tendencies pursuing a different goal. It is this fourth, "inferior" function which acts autonomously towards consciousness and cannot be harnessed to the latter's intentions. It lurks behind every neurotic dissociation and can only be annexed to consciousness if the corresponding unconscious contents are made conscious at the same time...(1969, pp. 197, 198)

But the shadow is merely somewhat inferior, primitive, unadapted, and awkward; not wholly bad. It even contains childish or primitive qualities which would in a way vitalize and embellish human existence, but—convention forbids! (1969, p. 78)

The personal unconscious is the shadow and the inferior function. (1970b, p. 199)

General Comments on Typology

So, too, there are four aspects of psychological orientation, beyond which nothing fundamental remains to be said. In order to orient ourselves, we must have a function which ascertains that something is there (sensation); a second function which establishes *what* it is (thinking); a third function which states whether it suits us or not (feeling); and a fourth function which indicates where it came from and where it is going (intuition). When this has been done there is nothing more to say. Scopenhauer proves that the "Principle of Sufficient Reason" has a fourfold root. This is so because the fourfold aspect is the minimum requirement for a complete judgment....(1969, p. 167)

One always has to answer people in their main function, otherwise no contact is established. (1976b, p. 140)

A typology is therefore designed, first and foremost, as an aid to a psychological critique of knowledge...the valuable thing here is the critical attempt to prevent oneself from taking one's own prejudices as the criterion of normality. Unfortunately, this happens only too easily; for instance, extraversion is "normal," but introversion is pathological auto-eroticism. (1970a, p. 471)

The reader should understand that these four criteria are just so many viewpoints among others, such as will-power, temperament, imagination, memory, morality, religiousness, etc. There is nothing dogmatic about them, nor do they claim to be the ultimate truth about psychology; but their basic nature recommends them as suitable principles of classification. Classification has little value if it does not provide a means of orientation and a practical terminology. I find classification into types particularly helpful when I am called upon to explain parents to children or husbands to wives, and vice versa. It is also useful in understanding one's own prejudices. (1976b, p. 219)

Other Comments

As a rule, the unconscious compensation does not run counter to consciousness, but is rather a balancing or supplementing of the conscious orientation. (1976a, p. 419)

A psychological theory, if it is to be more than a technical makeshift, must base itself on the theory of opposition; for without this it could only reestablish a neurotically unbalanced psyche. There is no balance, no system of self-regulation, without opposition. The psyche is just such a self-regulating system. (1966, p. 61)

I told you that unconscious things are very *relative*. When I am unconscious of a certain thing I am only relatively unconscious of it; in some respects I may know it. The contents of the personal unconscious are perfectly conscious in certain respects, but you do not know them under a *particular aspect* or at a *particular time*. (1976b, p. 57)

Neurotic phenomena are nothing but exaggerations of normal processes. (1959, p. 139)

To have overwhelming emotions is not in itself pathological, it is merely undesirable. We need not invent such a word as pathological for an undesirable thing, because there are other undesirable things in the world which are not pathological, for instance, tax collectors. (1976b, p. 24)

Notes

Chapter 1

1. Words in the text that appear in boldface type are defined in the Glossary at the back of this book.

2. For additional introductory material about psychological type theory, readers are referred to Myers (1980), Hirsh and Kummerow (1989), and other general introductory works.

3. Other personality theories must also explain out-of-character behavior. The most prevalent alternative theories, those based on personality traits, typically must add new traits or combinations of traits to account for these behaviors. One advantage of Jung's system lies in its *parsimony;* that is, it requires relatively few elements to explain a broad range of phenomena. For a detailed comparison of trait and type theories, see Quenk (1993).

4. This table is an adaptation of an exercise developed by Nancy Barger for MBTI training workshops.

5. This contrasts with Freud's *causal,* **reductive approach** that reduces behavior to its initial causes, most notably childhood traumatic events associated with sexual and aggressive instincts. The psychological repression (removal from consciousness) of such events causes neurotic symptoms. Freud saw only moderate opportunity for personality changes during adulthood.

Chapter 2

6. The distinctive features of consciousness are *permanence, regularity,* and *duration in time.* The conscious sphere operates on probabilities, and a conscious approach is flexible and can respond to contingencies; the unconscious has an all-or-none character. As a result, the variables of permanence, the regularity of predicting such things as cause and effect, and a sense of the extension of time into the past, present, and future are absent. The unconscious thus approaches life rigidly and responds in a fixed and automatic manner regardless of changing circumstances (A. Quenk, personal communication, 1992).

7. Readers unfamiliar with Myers' descriptions of the sixteen types will find them in Appendix A.

Chapter 3

8. Jung, though he did not deal explicitly with the attitude of either the auxiliary or tertiary functions, would probably have agreed with Myers. He sometimes described the

"auxiliary functions" or the "inferior functions" as having an opposite attitudinal "cast." Harold Grant (1983) proposed a more "balanced" approach, with the tertiary taking the attitude opposite the auxiliary, that is, the same attitude as the dominant. A third hypothesis that I have proposed is that given the somewhat borderline status of the tertiary function, it may take either attitude, depending on circumstances or other idiosyncratic factors. During the last year of her life, Isabel Myers reconsidered her earlier approach by suggesting that perhaps the tertiary, because it was not under a great deal of pressure, could take either attitude at different times (Katharine Myers, personal communication, 1992). Recent research by Mitchell (1992a) provides empirical support for this hypothesis.

Chapter 13

9. For a discussion of the effects of habitually using the auxiliary function as well as the dominant function in the preferred attitude, see N. L. Quenk (1985b).

Glossary

Adaptation: In Jungian psychology, "relating to, coming to terms with, and balancing internal and external factors....A vital aspect of individuation" (Samuels, Shorter, & Plaut, 1986).

Archetypes: Common human experiences and patterns of response to experiences such as birth, death, mother, father, hero, child, marriage, and so on. These themes link us to each other and to our ancestors, providing the vital connection to our past, present, and future as individuals and as a species.

Collective unconscious: The nonpersonal, objective layer of the unconscious that is the repository of the **archetypes**. Its sphere is larger than that of the **personal unconscious**.

Compensation: In Jungian psychology, the self-regulatory mechanism whereby the psyche regains the balance it has lost as a result of one-sidedness. It involves the "equal and opposite" discharge of unconscious psychic energy, which compensates a one-sided conscious approach.

Complex: In Jungian psychology, "a collection of images and ideas, clustered round a core derived from one or more archetypes, and characterized by a common emotional tone. When they come into play [become "constellated"], complexes contribute to behaviour and are marked by affect whether a person is conscious of them or not" (Samuels et al., 1986).

Consciousness: In Jungian psychology, the opposite of unconsciousness. Consciousness is characterized by a person's ability to control and direct psychological contents and to maintain full awareness of them and their effects.

Constellation: The clustering or grouping of elements together so that they emerge as an activated, unified whole. In Jung's theory, constellated mental contents usually cohere around a central core, often an archetypal image. Psychic elements such as complexes and the inferior function are constellated, or come into play, when certain conditions are present.

Differentiation: For Jung, "the development of differences, the separation of parts from the whole" (1976a, p. 424). According to Jung, psychological type functions must be differentiated into opposites in order for them to be used effectively by people. Without such differentiation, separate, distinct, opposite mental processes are absent.

Differentiated function: Sensing, intuition, thinking, or feeling that is separate and exists by itself, that is, it is not intermingled with one or more of the other functions and therefore can operate independently.

Individuation: In Jungian psychology, a process whereby a person becomes a complete individual, unique and distinct from other individuals and any group (collective). The process is lifelong and involves the gradual integration of unconscious elements (such as psychological type functions) into consciousness. Somewhat similar to the concept of self-actualization described by A. H. Maslow (1954).

Inferior function: "The opposite of the dominant function, also called the fourth or least preferred function. The inferior function is assumed to be nearest to the unconscious, the least differentiated, and a source of both problems and potential for growth" (Kummerow & Quenk, 1992, p. 63).

Midlife: A highly individual and therefore indeterminate period of time extending from the end of adulthood through the beginning of old age. For Jung, it is characterized by a shift of psychological focus from issues of personal and career identity to concerns with psychological completion through integration of previously neglected aspects of one's personality.

Personal unconscious: In Jungian psychology, the repository of an individual's repressed mental contents and personal information that has not yet become salient. These contents are largely subsumed within the **shadow**, the route to which is through the **inferior function**. The personal layer of the unconscious is in contrast to the objective, nonpersonal **collective unconscious.**

Projection: In Jungian psychology, a mechanism whereby a person's unconscious, unacknowledged psychological features are attributed to another person or other relevant object outside of him or herself. Typically, the person or object being projected upon has at least some of the quality being projected. For Jung, unconscious material, such as is associated with the inferior function, appears in projected form.

Prospective approach: Jung's focus on the purposes of behavior and symptoms, in contrast to Freud's causal, **reductive approach**. For Jung, the goal or end point of human development is individuation or psychological completeness.

Psyche: "The totality of all psychic processes, conscious as well as unconscious" (Jung, 1976a, p. 463). Included in Jung's encompassing term are all structures of **consciousness,** including the **differentiated** psychological type functions, as well as all structures of the personal unconscious (including the inferior function) and the collective unconscious.

Reductive approach: Jung's characterization of Freud's causal explanation of psychological symptoms, which reduces behavioral and psychological manifestations to their initial causes, often childhood traumas associated with sexual and aggressive instincts.

Self-regulating psyche: The ability of the psyche to regain its balance or equilibrium through the process of **compensation**. The psyche is thus designed both to correct itself when it is "out of balance," as well as to progress toward completion or **individuation.**

Shadow: In Jungian psychology, the negative, unacceptable part of the psyche, characteristically a major portion of the **personal unconscious**. It is the repository of all those things a person does not wish to acknowledge about him or herself. It often provides the content expressed when the inferior function has been constellated.

Trait: A human characteristic assumed to be distributed normally, that is, the majority (68%) of people have an "average" amount of the trait, with fewer people characterized by the extremes. Examples of traits are height, weight, intelligence, dominance, sociability, and assertiveness. Traits are universal, and people vary only in the amount of the trait they possess. Most personality theories are based on a trait approach.

Type (personality type): One of sixteen descriptive categories identified by the MBTI personality inventory composed of enduring preferences for one of each of four pairs of opposite mental processes (extraversion versus introversion, sensing versus intuition, thinking versus feeling, and judgment versus perception). The particular combination of the four preferences, along with their dynamic interplay, yields a unique category, which cannot be fully defined or adequately described by merely adding up its four component parts.

Type development: (See Differentiation and Differentiated function.)

Unconscious: In Jungian psychology, the opposite of conscious. The term identifies contents or material that is outside of the person's awareness and has the character of an instinct in that its manifestations are automatic and not under a person's control. Jung includes two spheres in his concept of the unconscious, the **personal unconscious** and the **collective unconscious**.

References

Druckman, D., and Bjork, R. A. (Eds.). *In the Mind's Eye, Enhancing Human Performance.* Washington, DC: National Academy Press, 1991.

Freud, S. *The Interpretation of Dreams.* New York: Basic Books, 1933.

Garden, A. M. "Burnout: The Effect of Jungian Type." *Journal of Psychological Type, 10* (1985): 3–10.

Garden, A. M. "Jungian Type, Occupation and Burnout: An Elaboration of an Earlier Study." *Journal of Psychological Type, 14* (1988): 2–14.

Grant, H. *From Image to Likeness.* New York: Paulist Press, 1983.

Hirsh, S., and Kummerow, J. *Lifetypes.* New York: Warner Books, 1989.

Hugo, V. *Wisdom of the Ages.* Dos 2.0 or greater. MCR Agency Inc., 1988.

Jung, C. G. "Psychology and Alchemy." In *Collected Works, Vol. 12,* translated by R. F. C. Hull. Princeton, NJ: Princeton University Press, 1953.

Jung, C. G. "The Practice of Psychotherapy." In *Collected Works, Vol. 16,* translated by R. F. C. Hull. Princeton, NJ: Princeton University Press, 1954.

Jung, C. G. "The Archetypes and the Collective Unconscious." In *Collected Works, Vol. 9i,* translated by R. F. C. Hull. Princeton, NJ: Princeton University Press, 1959.

Jung, C. G. "The Structure and Dynamics of the Psyche." In *Collected Works, Vol. 8,* translated by R. F. C. Hull. Princeton, NJ: Princeton University Press, 1960.

Jung, C. G. "Two Essays on Analytical Psychology." In *Collected Works, Vol. 7,* translated by R. F. C. Hull. Princeton, NJ: Princeton University Press, 1966.

Jung, C. G. "Psychology and Religion: West and East." In *Collected Works, Vol. 11,* translated by R. F. C. Hull. Princeton, NJ: Princeton University Press, 1969.

Jung, C. G. "Civilization in Transition." In *Collected Works, Vol. 10,* translated by R. F. C. Hull. Princeton, NJ: Princeton University Press, 1970a.

Jung, C. G. "Mysterium Coniunctionis." In *Collected Works, Vol. 14,* translated by R. F. C. Hull. Princeton, NJ: Princeton University Press, 1970b.

Jung, C. G. "Psychological Types." In *Collected Works, Vol. 6,* translated by R. F. C. Hull. Princeton, NJ: Princeton University Press, 1976a.

Jung, C. G. "The Symbolic Life." In *Collected Works, Vol. 18,* translated by R. F. C. Hull. Princeton, NJ: Princeton University Press, 1976b.

Jung, C. G. *The Visions Seminars.* New York: Spring Publications, 1976c.

Kummerow, J. M., and Quenk, N. L. *Interpretive Guide for the MBTI Expanded Analysis Report.* Palo Alto, CA: Consulting Psychologists Press, 1992.

Maslow, A. H. *Motivation and Personality.* New York: Harper, 1954.

McCrea, R. R., and Costa, P. T. "Reinterpreting the Myers-Briggs Type Indicator from the Perspective of the Five-Factor Model of Personality." *Journal of Personality, 57* (1989): 17–40.

Mitchell, W. D. Unpublished research, 1992a.

Mitchell, W. D. "Reconsidering a Classic Typology and its Measurement." Unpublished manuscript, 1992b.

Myers, I. B. *Gifts Differing.* Palo Alto, CA: Consulting Psychologists Press, 1980, 1990.

Myers, I. B. *Introduction to Type.* Palo Alto, CA: Consulting Psychologists Press, 1987.

Myers, I. B., and McCaulley, M. H. *Manual: A Guide to the Development and Use of the Myers-Briggs Type Indicator.* Palo Alto, CA: Consulting Psychologists Press, 1985.

Quenk, A. T., and Quenk, N. L. "The Use of Psychological Typology in Analysis." *Jungian Analysis,* edited by M. Stein. LaSalle, IL: Open Court, 1982.

Quenk, A. T. *Psychological Types and Psychotherapy.* Gainesville, FL: Center for Applications of Psychological Type, 1985.

Quenk, N. L. "The Inferior Function and the Shadow in Jungian Psychology." *MBTI News, 4* (1982).

Quenk, N. L. "The Dynamics of Type Development." *MBTI News, 7* (1984): 1–2.

Quenk, N. L. "Conflicts in Function Development." *MBTI News, 7* (1985a): 1–2.

Quenk, N. L. "Directionality of the Auxiliary Function." *MBTI News, 8* (1985b): 27–29.

Quenk, N. L. "Jung's Theory of Psychological Types and the Self-contained Patient." In *Psychotherapy and the Self-contained Patient,* edited by E. M. Stern. New York: Haworth Press, 1989.

Quenk, N. L. "Personality Types or Personality Traits: What Difference Does it Make?" *Bulletin of Psychological Type, 16* (1993).

Samuels, A., Shorter, B., & Plaut, F. *A Critical Dictionary of Jungian Analysis.* London: Routledge & Kegan Paul, 1986.

Spoto, A. *Jung's Typology in Perspective.* Boston: Sigo Press, 1989.

Thorne, A., and Gough, H. *Portraits of Type: An MBTI Research Compendium.* Palo Alto, CA: Consulting Psychologists Press, 1991.

Von Franz, M. L. "The Inferior Function." In *Jung's Typology,* by M. L. Von Franz and J. Hillman. New York: Spring Publications, 1971.

Wheelwright, J. B., Wheelwright, J. H., and Buehler, H. A. *Jungian Type Survey: The Gray-Wheelwright Test* (16th revision). San Francisco: Society of Jungian Analysts of Northern California, 1964.

Index